inspired faith

365 Days a Year

© Mark Gilroy Creative, LLC
www.markgilroy.com

Published by Simple Truths
1952 McDowell Road, Suite 300
Naperville, Illinois 60563

www.simpletruths.com
Toll Free 800-900-3427

All rights reserved. No portion of this publication may be reproduced, stored in a retrieval system or transmitted in any form by any means without the prior written permission of the publisher.

Inspired Faith is a registered trademark.

Unless otherwise noted, Scripture quotations are taken from the Holy Bible: New International Version® Copyright © 1973, 1978, 1984 by International Bible Society. Used by permission of Zondervan Publishing House. All rights reserved. Scripture quotations marked NKJV are taken from the Holy Bible, New King James Version. Copyright © 1979, 1980, 1982 by Thomas Nelson, Inc.

Content and Editorial Development: Mark Gilroy and Jessica Inman; research by Patti Hummell

Book Design: Thinkpen Design, www.thinkpendesign.com

Printed in China

ISBN: 978-1-60810-064-4

02 4CPG 11

Inspired Faith

365 Days a Year

simple truths®
Motivational & Inspirational Gifts

Table of Contents

Introduction

What a Difference a Day Makes

An apple a day keeps the doctor away.

The power of a daily habit is woven throughout our common-sense prescriptions for a better life. I don't know if an apple a day really keeps the doctor away, though I'm pretty certain that eating ten apples in one day is missing the point of the proverb. Some medicine does its work all at once, in one dose. But most of the important things in life—a marriage, raising a kid, a career, a reputation—require daily attention.

No wonder the power of our daily habits is woven throughout God's Word.

> *God's mercies are new every single day* (LAMENTATIONS 3:23)
> *God's strength is provided for us each day to meet the challenges of that particular day* (DEUTERONOMY 3:25)
> *We are advised to put each of our days in proper order* (PSALM 90:12)
> *Jesus calls us to follow Him daily* (LUKE 9:23)

If we were to list all the verses that talk about the importance of a single day and our daily activities, that list alone would fill up this book. That's why I'm so certain that spending time each day with God—in His Word, in prayer, in reflection of His love and plans for you—will make a tremendous positive difference in your life and spirit. Day by day.

Our prayer is that these Bible verses, short devotions, and prayer starters will be a special part of your time with God each day. And every day of the year.

January

New Beginnings

Hope for a New Year

Praise be to the God and Father of our Lord Jesus Christ!
In his great mercy he has given us new birth into a living hope
through the resurrection of Jesus Christ from the dead. 1 PETER 1:3

The beautiful thing about this adventure called faith is that
we can count on Him never to lead us astray. CHARLES SWINDOLL

We begin the New Year with resolutions only to leave them by the wayside by February. Unfulfilled promises and commitments leave us with feelings of guilt and failure for not living up to our own expectations. One obvious solution is to not try at all. It's probably wiser to frame our resolutions as goals, not promises.

But the real question is where we place our confidence. Is it in your own strength? Your own efforts? Start by accepting God's unconditional love. Allow Him to work through you. You might end up accomplishing more than you initially set out to do!

Your outlook for the year will be much brighter if you begin by asking God first for direction, then for strength to accomplish the tasks He sets before you. Jesus called Himself our Good Shepherd. When we follow Him, we find green pastures and an abundance of joy.

Lord, give me wisdom as I write out goals for this year.
Show me what You would have me accomplish.
And thank You for Your ever-present love and strength.

Pressing On

*Brothers, I do not consider myself yet to have taken hold of it.
But one thing I do: Forgetting what is behind and straining toward
what is ahead, I press on toward the goal to win the prize for which
God has called me heavenward in Christ Jesus.* PHILIPPIANS 3:13–14

Never be afraid to trust an unknown future to a known God. CORRIE TEN BOOM

Seventeenth-century hymnist Paul Gerhardt penned the following hymn to celebrate the New Year:

Above all else, Lord, send us Thy Spirit to attend us,
Within our hearts abiding,
To heaven our footsteps guiding.
All this Thy hand bestoweth,
Thou Life, whence our life floweth.
To all Thy name confessing
Grant, Lord, Thy New Year's blessing.

God is all knowing and able to direct our steps so we can press forward confidently—even when the future is uncertain. Since we are assured of His constant presence and help every day throughout the year, we should embrace the New Year—and each day—with a spirit of perseverance and confidence in our Heavenly Father.

Father, I want to begin this year—and each day of the year—by seeking Your guidance. Show me the plans You have for my life. Amen.

You Can Make a Difference

*Father, I thank you that you have heard me. I knew that you always
hear me, but I said this for the benefit of the people standing here,
that they may believe that you sent me.* John 11:41–42

*I have seen many men work without praying, though I have
never seen any good come out of it; but I have never seen a
man pray without working.* James Hudson Taylor

A Classic Devotional from D. L. Moody

Those who have left the deepest impression on this sin-cursed earth have been
men and women of prayer. You will find that prayer has been the mighty power
that has moved not only God, but man also.

We read that Elijah brought fire down on Mount Carmel (see 1 Kings 18:17–
39). The prophets of Baal cried long and loud, but no answer came. The God of
Elijah heard and answered his prayer. Let us remember that the God of Elijah
still lives. As we go to the throne of grace, let us always remember that God
answers prayer.

All through the Scriptures you will find that when believing prayer went up to
God, the answer came down.

Lord, I can't do anything apart from You. I ask You to work
through me to make a difference in the world. Amen.

Patiently Waiting

Guide me in your truth and teach me,
for you are God my Savior,
and my hope is in you all day long. Psalm 25:5

How we spend our days is, of course, how we spend our lives. Annie Dillard

Waiting is difficult—crawling behind a car that is going well below the speed limit in a no-passing zone, tapping your foot in line at the coffee shop as someone scrounges up exact change, anxiously waiting for the mailman so you can get your hands on that check that was promised weeks ago, and, of course, trying to keep a great attitude in church on the very Sunday that you planned to meet friends for lunch at 12:30 and your pastor decides to include next week's sermon in with this week's. Maybe the toughest waiting is when we ask God for direction on an important life decision.

No, waiting is not easy, but God tells us to wait patiently for Him: His choices, His answers, His news, His guidance, His perfect spouse for us, His desire for our vocation, His love, and yes, even His coming again. Waiting patiently means trusting God knows what is best for us because we are His children. God desires us to wait for Him because when we acknowledge Him in all our decisions, we truly begin to walk in wisdom.

Dear God, help me to overcome doubts and the temptation of impatience. Help me to trust You with the choices and decisions of my life because You know what is best for me. Amen.

A Ready Vessel

Seek the LORD while he may be found;
call on him while he is near. ISAIAH 55:6

Faith asks us neither to destroy nor to exalt human desire but to
gather it into an even greater desire: the thirst for God. AUTHOR UNKNOWN

A Classic Devotional from A. W. Tozer

Pick at random a score of great saints whose lives and testimonies are widely known. Let them be Bible characters or well-known Christians of post-biblical times. You will be struck instantly with the fact that the saints were not alike. Sometimes the dissimilarities were so great as to be positively glaring. The differences are as wide as human life itself—differences of race, nationality, education, temperament, habit and personal qualities. Yet they all walked, each in his day, upon a high road of spiritual living far above the common way.

I venture to suggest that the one vital quality which they had in common was *spiritual receptivity*. Something in them was open to heaven, something which urged them Godward. I shall say simply that they had spiritual awareness and that they went on to cultivate it until it became the biggest thing in their lives.

Lord, I ask that You would help me be open to You.
Help me to hear Your voice and do Your will. Amen.

God's Strength

That is why, for Christ's sake, I delight in weaknesses,
in insults, in hardships, in persecutions, in difficulties.
For when I am weak, then I am strong. 2 CORINTHIANS 12:10

Feed on Christ, and then go and live your life, and it is Christ
in you that lives your life, that helps the poor, that tells the truth,
that fights the battle, and that wins the crown. PHILLIPS BROOKS

It's true that God is mighty, that He can do anything. And yet, Scripture also tells us that God often uses humble means of exercising His power. In 2 Corinthians 4:7, Paul tells us that God can use imperfect people to do His will: "We have this treasure in earthen vessels, that the excellence of the power may be of God and not of us." And Jesus taught us that if we want to be great, we must serve. Philippians 2:7 tells us that Jesus Himself "made Himself of no reputation, taking the form of a bondservant, and coming in the likeness of men."

So if you're feeling not-so-powerful or unsure of what contributions you can make, take heart. God in you is more powerful than you could ever be on your own, and He has prepared great things for you to do.

Dear Lord, thank You for working in and through me.
Thank You for Your will for me.
Help me accomplish all that You want me to do. Amen.

His Faithfulness

God, who has called you into fellowship with his
Son Jesus Christ our Lord, is faithful. 1 CORINTHIANS 1:9

The promises of God which are made through Christ relate to
the pardon of sin to the penitent; the sanctification of His people;
support in temptation and trial; guidance in perplexity;
peace in death, and eternal glory beyond the grave. All of these
are made through a Redeemer, and none of these shall fail. ALBERT BARNES

Even if people haven't kept their promises to you; even if no one else in the world is faithful and true; even if you feel let down by others; there is One who is faithful and true to His Word.

God has never turned away anyone who has asked Him for forgiveness. God has never left the side of any of His followers—even if they were untrue to Him. God will never withhold the hope of glory and heaven from one who seeks Him.

What greater promises can we receive? What else do we truly need? No wonder the hymnist Thomas O. Chisholm declared: Great is thy faithfulness!

Father, thank You for Your continuous presence,
for Your commitment to me as Your child.
Help me live in the light of Your love. Amen.

A Real Home

God sets the lonely in families. Psalm 68:6

A home is a house with a heart inside. Author Unknown

She was a single mother with a five-year-old son and a ton of bills. Just to stay afloat, she rented a musty, cramped camper at a local RV park. She was embarrassed and discouraged by her surroundings. She cringed one day as she overheard someone ask her little boy if he wished they had a real home. But her grimace was replaced with a tear and a smile when she heard him give this reply: "We do have a real home; we just don't have a house to put it in."

Maybe you're not happy where you are. But no matter how bad things look, don't get so focused on where you want to go that you miss the good things you have right now. God has a good plan for your future—but He has also sprinkled gifts and blessings in the life you have now.

Make sure your eyes—and heart—are open to see them.

Dear Father, thank You for bringing me into
Your family and thank You for those intangible
blessings that make life wonderful. Amen.

Rest for the Weary

My soul clings to you;
your right hand upholds me.
PSALM 63:8

Pray, and let God worry.
MARTIN LUTHER

A badly broken foot a few months ago landed Patti in a wheelchair on an international trip. Instead of sightseeing, she spent her time in a hospital bed—definitely not where she wanted to be. But Patti found that because she wasn't able to be as active, she had more time to spend with the Lord and listen to His message for her life:

"I had the opportunity to rest in Him and rely on Him for healing in my soul as well as my body. God used the nine months of recovery and physical therapy to draw my heart near to His."

The Bible tells us that we will experience trials and tribulations in life and that when we do, we have a choice to make. We can either endure the time by basking in pity—or we can look upon the trial as an opportunity to invite Christ to do new work in our heart. The latter brings with it joy and peace and a sense of satisfaction in knowing even tough times are not wasted.

Father, thank You for helping me respond to
You when life is tough—and for making this a time
to grow into the person You want me to be. Amen.

The Second Birth

*Therefore, if anyone is in Christ, he is a new creation; the old has gone,
the new has come! All this is from God, who reconciled us to himself through
Christ and gave us the ministry of reconciliation.* 2 CORINTHIANS 5:17–18

Will-power does not change men. Time does not change men. Christ does.
HENRY DRUMMOND

Think about it: you can be made new! Even if you have failed in business.
Even if you have experienced broken relationships. Even if you turned your back
on God and did exactly what you wanted to do—even though you knew those
things were wrong.

Everyone living has experienced a natural birth. But just as Jesus promised
Nicodemus in a late night meeting (see John 2), we can also be reborn, born into
the Kingdom of God, becoming His children by spiritual rebirth. What a gift!

With this new status as children of God, we receive a new purpose, a new
mission in life. In Matthew 28:19–20, Jesus tells His disciples—and us—to take
the good news of forgiveness and new beginnings throughout the world: to
our own family and friends, to our next-door neighbors, to our co-workers, and
every other person we know and meet. We become ambassadors for Christ's
message of new life, sharing this message of hope with a world that desperately
needs hope!

Lord, thank You for saving me and for giving
me the precious opportunity of sharing the love
You have given to me with others. Amen.

In the Beginning

In the beginning God created the heavens and the earth.
GENESIS 1:1

All glory comes from daring to begin.
EUGENE F. WARE

When we discuss the economy and new jobs, invariably entrepreneurs and small business owners are mentioned. Those brave souls who leave the security of an established company—and regular paycheck—to start a new venture.

We can admire men and women who dare a bold new beginning, but the ultimate Entrepreneur, the original Entrepreneur, the One who gave the most to accomplish the most is none other than God, the Creator of the universe and all that is. Now that's a business story, a love story, and a grand adventure rolled into one.

When was the last time you praised God the Creator? When was the last time you thanked God for creating *you*?

God, I'm in awe of Your creativity. I ask You for a
heart of gratitude for the world You have given me
and for creating me the way You did. Amen.

New Beginnings

Forget the former things; do not dwell on the past. See, I am doing a new thing! Now it springs up; do you not perceive it? I am making a way in the desert and streams in the wasteland. Isaiah 43:18–19

Always bear in mind that your own resolution to succeed is more important than any one thing. Abraham Lincoln

God promised that He will transform us when we become part of His family. He will do a new thing in us and He will continue to bring forth change that will be for our good and His highest.

God is able to make rivers spring forth in the desert. If He can do that, He can be trusted to cover the messes we made in our past—and supply everything we need for a bright new future. That's the kind of God He is. He is the One who is able to take broken, worn out, failed, dusty experiences—and plant a beautiful garden.

If we want to experience all that He has for us, we must begin with the simple belief that He loves us and wants to do something special in us—no matter what has transpired up to this very moment. One of the ways you show that belief is by seeking His will for your life, trusting Him for His wisdom to make right choices and go in the right direction.

Ready for a fresh start? A new start? Turn to God. He is faithful to guide you to a brand new beginning!

Thank You, God, for Your love that draws me back to You when I've made a mess of my life and for showing me Your power to produce flowing rivers in the desert of life. Amen.

Learning to Wait for God's Best

*The LORD bestows favor and honor; no good thing does he withhold
from those whose walk is blameless. O LORD Almighty, blessed
is the man who trusts in you.* PSALM 84:11–12

*God has wisely kept us in the dark concerning future events and reserved for
himself the knowledge of them that he may train us up in a dependence upon
himself and a continued readiness for every event.* MATTHEW HENRY

Children can be impulsive and often want everything "now!" (So can grown-ups!) It is the wise parent who does not give in to every demand, but rather keeps some things on hold until the time is right.

God deals with us the same way. He makes every good thing available to His children—but only in the right time. As our Father, He loves to prepare us for all that He has for us to know and enjoy. But out of fatherly wisdom, He trains us to trust Him—even when we want something right now—so that we will become mature, Christ-like adults, who are better able to appreciate and enjoy His blessings. He also keeps us from greedy self-centeredness by answering some of our requests with a firm "no."

To try and move ahead of God's perfect plan for us is to deny Him the privilege of teaching us and watching us grow to be like Him.

Father, God, how grateful I am for the good things you have
brought into my life, but even more so, for the blessing of Your
hand of guidance. Help me to wait for You. Amen.

Your Best You

Whatever you do, do it all for the glory of God.
1 CORINTHIANS 10:31

And in the end, it's not the years in your life that count.
It's the life in your years. ABRAHAM LINCOLN

All good things we have are gifts from God. Even the faith with which we respond to God's grace is a gift from Him. All talents and strengths are from Him.

Yet God calls us to use what He has given us. He calls for us to work, acquire, learn, plan, and dream. Some of us aren't comfortable with the thought that God just might be calling us to be ambitious. That doesn't sound godly!

Kindness, love, and service all come first. But what is God telling you to get started, to work on in your life now?

Are you moving forward—or sitting back and relaxing?

Lord, help me walk forward in all that You have for me to do.
Thank You for a bright future! Amen.

Ready for Anything

*That is how it continued to be; the cloud covered it,
and at night it looked like fire.* NUMBERS 9:16

*Faith and obedience are inescapably related. There is no saving
faith in God apart from obedience to God, and there can be no godly
obedience without godly faith.* JOHN MACARTHUR

A Classic Devotional from Alexander MacLaren

We need to hold the present with a slack hand, so as to be ready to fold our tents and take to the road if God will. We must not reckon on continuance, nor strike our roots so deep that it needs a hurricane to remove us. To those who set their gaze on Christ, no present from which He wishes them to remove can be so good for them as the new conditions into which He would have them pass. It is hard to leave the spot, though it be in the desert, where we have so long encamped that it has come to look like home. But we must set ourselves to meet the God appointed change cheerfully, in the confidence that nothing will be left behind which it is not good to lose, nor anything met, which does not bring a blessing, however its first aspect may be harsh or sad.

Heavenly Father, help me to not get so comfortable with my life that I can't move on to new opportunities You set before me. Give me the kind of faith that is ready to go when You call my name! Amen.

The Great Race

*Commit to the L*ORD *whatever you do,*
and your plans will succeed.
PROVERBS 16:3

God has a great race for you to run. Under His care, you'll go
where you've never been and serve in ways you've never dreamed.
But you have to release your burdens. MAX LUCADO

Life has often been compared to a race, and it is often a test of our will, our endurance, and our resilience in the same way a physical race is.

What's the secret of making it to the finish line? Is it determination? Is it trying harder? Is it mustering every ounce of courage we can find? Is it asking great people to help us? Those things all sound great, but we'll never make it to the finish line on our own efforts—even if others help us. In this way the Christian race is different from a marathon or mad sprint.

The Christian life has always been and will always be about trusting God and relying on His power and help, not just to bring us salvation, but to help us take each step of our life journey. That victorious finish will not come by trying harder—but by trusting Him more!

Dear God, I know I can't win the race of life on my own.
I need Your help and guidance every step of the way.
Thank You for being there for me! Amen.

Ask for What You Need

"What do you want me to do for you?" Jesus asked him. MARK 10:51

Children do not find it difficult or complicated to talk to their parents, nor do they feel embarrassed to bring the simplest need to their attention. Neither should we hesitate to bring the simplest requests confidently to the Father.
RICHARD J. FOSTER

A Classic Devotional from Andrew Murray

Our prayers must be a distinct expression of definite need, not a vague appeal to His mercy or an indefinite cry for blessing. It isn't that His loving heart does not understand or is not ready to hear our cry. Rather, Jesus desires such definite prayer for our own sakes because it teaches us to know our own needs better. Time, thought, and self-scrutiny are required to find out what our greatest need really is.

Our desires are put to the test to see whether they are honest and real and are according to God's Word. We also consider whether we really believe we will receive the things we ask. Such reflective prayer helps us to wait for the special answer and to mark it when it comes.

Dear Father, You know my needs at this time in my life.
Help me to fully bring them to You and please
teach me to pray, Holy Spirit. Amen.

I Packed Your Parachute

And whatever you do, whether in word or deed, do it all in the name of the Lord Jesus, giving thanks to God the Father through him. Colossians 3:17

God has created me to do him some definite service; he has committed some work to me which he has not committed to another. I have my mission. I never may know it in this life, but I shall be told it in the next. John Henry Newman

Charles Plumb was a U.S. Navy jet pilot in Vietnam. After seventy-five combat missions, his plane was shot down, and Plumb parachuted into enemy territory, becoming a POW. He survived his ordeal, however, and eventually returned home. While eating in a restaurant one day, he was approached by a scruffy-looking man who said, "You're Plumb! You flew jet fighters in Vietnam and were shot down!"

"How did you know that?" asked Plumb.

"I packed your parachute," the man replied. "I guess it worked!"

Plumb couldn't sleep that night, thinking about the unknown man who'd saved his life. From that day on, he determined to always take notice of—and say thank you to—those who "pack his parachute" each day.

Make the most of each day by thanking those who "pack your parachute" and by making an effort to do the same for someone else.

Father, I know that You can use even the smallest gestures and efforts. Thank You for all the little things people do for me, and help me to be an encouragement to someone else today. Amen.

The God of the Living

He is not the God of the dead, but of the living, for to him all are alive.
LUKE 20:38

I cannot make a new me or a new you, but Christ can make you new and me new, as well, if we decide for Him. FRANK HARRINGTON

Skeptics hounded Jesus with questions and objections to His teachings and ministry. Some undoubtedly had honest questions to discuss; others were simply trying to catch Him in error and undermine Him.

A Sadducee, a teacher who didn't believe in the afterlife, tried to make Jesus look foolish by asking who a woman would be married to in heaven if her first husband died and she had taken a second husband (see Luke 20:27–39).

Jesus simply hijacked the question and made the bold proclamation that all that really matters is whether you—that Sadducee, the other listeners, and each of us reading His words today—have been made new and have personally experienced the power of the Resurrection.

That doesn't happen through having devotions or being a good person. It's a miracle we must ask for and receive as a gift from God.

Have you been made alive?

Father, I pray that You would make me alive through
the power of Christ's resurrection. Amen.

On Top of the World

Every good and perfect gift is from above, coming down from the Father of the heavenly lights, who does not change like shifting shadows. JAMES 1:17

His command is the sure guarantee that He will give what He desires us to possess. ANDREW MURRAY

The highest peak in the country of Wales is affectionately called "the Top of the World." On a visit one summer, the wind blew and the clouds billowed, and all around as far as the eye could see were white spots—sheep dotting every pasture all the way to the lowest valley below. It was a breathtaking sight. No one on earth could create such a scene, not even the best set designer in all of Hollywood. Nothing compares to the intensity and exhilaration we feel when we are actually on top of a mountain.

We will experience mountaintop highs in life—and we will walk through some deep valleys as well. We can't always experience life on top of the world, but the mountaintop moments God grants us—spiritually and through the splendor of his world—will give us reminders of His love when we walk the inevitable valleys that are part of the human journey.

Take time to remember some of those special moments God has brought into your life and be ready to face anything with optimism, hope, and confidence!

Father, thank You for the moments in my life that bring me joy—and thank You for great memories to help me get through those moments that cause me pain. Help me to lean on You when I'm top of the world or walking through the valley. Amen.

God With Us

The LORD your God is with you, he is mighty to save. He will take great delight in you, he will quiet you with his love, he will rejoice over you with singing.
ZEPHANIAH 3:17

The God of Abraham, the God of Isaac, the God of Jacob, the God of Christians is a God of love and comfort, a God who fills the soul and heart of those whom he possesses, a God who makes them conscious of their inward wretchedness, and his infinite mercy. BLAISE PASCAL

We live in a fast-paced, busy, media-saturated, noisy world. Is it any wonder that we really do need a quiet time every day? A time for prayer and God's Word? Because it's too easy to let the noise and activity of modern life cloud and obscure the reality that God is present and in our midst.

How different our lives would be if we walked each step and breathed each breath with the knowledge that God is right beside us. Rejoicing with us. Correcting us. Encouraging us. Loving us.

Do you slow down long enough to sense God's nearness to you?

Lord, thank You for being there for me, for being present in all the moments of my life. Forgive me when I get too busy to acknowledge You. Amen.

A New Song

*Sing to the L*ORD *a new song; sing to the L*ORD*, all the earth.*
*Sing to the L*ORD*, praise his name; proclaim his salvation day after day.*

PSALM 96:1–2

Rejoice, my heart, be glad and sing, A cheerful trust maintain;
For God, the Source of everything, Thy portion shall remain.

PAUL GERHARDT

A Classic Devotional from St. Augustine

Sing to the Lord a new song; his praise is in the assembly of the saints. We are urged to sing a new song to the Lord, as new men who have learned a new song. A song is a thing of joy; more profoundly, it is a thing of love. Anyone, therefore, who has learned to love the new life, has learned to sing a new song, and the new song reminds us of our new life.

The new man, the new song, the new covenant, all belong to the one kingdom of God, and so the new man will sing a new song and will belong to the new covenant.

Lord, You have given me a blessed new life.
May my every word and action be a song of praise to You. Amen.

Praying People

And pray in the Spirit on all occasions with all kinds of prayers and requests.
With this in mind, be alert and always keep on praying for all the saints.
EPHESIANS 6:18

He who has learned to pray has learned the
greatest secret of a holy and happy life. WILLIAM LAW

A Classic Devotional from E. M. Bounds

The people who are so greatly needed in this age of the church are those who have learned the business of praying—learned it on their knees, learned it in the need and agony of their own hearts. Praying people are the one commanding need of this day, as of all other days, if God is to intervene in the world.

In doing God's work there is no substitute for praying. People of prayer cannot be replaced with other kinds of people. People of financial skill, people of education, people of worldly influence—none of these can possibly substitute for people of prayer.

The people to whom Jesus Christ committed the fortunes and destiny of His church were people of prayer. To no other kind of people has God ever committed Himself.

Lord, I don't know what You have in store for me,
but teach me to prepare myself for what's next
through prayer and communion with You. Amen.

What Makes the Difference

Look to the LORD and his strength; seek his face always. 1 CHRONICLES 16:11

Reach boldly for the miracle. God knows your gifts, your hindrances, and the condition you're in at every moment. BRUCE WILKINSON

Already know what you need to do? Already feel a sense of purpose? Already have your eyes on a project or endeavor in your work? Your home life? Your personal development? Your spiritual journey?

Do you already have something to accomplish but fear how you are going to get it done? Whether you will be successful? Whether you have the strength and abilities?

Good! You're in a wonderful place to get started. And there is only one place to start. Turn to God. Tell Him your fears. Tell Him you are not sure you have what it takes. Then ask Him to provide you with His strength, encouragement, and wisdom to get the task done.

Maybe you don't have what it takes. But God does. And that makes all the difference!

Father, thank You for Your strength that meets me where I am.
Please continue to give me grace as I press forward. Amen.

True Confidence

Have I not commanded you? Be strong and courageous. Do not be terrified; do not be discouraged, for the LORD your God will be with you wherever you go.
JOSHUA 1:9

You don't have to be great to start, but you have to start to be great.
ZIG ZIGLAR

Confidence is . . .

Diving off the high dive.

Introducing yourself to someone new in a social gathering.

Attending a workshop or seminar not because it's required at work, but "just because."

Visiting patients in a hospital—or prisoners in a jail—even though you've never met them before.

Looking at someone who has told you about a difficulty he or she is experiencing and asking them, "Can I pray for you right now?"

Confidence means taking bold steps. And each of us can do just that, even if we don't consider ourselves to be very confident. Why? Because God is with us wherever we go.

Lord, help me to do the best job I can for You. Amen.

The Future Is Bright

No eye has seen,
no ear has heard,
no mind has conceived
what God has prepared for those who love him.
1 CORINTHIANS 2:9

The future is as bright as the promises of God.
ADONIRAM JUDSON

No one knows the future. Oh, some economists are better than others at predicting tomorrow's economic conditions; some technology experts are better at predicting what tools we will be using in the days to come; some sociologists are better at predicting societal changes and shifts that are ahead. But no one knows the future.

Except for God. And He knows the plans He has for you. Some of which are greater and more exciting than you can imagine today.

Yes, we should plan appropriately for the future. But we aren't to think about the future with fear and anxiety.

What lies ahead? You already know the answer. With an open and obedient heart, great works and great moments that God has planned specially, just for you!

Dear God, thank You for Your promise of a bright,
meaningful, and surprising future. Amen.

Live Smart

Teach us to number our days aright, that we may gain a heart of wisdom.
PSALM 90:12

*As we trust God to give us wisdom for today's decisions, He will lead us
a step at a time into what He wants us to be doing in the future.*
THEODORE EPP

Some troubles come though we have done nothing to deserve them. An illness. An accident. A betrayal. An act of evil.

But other troubles run our way because we call for them through carelessness, questionable decisions, and sin.

In Psalm 90, David catalogs how hard life can be, how many woes befall us. He would know. He experienced troubles that were not of his own making, but he also experienced heartache and woe that he brought on himself. No wonder he tells us to live, order, walk our days "rightly" (v. 12). We are wise to heed the words of one who knows.

Are there thoughts or deeds in your life that are inviting trouble?

Oh God, help me to walk with wisdom and
righteousness every day of my life. Amen.

A New Heart

I will give you a new heart and put a new spirit in you; I will remove
from you your heart of stone and give you a heart of flesh.
EZEKIEL 36:26

God became man to turn creatures into sons: not simply to produce
better men of the old kind but to produce a new kind of man.
C. S. LEWIS

Near death, the word came through that a new heart was available. A young man was killed in a motorcycle accident. The older man had his transplant surgery that same week.

With the surgeries came a new life for him. He was suddenly healthier than he had been in years. He regained energy that had been drained. He was joyful and excited about life. And he understood the sacrifice that was made so that he could truly live again.

His comment: "As a Christian, this tragic and joyous experience made me more fully understand that God gave His only Son so that I could have new life, not just here on earth but for eternity. I am grateful to God for the gift of life and the sacrifice that brought this to me."

God gives us new beginnings, but His very best gift of life is the one we will experience throughout eternity.

Father, thank You for the new life You have given me in Christ. Amen.

A Bold Move

Let us run with perseverance the race marked out for us.
HEBREWS 12:1

Why wilt thou defer thy good purpose from day to day? Arise, and begin in this very instant, and say, "Now is the time to be doing; now is the time to be striving; now is the fit time to amend myself." Unless thou dost earnestly force thyself, thou shalt never get the victory over sin. THOMAS À KEMPIS

The easiest step and the hardest step is the first step.

What's keeping you from getting started? Why are you wallowing in a self-destructive attitude or habit that deep down you want to be rid of?

- Someone you won't forgive
- A temptation you run toward rather than away from
- An area of your life that is weak and needs strengthening
- A sin from your past that needs restitution

Is it laziness? Is it procrastination? Is it stubborn pride? Is it a sense of defeat before you even start?

Today is your day. It won't be easy. But you can succeed, with God's help. But you must take the first step.

Lord, I've lived with defeat too long. Please help me make the move, the first step toward recovery and new life. Amen.

Turnaround

I tell you, no! But unless you repent, you too will all perish. LUKE 13:3

A pessimist sees the difficulty in every opportunity;
an optimist sees the opportunity of every difficulty.
WINSTON CHURCHILL

Is it fair to say we live in a lax, permissive, indulgent age? That doesn't include everybody, of course, but many of us put pleasure before discipline in our own habits, our child rearing, and our attitudes toward the behavior of others.

Part of this prevailing attitude is due to our desire not to be judgmental. That is a good impulse. But some of it comes from being too comfortable in our relative wealth and easy lifestyle!

Repentance is turning away from sin and going in an opposite direction. Not all of our choices deal with sin, but nevertheless, the wise person incorporates discipline and even self-denial to grow toward maturity.

In what ways do you need more discipline in your life?

Dear God, it is by Your grace I am saved, but thank
You for giving me the power to make decisions that
help me grow and become stronger. Amen.

A New You

*If we have been united with him like this in his death, we will certainly
also be united with him in his resurrection. For we know that our
old self was crucified with him so that the body of sin might be
done away with, that we should no longer be slaves to sin.*

ROMANS 6:5–6

*God specializes in things fresh and firsthand. His plans for you this
year may outshine those of the past. He's preparing to fill your
days with reasons to give Him praise.*

JONI EARECKSON TADA

Life is filled with experiences where two things—positive and negative—
happen at once.

We move to a new location and leave an old location behind.

A young couple walks down the aisle and exchanges wedding vows, leaving
behind their primary family relationships.

A graduate makes new friends at college but says goodbye to high school
classmates.

Some of these experiences become bittersweet. But one experience that includes
a negative is only positive: salvation. When we receive new life in Christ, something
else, our "old man," that part of us that rebelled against God, is destroyed.

That is one goodbye we will never regret.

Father, thank You for Your redemption and restoration,
for making my heart brand-new. Amen.

February

LOVE

Love Beyond Reason

You did not choose me, but I chose you. JOHN 15:16

He chose us because He loves us, and He loves us because He loves us. He does not love us because we are lovable, but only because He is love. JOHN STOTT

Throughout the Old Testament, God spoke to His people through prophets. Some of the prophets were great orators. Others, like Hosea, communicated truth about God's love and judgment through dramatic events in their own lives.

Hosea was married to an unfaithful wife. She bore the sons of other men. She left him and lived as a prostitute. When she lost her beauty and charm and was sold into slavery, what did Hosea do?

The unthinkable, of course. He acted like God.

He went to the market to redeem her. He bought her not as a slave, but to make her his wife once again. In this act of supreme commitment and mercy, Hosea showed God's people that God still loved them—even though they were not faithful to Him. He loves us the same way, too!

Heavenly Father, Your love never fails. Thank You for redeeming me when I was not faithful to You. Amen.

Love Is a Verb

*Dear children, let us not love with words or tongue
but with actions and in truth.* 1 JOHN 3:18

You learn to love by loving.
FRANCIS DE SALES

If love is a mere emotion, then our love for a spouse, children, even God, is dependent on how we feel about them at a given moment. But feelings are fickle and can be up or down based on factors as simple and mundane as the amount of sleep we've had or whether or not we exercised today.

No wonder people fall in and out of love so much. They are treating love as an emotion or feeling rather than what it really is, an active verb.

God demonstrated His love for us by sending His Son to redeem us. That's no mere act of emotion, but an act that lives out love. Ultimately, we, too, love God and those around us when we actively demonstrate it.

Have you shown someone you love them today?

Dear God, I marvel at how much You love me and at how
You came to redeem me. Help me to love as You do,
with actions as well as words. Amen.

A Deep, Deep Love

And I pray that you, being rooted and established in love,
may have power, together with all the saints, to grasp how wide
and long and high and deep is the love of Christ. EPHESIANS 3:17–19

> *O the deep, deep love of Jesus!*
> *'Tis a heav'n of heav'ns to me;*
> *And it lifts me up to glory,*
> *With You evermore to be.*
> SAMUEL FRANCIS

When everything around us crumbles, we will always have the love of God. No matter how bad we mess up, no matter how unloved—or unlovable—we've been, His love endures forever. His love is so deep that it's incomprehensible. Sometimes the lack of love we give and receive makes it hard for us to accept and understand that God truly loves us. But He does, and His grace can help us understand and live out the loving affection our Father has for us.

The song "O the Deep, Deep Love of Jesus," penned by Samuel Francis in the 1800s, describes this vast love of God. Find comfort in the knowledge that God's love is unconditional and irresistible:

'Tis an ocean vast of blessing,

'Tis a haven sweet of rest.

Father, I know that You love me, but sometimes that
reality is hard to accept. Help me live in Your love today,
and help me share it with others. Amen.

A Beloved Bride

And so we know and rely on the love God has for us. 1 John 4:16

We are His beloved. Let us but feel that He has set His love upon us, that He is watching us from those heavens with tender interest, that He is working out the mystery of our lives with solicitude and fondness. A. B. Simpson

Evangelist and philanthropist George Mueller once said that not once in his marriage did he pass his wife or see her enter a room without love filling his heart. He always saw her as a gift from God, and his love intensified each time they were near each other.

The kind of love between Mueller and his wife is perhaps rare, but still stands as a marker, a reminder, of what God intends between husband and wife.

But what's most amazing is that the Bible refers to Christ's church as His bride. He loves us more tenderly, deeply, and devotedly than the best husband on earth could ever cherish his beloved.

Life suddenly becomes more wonderful when we live in the knowledge that we are as precious to God as a beloved bride.

Thank You, Lord, for Your love for me, Your child.
Help me allow Your love to fill my life with joy,
and help me spread that joy everywhere I go. Amen.

From the Beginning of Time

For God so loved the world that he gave his one and only Son,
that whoever believes in him shall not perish but have eternal life.
JOHN 3:16

The work of Christ on the cross did not influence God to love us, did not
increase that love by one degree, and did not open any fount of grace or mercy
in His heart. He had loved us from eternity, and needed nothing to stimulate
that love. The cross is not responsible for God's love; rather it was His love
which conceived the cross as the one method by which we could be saved.
A. W. TOZER

Mothers love their children before they are even born. Why else would they have names picked out? Rooms brightly painted? Clothes neatly folded and books picked out to read? Rarely does a mother need to be told to love her newborn infant. Even during the terrible twos and the tumultuous teens, mothers steadfastly love their children.

God has loved us—has loved you—from the foundation of the world. You could never be a mere accident or unexpected surprise to Him. He loved you in your mother's womb and He loves you today.

Heavenly Father, I stand in awe of Your love for me.
Thank You for Your never-ending love. Amen.

God Still Speaks

My sheep listen to my voice; I know them, and they follow me.
JOHN 10:27

Stay within whispering distance. If you stray, you won't hear His voice.
AUTHOR UNKNOWN

Throughout the Bible, God interacts intently, intimately with those who seek after Him. He whispered to the prophet Samuel as a young boy. He spoke directly to and through the prophets. He wrestled with Jacob. He called David a man after His own heart and greeted Mary as someone "highly favored." And in Jesus He walked among us, just as He did with Adam and Eve in the Garden of Eden.

Thousands of years later, God is still speaking. He longs to hear from us, His children, in prayer, and He wants to speak back to us. Relationships thrive on communication—regular, quality communication. Through prayer and listening to God through His word, we can experience a loving, thriving relationship with none other than God Himself.

Lord, thank You that You speak to us and seek us out. Thank You for knowing me. Teach me to listen to and follow You. Amen.

You've Been Sent

Moses said to God, "Suppose I go to the Israelites and say to them,
'The God of your fathers has sent me to you,' and they ask me, 'What is his
name?' Then what shall I tell them?" God said to Moses, "I am who I am.
This is what you are to say to the Israelites: 'I AM has sent me to you.'"
EXODUS 3:13–14

Lord, make my life a window for Your light to shine through and
a mirror to reflect Your love to all I meet. ROBERT SCHULLER

Moses was raised and educated in Pharaoh's court as a young nobleman. But when God called him to lead his people from slavery he was terrified. He was afraid to speak, much less lead. He had good excuses. He stuttered. He had a criminal past. He had been abandoned by his mother as a baby.

But then he saw God in a burning bush. One by one his excuses were stripped away. His doubts and questions were answered as only God can answer. And he, a refugee far from home, was sent with a message from God.

You've been sent too. With a message from God. No excuses. No giving in to fear. Are you ready to say yes?

Dear God, I want to be willing to heed Your call. Show me what You would have me do to share Your love with the world. Amen.

God's Love Commended to Us

But God demonstrates his own love for us in this:
While we were still sinners, Christ died for us.

ROMANS 5:8

If we want proof of God's love for us, then we must look first at the Cross where
God offered up His Son as a sacrifice for our sins. Calvary is the one objective,
absolute, irrefutable proof of God's love for us. JERRY BRIDGES

A Classic Devotional from Charles Grandison Finney

So long as we think of God only as One to be feared, not to be loved, there will be a prejudice against Him as more an enemy than a friend. Yet, God would lead us to serve Him in love and not in bondage. He would draw us forth into the liberty of the sons of God. He loves to see the obedience of the heart. He would inspire love enough to make all our service free and cheerful and full of joy.

If you wish to make others love you, you must give them your love. Show your servants the love of your heart, so will you break their bondage, and make their service one of love. In this way God commends His love towards us in order to win our hearts to Himself, and thus get us ready and fit to dwell forever in His eternal home.

His ultimate aim is to save us from our sins that He may fill us forever with His own joy and peace.

Lord, thank You for loving me. Help me to serve You with joy. Amen.

The Unlovables

Therefore, as God's chosen people, holy and dearly loved, clothe
yourselves with compassion, kindness, humility, gentleness and patience.
Bear with each other and forgive whatever grievances you may have against
one another. Forgive as the Lord forgave you. COLOSSIANS 3:12–13

Love means to love that which is unlovable; or it is no virtue at all.
GILBERT K. CHESTERTON

Every living creature has been blessed by God with a way to protect itself. When a sand particle gets inside the oyster's shell, for example, that tiny abrasive becomes life-threatening to the oyster due to its soft, porous tissue. But the oyster secretes an essence from its own life to create a pearl from the grain of sand.

What would happen if we, like the oyster, didn't try to discard the abrasive and unlovable people from our lives—even when we feel threatened—but rather welcomed them as opportunities for God's love to create something beautiful inside us?

Those bothersome people might need you to help them experience God's new life. Likewise, you might need them to develop your patience and godly love. So don't automatically expel difficult people from your life; ask God to help you turn an annoyance into a pearl.

Lord, I want to allow You to work in my life through
any circumstances, even the unpleasant ones.
Teach me to love with Your love. Amen.

Love for God

Your love, O LORD, reaches to the heavens,
your faithfulness to the skies.
PSALM 36:5

Though our feelings come and go, God's love for us does not.
C. S. LEWIS

The young woman sobbed as she told her small group of friends of the divorce she had gone through years before. Remarried and in love with a wonderful man, she had never been treated better in her life. But she could not get over feelings of abandonment from her first marriage and lived in constant fear that once again someone she loved deeply would leave her.

Healing didn't take place all at once but it began in a profound way when one of the women said to her:

"I can't promise you that your husband will be faithful to you and never leave you. I can't even promise you that I'll always be here for you. Humans are not always true. But God is One who will never leave you alone. If you can't trust your husband right now, don't worry about that, and start learning to trust God more. Everything else will fall into place."

Thank You, Lord, for Your faithful love, the anchor of my life. May my entire day be a song of gratitude for Your loving kindness. Amen.

Out of Love

Therefore go and make disciples of all nations, baptizing them in the name of the Father and of the Son and of the Holy Spirit, and teaching them to obey everything I have commanded you. And surely I am with you always, to the very end of the age. MATTHEW 28:19–20

Missionary zeal does not grow out of intellectual beliefs, nor out of theological arguments, but out of love. ROLAND ALLEN

It was a huge pop hit in the 1960s sung by Jackie DeShannon, and was a huge hit again in the 1970s as sung by Dionne Warwick. The Hal David lyrics asserted, "What the world needs now is love, sweet love—no, not just for some, but for everyone." Even if you weren't born yet when the song was a hit in either decade, chances are you know the tune and at least some of the words.

Sentimental and sappy? Maybe. Okay, probably. But perhaps the song was such a hit because it expressed a powerful truth.

We do live in a lost and hurting world. People run to addictions and entertainment to numb their pain. But the heartfelt cry of every human heart is to be loved.

How is God's love shared? Simple. From the heart, words, and service of His people. And what makes that happen is "love, sweet love."

Lord, please give me a heart that longs
to reach others with Your love. Amen.

Pray for Others

As for me, far be it from me that I should sin against the LORD by failing to pray for you. And I will teach you the way that is good and right.

1 SAMUEL 12:23

If we truly love people, we will desire for them far more than it is within our power to give them, and this will lead us to prayer: Intercession is a way of loving others. RICHARD J. FOSTER

A Classic Devotional from E. M. Bounds

People must pray, and people must be prayed for. The Christian must pray for all things, of course, but prayers for people are infinitely more important, just as people are infinitely more important than things. Also, prayers for people are far more important than prayers for things because people more deeply involve God's will and the work of Jesus Christ. People are to be cared for, sympathized with, and prayed for, because sympathy, pity, compassion, and care accompany and precede prayer for people.

Our praying concerns not only ourselves, but all people and their greatest interests, and even the salvation of their immortal souls. Praying is a business that takes hold of eternity and the things beyond the grave. It is a business that involves earth and heaven. All worlds are touched by prayer, and all worlds are influenced by prayer.

Father, thank You for the people in my life, and thank You for knowing their needs. Help me to love others by praying for them. Amen.

Love Sees No Color

There is neither Jew nor Greek, slave nor free,
male nor female, for you are all one in Christ Jesus.
GALATIANS 3:28

Hatred paralyzes life; love releases it. Hatred confuses life;
love harmonizes it. Hatred darkens life; love illuminates it.
MARTIN LUTHER KING, JR.

It has been said that Sunday morning is the most racially segregated time of the week in America. Whether true or not, and even as far as we've come as a nation in turning from racism, all of us as individuals still have room to grow in our love for those who are superficially different from us. God makes no distinction among colors, races, or nationalities. God loves all types of people, and He has given everyone on earth the opportunity to experience salvation and follow Him. When Christ looks at someone, He sees the heart, not color or nationality.

Jesus commanded us to love as He loves. He said that our love for each other will serve as proof that we are His disciples. The only way to love as Christ loves is to love without barriers. It might take a little extra effort to get to know people of other backgrounds and love them with God's love, but the rewards are rich.

Lord, help me to love everyone with Your love, and give me
courage to build bridges in my sphere of influence. Amen.

Valentine's Day

How great is the love the Father has lavished on us,
that we should be called children of God! And that is what we are!
The reason the world does not know us is that it did not know him.
1 JOHN 3:1

You can give without loving, but you cannot love without giving.
AMY CARMICHAEL

Plush teddy bears, extravagant flower arrangements, rich velvety chocolates—the signs of Valentine's Day are inescapable in the middle of February. Some think that this particular holiday is not for Christians, that it's a completely secular and commercial occasion. But if God is love—and we know that He is—and if love is a beautiful sign of His work in the world, then maybe we should put even more emphasis on a holiday set apart for celebrating love.

Of course, the love proclaimed on Valentine's Day can stray far from the pure love of God—it can be tawdry, cheap, and conditional. But if you get creative and ask for help from God, you just might find ways to share His unrelenting love with those around you.

Lord, help me to be salt and light in my world,
sharing Your love with others. Amen.

Tough Love

My son, do not despise the Lord's discipline and do not resent his rebuke, because the Lord disciplines those he loves, as a father the son he delights in. Proverbs 3:11–12

God had one Son without sin, but not a single child without the rod. C. H. Spurgeon

Discipline is a somewhat lost concept in our culture. Nowhere is that more evident than in how we raise our children. Those of us who are a little older can remember Dad—or even a teacher—getting out the "board of education" when we got in trouble. It was far from pleasant, but it certainly got the point across.

Solomon, the wisest man who ever lived, tells his son not to be resentful over discipline received from God. He says that a father's discipline is actually a sign of love. Perhaps Solomon was thinking about his own childhood. His father, King David, was a mighty warrior—but was also known to be somewhat indulgent with his children. Maybe Solomon was reflecting on whether a firmer hand of parental discipline would have benefited him in his own life!

Discipline yourself—or leave it to someone else to do that for you. Even if a boss, parent, spouse, friend, or customer won't step up and hold us accountable for our decisions, the good news is we have a Heavenly Father who cares too much about our actions and the state of our heart to just ignore things we do wrong. That's His tough love.

Have you experienced God's chastening? Did you respond with resentment or with an open heart?

Dear God, I don't like to experience discipline in my
life and I too easily get resentful. Help me to learn what
You have to teach me in moments of correction. Amen.

The Language of Love

Carry each other's burdens, and in this way you will fulfill the law of Christ.
GALATIANS 6:2

I have found the paradox that if I love until it hurts,
then there is no hurt, but only more love.
MOTHER TERESA

Author Leo Buscaglia told about a contest he was asked to judge. The purpose of the contest was to find the most caring child.

The winner was a four-year-old child whose elderly next-door neighbor had recently lost his wife. Upon seeing the man cry, the little boy went into the old gentleman's yard, climbed onto his lap, and just sat there.

When his mother asked him what he had said to the neighbor, the little boy said, "Nothing, I just helped him cry."

The Bible tells us to mourn with those who mourn and rejoice with those who rejoice (Romans 12:15). We all have burdens to bear. But one of the ways God helps us bear them is to send us the loving comfort of other people. If you want to experience and live out God's love for you, make your heart available both to receive love and companionship from others and to be a loving presence in someone else's life.

Father, thank You for the gift of love that You bring through others.
Send me to someone I can encourage today. Amen.

A Loving Family

Dear friends, since God so loved us, we also ought to love one another. 1 John 4:11

Let your love grow as God wants it to grow. Seek goodness in others. Love more persons more. Love them more impersonally, more unselfishly, without thought of return. The return, never fear, will take care of itself. Henry Drummond

Have you ever noticed that we tend to be at our very best—charming, kind, considerate—with casual acquaintances and even complete strangers? And then we act our absolute worst—rude, impatient, moody, ungrateful—with those who are closest to us, our family? We fall into the trap of taking for granted those who love us the most.

The good news is that it doesn't have to be that way! In fact, there are two simple steps that will cure the majority of family conflicts—and make any family stronger.

The first step is cultivating a spirit of gratitude. When was the last time you felt thankful for the people living in your home—and said thank you? The second step is simply demonstrating your love. How can you show those in your home through actions that you truly love them? The Apostle James said that faith without works is dead (James 2:17), and in the same way love without actions is empty.

Relationships are among the best of God's gifts to us. We can be good stewards of those gifts by practicing love toward those closest to us.

Heavenly Father, thank You for my family. Help me to express the love I truly have for them. Amen.

A God Who Forgives

Have mercy on me, O God, according to your unfailing love;
according to your great compassion blot out my transgressions.
Wash away all my iniquity and cleanse me from my sin. Psalm 51:1–2

Our Savior kneels down and gazes upon the darkest acts of our lives.
But rather than recoil in horror, he reaches out in kindness and says,
"I can clean that if you want." And from the basin of his grace,
he scoops a palm full of mercy and washes our sin. Max Lucado

A granddaughter timidly approached her grandmother to tell her of something she had done wrong. The two hugged and cried and prayed together. The granddaughter asked for forgiveness and repented of the sin in her life right then. After asking for forgiveness, she promised her grandmother she would never act that way again. Ever.

Her grandmother forgave her and told her how much she appreciated her heart and her intentions. But then she added that she might not be able to keep her promise because as long as we live on earth we will struggle with sin. Then she told her the story of King David and how he had to repent from sin numerous times—even though he was known as a man "after God's heart."

Jesus saves us from our sins. He wants us not to sin. But if we do, we are to confess, repent, and ask for forgiveness, and He says that He is faithful to forgive us.

God's love is a forgiving love and a nurturing love. He delights in seeing His children get it right, even after we have gotten it wrong.

Father, thank You for Your love that always welcomes me back home and helps me find the right path. May my life be pleasing to You today. Amen.

The Healer of a Broken Heart

He heals the brokenhearted and binds up their wounds. PSALM 147:3

In this crazy world, there's an enormous distinction between good times and bad, between sorrow and joy. But in the eyes of God, they're never separated. Where there is pain, there is healing. Where there is mourning, there is dancing. Where there is poverty, there is the kingdom. HENRI NOUWEN

A Classic Devotional from C. H. Spurgeon

There are many sorts of broken hearts, and Christ is good at healing them all. The patients of the great Physician are those whose hearts are broken through sorrow. Hearts are broken through disappointment. Hearts are broken through bereavement. Hearts are broken in ten thousand ways, for this is a heart-breaking world; and Christ is good at healing all manner of heart-breaks.

I would encourage every person here, even though his heart-break may not be of a spiritual kind, to make an application to him who healed the broken in heart. Come hither, ye that are burdened, all ye that labor and are heavy laden; come hither, all ye that sorrow, be your sorrow what it may; come hither, all ye whose hearts are broken, be the heart-break what it may, for he healeth the broken in heart.

God, I know that You can heal my broken heart.
Help me experience Your healing touch today. Amen.

A Loving Touch

Filled with compassion, Jesus reached out his hand and touched the man. MARK 1:41

Our God is not made of stone. His heart is the most sensitive and tender of all. No act goes unnoticed, no matter how insignificant or small. A cup of cold water is enough to put tears in the eyes of God. God celebrates our feeble expressions of gratitude. RICHARD J. FOSTER

For many of us, God is more an idea, a principle, a concept, a distant thought than He is a Person. A real, live, feeling Person.

No wonder we forget that God loves us not in principle—but with feeling! Think back to childhood; to climbing up on your father's lap and experiencing the strength and warmth of his arms as he held you and read to you or asked about your day at school. Even if that wasn't your exact experience, you get the picture. How lovely to know that our Heavenly Father cares that much.

There are many stories throughout the Gospels about people being touched by the Lord: Jesus feeding the five thousand and calming the storm; Jesus healing a boy who was paralyzed; Jesus raising Jairus' daughter from her deathbed; and Jesus healing the blind man are just a few. The examples of Him reaching out and touching people demonstrate His personality and passion. And He continues to touch His children in a multitude of ways today.

Our God isn't an abstract principle, but He is definitely a "hands-on" God!

Lord Jesus, how blessed I am to have a Savior who came down from heaven and walked among His people. Thank You for being available to me, for loving me in so many practical ways. I love You. Amen.

Love Is Costly

My command is this: Love each other as I have loved you.
JOHN 15:12

Whoever loves much, does much.
THOMAS À KEMPIS

He had little himself, but he knew that the young Chinese mother he encountered had nothing at all. The woman looked so weak from starvation. He wondered if she would live through the night. She held a tiny baby girl in her arms. He handed the mother all the food he had, a cooked sweet potato. The young mother took a bite of the potato, chewed it carefully—and then pressed the warm food into her baby's mouth. She repeated the process again and again, not keeping a single bite for herself. Sadly, the mother died during the night. But the little girl lived.

Jesus said, "Greater love has no one than this, than to lay down one's life for his friends" (John 15:13). He Himself went on to give His life so that we could live eternally with Him. We may never have to die for someone we love. But with God's help, we can learn to love others sacrificially, reflecting His perfect love.

Dear Lord, help me love others the way You have loved me. Amen.

What Matters Most

Jesus replied: "'Love the Lord your God with all your heart and with all your soul and with all your mind.' This is the first and greatest commandment. And the second is like it: 'Love your neighbor as yourself.'" MATTHEW 22:37–39

Let your religion be less of a theory and more of a love affair. G. K. CHESTERTON

Some people claim to love God but have a strong aversion to "religion." But we are called to be part of the body of Christ, so an isolated faith isn't part of God's plan. However, the desire to keep things simple isn't so bad. When the religious leaders of His day asked Jesus what matters most, He was able to summarize the Ten Commandments and the entire body of religious law into two simple commands:

Love God with all your heart.
Love your neighbor as yourself.

What more is there? It doesn't get any simpler than that. But don't mistake "simple" for "easy." Jesus Himself showed us the true cost of loving God and others!

Dear God, I do love You with all my heart.
Help me to love my neighbors as You love them. Amen.

For God So Loved You

For God so loved the world that he gave his one and only son, that whoever believes in him shall not perish but have eternal life. John 3:16

God loves each of us as if there was only one of us. St. Augustine

Very few people question that God is loving. But many of these very same people question whether God truly loves—could ever love—him or her. They are certain God hears the prayers of others, forgives others, has plans for others, is patient and loving with others—but not for them.

How about you? Do you know that God not only loves the world but that He loves you? Personally. On a first name basis.

One simple activity that might bring that point home to you in a crystal clear way is to write out John 3:16 but in place of the word "world" insert your own name. For God so loved Lynne ... Amy ... Jessica ... Greg ... Nathan ... Troy ... Then read the verse out loud several times today—and tomorrow. In fact, you might try that right now.

Our life changes when we experience for ourselves the reality that God loves the world—and each individual in it.

Thank You Heavenly Father for loving me so much that if I was the only lost person in the world, You would still die for me. Amen.

The Still, Small Voice

*But I have stilled and quieted my soul; like a weaned child
with its mother, like a weaned child is my soul within me.*

PSALM 131:2

*Are you weak? Weary? Confused? Troubled? Pressured? How is your
relationship with God? Is it held in its place of priority? I believe the greater
the pressure, the greater your need for time alone with Him.* KAY ARTHUR

A Classic Devotional from A. B. Simpson

God said, "Be still, and know that I am God." Then came the conflict of
thoughts for tomorrow, and its duties and cares; but God said, "Be still." As I
listened, it became to me the voice of prayer, the voice of wisdom, the voice of
duty, and I did not need to think so hard, or pray so hard, or trust so hard; but
that "still small voice" of the Holy Spirit in my heart was God's prayer in my
secret soul, was God's answer to all my questions, was God's life and strength for
soul and body, and became the substance of all knowledge, and all prayer and all
blessing: for it was the living GOD Himself as my life, my all.

It is thus that our spirit drinks in the life of our risen Lord, and we go forth
to life's conflicts and duties like a flower that has drunk in, through the shades
of night, the cool and crystal drops of dew. But as dew never falls on a stormy
night, so the dews of His grace never come to the restless soul.

Dear Lord, teach me to quiet my soul so that I can hear Your still,
small voice. Thank You for the peace of Your presence. Amen.

Love Is the Winner

But I tell you: Love your enemies and pray for those who persecute you.
MATTHEW 5:44

Nature teaches us to love our friends, but religion our enemies.
THOMAS FULLER

David Wilkerson's bestselling book, *The Cross and the Switchblade*, is the account of his dramatic and sometimes traumatic encounters with Nicky Cruz, leader of a notorious New York City gang of thugs, the Mau Maus. Ultimately, it was a story of love winning over hate.

One night, when Cruz threatened to use his knife to cut up Wilkerson, he was shocked to hear the preacher tell him that if he did, every piece of his body would scream out how much God and Reverend Wilkerson loved him. That message of love in the face of the hate that ruled his life would not leave the heart and mind of Cruz. And now, for more than fifty years he has walked with God, serving in ministry, telling thousands upon thousands about the power of God's love and how it can transform even the wickedest of sinners.

Hate is powerful and destructive. But love truly is the winner.

Lord, Your love can transform anyone—and I'm grateful
that it has transformed me. Help me be a conduit of Your
love in someone's life this week. Amen.

All My Songs Are Wonderful

I praise you because I am fearfully and wonderfully made;
your works are wonderful, I know that full well. PSALM 139:10

The Good News first of all is that you and I are accepted and loved by God.
From all eternity you and I have been in the mind of God. God's love for us is
utterly reliable and has no conditions whatsoever. CYRIL BROOKS

Irving Berlin has been one of America's best-loved composers with more than one thousand songs in his catalog. In addition to the familiar favorites, "God Bless America," "Anything You Can Do I Can Do Better," and "Easter Parade," he wrote, "I'm Dreaming of a White Christmas," the world's all-time bestselling musical score.

In an interview when he was in his nineties, Berlin was asked, "Is there any question that you've never been asked, but that you would like to be asked?"

"Well, yes, there is one," he replied. "'What do you think of the many songs you've written that didn't become hits?' My reply would be that I still think they are wonderful."

God, too, has an unshakable delight in the things—and people—He has made. Whether or not they're a "hit" in the eyes of others, He thinks each of His children is wonderful!

How might your life be different if you begin to see yourself as a delight to God?

Lord, it boggles my mind that You made me and delight in me.
I pray that this knowledge would sink deep into my heart. Amen.

One Love

*Make my joy complete by being like-minded, having the same love,
being one in spirit and purpose. Do nothing out of selfish ambition or vain
conceit, but in humility consider others better than yourselves. Each of you
should look not only to your own interests, but also to the interests of others.*

PHILIPPIANS 2:2–4

He who is filled with love is filled with God Himself. St. Augustine

There is no "new and improved" magical formula that will make your marriage better in only seven days. It is only when both husband and wife begin to practice the biblical principle of "mutual submission" (see the words of the Apostle Paul in Ephesians 5:17) that love and a marriage can soar. Submission, one of the most difficult habits to cultivate in our self-centered society, simply means: I love you so much, I will look out for your interests before I look out for mine.

God's plan for your life includes personal fulfillment, success, and happiness. But He also asks His children to be strong enough to take the initiative in loving and serving others. Even your spouse! And if you're not married, there are still many people in your life whom you can serve in love.

The good news is that love is still the most poignant and powerful force in the world. So whether your marriage is healthy and thriving, in need of some fine tuning, or in a serious crisis, express to your spouse the love that God has so generously lavished on you—and watch God rekindle the flames of love and romance.

Lord, You love the church—your children—as a husband loves his bride. Help me to love those closest to me with Your love. Amen.

The Greatest of These

And now these three remain: faith, hope and love.
But the greatest of these is love. 1 CORINTHIANS 13:13

All the fruits of the Spirit . . . are summed up in charity, or Christian love;
because this is the sum of all grace. JONATHAN EDWARDS

Some scripture is so clear it needs no interpretation or comment! The focus of the devotions for February has been love. What better way to wrap up the month than to read the famous "love chapter" from the Apostle Paul!

If I speak in the tongues of men and of angels, but have not love,
I am only a resounding gong or a clanging cymbal. If I have the gift of
prophecy and can fathom all mysteries and all knowledge, and if I have a
faith that can move mountains, but have not love, I am nothing. If I give all I
possess to the poor and surrender my body to the flames, but have not love, I
gain nothing. Love is patient, love is kind. It does not envy, it does not boast, it
is not proud. It is not rude, it is not self-seeking, it is not easily angered, it keeps
no record of wrongs. Love does not delight in evil but rejoices with the truth. It
always protects, always trusts, always hopes, always perseveres.
1 CORINTHIANS 13:1–7

Dear God, thank You for all the talents and gifts
You have given me. But thank You most of all for love.
Help love to grow in me every day. Amen.

March

Hope

Falling Stars and Fairies

He who began a good work in you will carry it on to completion until the day of Christ Jesus. PHILIPPIANS 1:6

What gives me the most hope every day is God's grace; knowing that his grace is going to give me the strength for whatever I face, knowing that nothing is a surprise to God. RICK WARREN

Jiminy Cricket told us that we should wish upon a falling star. Peter Pan said that we just need to believe in fairies. Sleeping Beauty knew everything would turn out all right with the kiss of Prince Charming.

We know that we can't really place our hope in a fairy tale. But sometimes we do seem a bit naïve—maybe even childlike—in the things on which we set our hope. The stock market might be a good investment, but it's no place to build your hopes. Jesus warned us against building our houses on sand (Matthew 7:24–27). Likewise, a strong army and defense systems can be comforting, but can we really find total security in military might? God told Zerubbabel that it's not by might but by His Spirit that the world changes (Zechariah 4:6). A pastor? A spouse? A parent? A friend? Again, it's great to have people we can truly count on. But can we truly place all our hopes in people?

There is only one sure foundation we can build our life on, and that is a relationship with God. With God beside you, your life is never hopeless.

Lord, thank You for walking beside me every
step of my journey. Thank You for Your daily grace
that makes all the difference in my life. Amen.

A Sure Foundation

Those who trust in the LORD are like Mount Zion,
which cannot be shaken but endures forever.
PSALM 125:1

God is the only one who can make the valley of trouble a door of hope.
CATHERINE MARSHALL

During the Great Depression many people lost hope in the government, their churches, their families, and even God as the downward spiral of economic disaster engulfed everything they owned. People who had previously been considered upper middle class found themselves standing in soup lines. Those who had ordered their lives around money faced dismal futures, and suicides became common.

Sound familiar? Is it possible that living in a prosperous society tempts us to put our hope in the wrong things?

The truth is that no earthly thing deserves our trust; recent economic woes and front page scandals demonstrate once again that even the most stable institution, person, or system can fail. But when we place our hope in God, we find His protection and renewal even in the deepest valleys of our lives on earth. He alone is a worthy foundation on which to build our lives.

Lord, You are the One who holds my life in Your hands.
Today I put my trust in You. Amen.

All Spiritual Blessings

Praise be to the God and Father of our Lord Jesus Christ, who has blessed us in the heavenly realms with every spiritual blessing in Christ.
EPHESIANS 1:3

Those blessings are sweetest that are won with prayers and worn with thanks.
THOMAS GOODWIN

A Classic Devotional from R. A. Torrey

Jesus Christ, by His atoning death and by His resurrection and ascension to the right hand of the Father, has obtained for every believer in Him every possible spiritual blessing. There is no spiritual blessing that any believer enjoys that may not be yours. It belongs to you now; Christ purchased it by His atoning death, and God has provided it in Him. It is there for you; but it is your part to claim it, to put out your hand and take it. God's appointed way of claiming blessings, or putting out your hand and taking hold of the blessings that are procured for you by the atoning death of Jesus Christ, is by prayer. Prayer is the hand that takes to ourselves the blessings that God has already provided in His Son.

Lord, thank You for Your abundant blessings—including the ones I have yet to experience. Teach me to ask You for what I need. Amen.

A Courageous Hope

Be of good courage,
And He shall strengthen your heart,
All you who hope in the Lord.
PSALM 31:24 NKJV

We can walk without fear, full of hope and courage and strength
to do His will, waiting for the endless good which He is always giving
as fast as He can get us able to take it in. GEORGE MACDONALD

What keeps us from attempting—let alone accomplishing—great things? None other than fear! No wonder the phrase "fear not" is found more than 100 times throughout the Bible. The opposite of fear is courage. But how do you get courage if you're afraid? Unlike the Cowardly Lion, it's not like we can follow the Yellow Brick Road with Dorothy and Toto to see if a wizard will bestow courage on us.

The psalmist tells us that there is something we can do to build our courage: hope in the Lord (Psalm 31:24). There's no other starting point. It's the only thing that enabled David to face Goliath (1 Samuel 17:1–51); Gideon to lead a small rag-tag army against the might Midianites (Judges 6:1–7:25); Joshua to cross the Jordan River and later conquer Jericho (Joshua 3:1–17); Peter to walk on water (Matthew 14:22–29). And it's the only thing that enables you and me to face any giants and challenges that come our way.

Is your hope in God?

Oh Lord, I do put my hope in you this day. Give me the courage and strengthen my heart so I can do something great for You. Amen.

A Glorious Hope

No two Christians will ever meet for the last time.
AUTHOR UNKNOWN

He will wipe every tear from their eyes. There will be no more death or mourning or crying or pain, for the old order of things has passed away.
REVELATION 21:4

Death is not the end for Christians. Oh, no doubt, it is still a time of sharp loss, acute pain, and a throbbing ache that lingers for years and sometimes a lifetime. Perhaps there is no greater sorrow than what is felt over the death of a child.

But woven into the heartache, there is a glorious hope for all who know God and have been redeemed by the blood of Jesus Christ. Death is not the final chapter of life, but rather a doorway into an eternity with God, where every longing of the human spirit is met and fulfilled.

Heaven is a place of no more tears. Death truly is different for God's children.

Father, thank You for the gift of eternal life and the promise of being face-to-face with You in heaven. Amen.

Praying Scripture

I pray also that the eyes of your heart may be enlightened in order that you may know the hope to which he has called you, the riches of his glorious inheritance in the saints. EPHESIANS 1:18

The richness of God's Word ought to determine our prayer, not the poverty of our heart. DIETRICH BONHOEFFER

James, the brother of Jesus, tells us, "The effective, fervent prayer of a righteous man avails much" (5:16). When we face hard times, prayer can sustain us like nothing else—both the prayers of others and the continual prayers we offer for our own situation.

Perhaps one of the most effective ways to pray powerfully is to pray the words of Scripture. Just as Jesus responded to temptation with Scripture, so we can experience spiritual victory with the Word of God.

Pray God's promises and ask for their fulfillment in your life. Pray that those close to you would follow God's path for them. Pray for His kingdom to come, His will to be done on earth as it is in heaven. There can be no better words of comfort, strength, healing, love, and hope than the very words and thoughts of God as revealed in His Word.

Father, God, thank You for Your Word, which is powerful.
I pray that my prayer life would become more powerful and effective.
May my prayers move hearts and mountains. Amen.

Invisible Reality

Hope that is seen is no hope at all. Who hopes for what he already has? But if we hope for what we do not yet have, we wait for it patiently. ROMANS 8:24–25

I believe in the sun even if it isn't shining. I believe in love even when I am alone. I believe in God even when He is silent. AUTHOR UNKNOWN

How can you prove God is real?

The truth is, even though there are wonderful arguments for the existence of God, you cannot prove His existence. You can point to His world and His works, but He is invisible. Some have heard Him speak in an audible voice, but again, no one has caught God on an audio recorder.

Is this a problem? Is it troubling? Not at all! If God could be seen through a telescope or under a microscope, would He be the Almighty God proclaimed in His Word? He's the Creator and as such cannot be studied in the same way as His creation.

Paul asks, "who hopes for what he already has?" He also says, "hope that is seen is no hope at all." Hope is for the deeper, more profound realities that require open hearts and eyes.

Lord, thank You for revealing Yourself to me in my
heart and for the faith to see You. Amen.

Christ Is All

Christ is all, and is in all.
Colossians 3:11

We Recognize No Sovereign but God, and no King but Jesus!
John Adams and John Hancock

A Classic Devotional from C. H. Spurgeon

Christ must be all, as your principal object in life—your chief good. Your great aim must be to glorify Christ on the earth, in the hope and expectation of enjoying Him for ever above. The true Christian will say, "I know that I am bound to be diligent in business; but I want to work for eternity as well as for time. I need something besides earthly riches; I want an inheritance not made with hands, a mansion not built by man, a possession in the skies."

If you can say that Christ is your all, then your treasure will never be gone; for He will never leave you, nor forsake you. Not only in this world, but also in that which is come, you shall be happy and blessed, for you shall be crowned with glory, and made to sit with Christ on His throne for ever.

Help me, Lord, to do everything for You, and thank You for the joy and fulfillment of following closely after You. Amen.

The Value of Hard Work

The plans of the diligent lead to profit.
PROVERBS 21:5

He who labors diligently need never despair,
for all things are accomplished by diligence and labor.
MENANDER

Scripture tells us to rely on God and wait for Him. It tells us that He has blessings for us that we can't earn and that He loves to give gifts to His children.

But there's another principle in the Bible that we shouldn't ignore: the principle of hard work. The book of Proverbs instructs us to look to the ant, who has no "overseer or ruler, yet it stores its provisions in summer and gathers its food at harvest" (6:7–8). If we want a bright future—if we want to enjoy benefits in the short-term as well as the long-term—we have to put our nose to the grindstone and do some work.

So while it's important to wait on God and look to Him for provision, perhaps one of the best things to do while we're waiting is work hard.

Dear Lord, thank You for the blessings in my life. Give me a spirit of diligence and commitment to the tasks in front of me. Amen.

A Shared Hope

And let us consider how we may spur one another on toward love and good deeds.
Let us not give up meeting together, as some are in the habit of doing, but let us
encourage one another—and all the more as you see the Day approaching.
HEBREWS 10:24–25

The Bible knows nothing of solitary religion. JOHN WESLEY

Church attendance is down in America. Fewer people attend and those who attend do so less often. A number of reasons are given, including:

There are more Sunday morning options—golfing, fishing, lake houses, kids' sports, professional sports, television programming, work demands, and more—than there were in a simpler day when more people attended.

The church isn't meeting the needs of people today and isn't relevant.

People have become complacent and comfortable and aren't committed to growing their faith, much less committed to church.

America is changing and is not a Christian nation any longer.

Whether you agree or disagree with any of the reasons given above, one thing is certain: the writer to the Hebrews said that meeting together is essential for the spiritual vitality of believers. He says we need to encourage one another and spur one another on to good deeds.

Do you have a weekly place where you meet with other believers for spiritual growth and encouragement?

Dear Father, help me to commit myself to the body of Christ and help others to grow in their faith—while I grow in my faith, too. Amen.

Prayer Changes Things

Nothing is impossible with God. Luke 1:37

*When we call on God, He bends down His ear to listen, as a father
bends down to listen to his little child.* Elizabeth Charles

A Classic Devotional from Oswald Chambers

We grouse before God, we are apologetic or apathetic, but we ask very few
things. Yet what a splendid audacity a childlike child has! Our Lord says—"Except
ye become as little children." Ask, and God will do. Give Jesus Christ a chance,
give Him elbow room, and no man will ever do this unless he is at his wits' end.
When a man is at his wits' end it is not a cowardly thing to pray, it is the only
way he can get into touch with Reality. Be yourself before God and present your
problems, the things you know you have come to your wits' end over.

It is not so true that "prayer changes things" as that prayer changes me and
I change things. God has so constituted things that prayer on the basis of
Redemption alters the way in which a man looks at things. Prayer is not a ques-
tion of altering things externally, but of working wonders in a man's disposition.

Lord, sometimes I feel overwhelmed and unsure of how things
are going to turn out. But I know that You hear my cries to You.
Help me bring problems to You completely. Amen.

The Secret of Life

The mystery that has been kept hidden for ages and generations, but is now disclosed to the saints. To them God has chosen to make known among the Gentiles the glorious riches of this mystery, which is Christ in you, the hope of glory.

COLOSSIANS 1:26–27

Follow hard after Him, and He will never fail you. C. H. SPURGEON

Mysteries and lost codes have never been more popular than in today's popular entertainment culture. Prophecies, cryptic clues, secret societies, dangerous searches, untapped divine power, buried treasures—all the components of an entertaining thriller.

The world Paul preached to was similar. There was a fascination with mysteries that unlocked godlike power and riches for humans inquisitive enough to solve the difficult and arcane riddles.

Paul wasn't a man to keep a powerful secret for just a few select individuals, to be hidden and protected from the masses. Instead he revealed the identity of the mystery that had eluded humans for generations: Jesus. The mystery solved is Jesus inside your life.

Have you experienced the glory and power of God inside you? You don't even have to search for God. He will find you!

God, I am so grateful that I have discovered
the answer for life in Jesus Christ. Amen.

We Can Trust God

How great is your goodness,
which you have stored up for those who fear you,
which you bestow in the sight of men
on those who take refuge in you.

PSALM 31:19

God has wisely kept us in the dark concerning future events and
reserved for himself the knowledge of them, that he may train us up in a
dependence upon himself and a continued readiness for every event.

MATTHEW HENRY

A Classic Devotional from Samuel Rutherford

Duties are ours, events are God's; When our faith goes to meddle with events, and to hold account upon God's Providence, and beginneth to say, "How wilt Thou do this or that?" we lose ground; we have nothing to do there; it is our part to let the Almighty exercise His own office, and steer His own helm; there is nothing left for us, but to see how we may be approved of Him, and how we roll the weight of our weak souls upon Him who is God omnipotent, and when we thus essay miscarrieth, it shall be neither our sin nor our cross.

Lord, I know there are so many things I can't control—but You can.
Help me to do Your will and entrust myself to Your care. Amen.

The Right Armor

But since we belong to the day, let us be self-controlled, putting on faith and
love as a breastplate, and the hope of salvation as a helmet.
1 THESSALONIANS 5:8

God hath in Himself all power to defend you, all wisdom to direct you,
all mercy to pardon you, all grace to enrich you, all righteousness to clothe you,
all goodness to supply you, and all happiness to crown you.
THOMAS BROOKS

God sees us in our need, saves us from our sins, and puts us on the right path.
Our life changes for the better. We are thankful. But sometimes we get proud.
And we begin to feel self-sufficient. And we forget that God is the One who
turned our lives around in the first place. We make a mess of things. But God
sees us, hears our call for help, redeems us, and puts us on solid ground again.
And oftentimes, again.

Rather than live in a cycle of defeat, wouldn't it be better to remember—to
never forget—that God is the source of our salvation and strength?

Are you facing life with your own sufficiency? Or are you wearing His armor?

Lord, I acknowledge my need for You. You are my strength
and salvation. Help me to walk humbly with You. Amen.

A Future Hope Changes the Present

*We have heard of your faith in Christ Jesus and of the love you
have for all the saints— the faith and love that spring from the hope
that is stored up for you in heaven and that you have already
heard about in the word of truth, the gospel.*

COLOSSIANS 1:4–5

*In the midst of an ever-changing world, the good news is that the life of faith is
anchored by the power, provisions, and promises of God. Circumstances may
change, but the future is as sure as the character of God himself. No matter
what happens, those who trust in God hope in his word.*

SCOTT HAFEMANN

A Classic Devotional from C. H. Spurgeon

Our hope in Christ will animate our hearts to think often of heaven, for all
that we can desire is promised there. Nevertheless let it never be said of us, that
we are dreaming about the future and forgetting the present, let the future sanctify the present to highest uses. Through the Spirit of God the hope of heaven is
the most potent force for the product of virtue; it is a fountain of joyous effort, it
is the corner stone of cheerful holiness. The man who has this hope in him goes
about his work with vigor, for the joy of the Lord is his strength.

May my hope be only in You, Lord. Amen.

A Beautiful Perseverance

So we fix our eyes not on what is seen, but on what is unseen.
For what is seen is temporary, but what is unseen is eternal.
2 Corinthians 4:18

By perseverance the snail reached the ark.
C. H. Spurgeon

A woman planted a rare rosebush, fussed over it, fertilized it, watered it, and was incredibly disappointed when she saw no reward of her labors. The rose bush simply wouldn't grow.

Then one day she visited her neighbor and discovered that shoots from this bush had pushed through to the other side of the fence and were blooming in splendid beauty there. She thought to herself of some recent disappointments in her prayer life and realized that faith in God is much like her rose bush. You can't always see the results of what God is doing in your life, but if you have patience and perseverance, you will discover that He was creating something beautiful in you all along.

Hope requires perseverance. The rewards found inside us and that await us in heaven are worth any struggles we face here on earth.

God, thank You for giving me so much to look forward to.
Please strengthen my spirit and help me persevere. Amen.

No Worries

*Are not two sparrows sold for a penny? Yet not one of them will
fall to the ground apart from the will of your Father. And even the
very hairs of your head are all numbered. So don't be afraid;
you are worth more than many sparrows.*

MATTHEW 10:29–31

*Every evening I turn my worries over to God.
He's going to be up all night anyway.*

MARY C. CROWLEY

It is believed by some that worrying is a sin. Do you believe that? How could
such a natural and common emotion be a violation of God's will?

Without attempting to answer that question, all of us can argue that worry is rarely,
if ever, helpful—and it is usually detrimental to our quality of life. Worry is bad for
our physical health, bad for our mental health, and it doesn't change anything.

Fundamentally, worry is a lack of faith in God and His protection and provision in our lives. That's why some call it a sin. It is true He doesn't promise to
make everything turn out like we want it to. But He does promise to meet all our
needs and to never forsake us.

Will you believe Him? If so why worry? With God beside us, there are no real
worries.

God You clothe and feed all the birds outside my window,
so I know You care for me. Amen.

A Delayed Hope

*These were all commended for their faith, yet none of them received
what had been promised. God had planned something better for
us so that only together with us would they be made perfect.*
HEBREWS 11:39–40

*It takes some of us a lifetime to learn that Christ, our Good Shepherd,
knows exactly what He is doing with us. He understands us perfectly.*
PHILLIP KELLER

When you were a child or teen, did you ever hope for something with seemingly all of your heart—but it never came to pass? A particular toy. A part in the musical. A certain someone to be your boyfriend or girlfriend.

Even when it comes to temporal desires, Solomon says that, "Hope deferred makes the heart sick, but a longing fulfilled is a tree of life" (Proverbs 13:12). How are we supposed to handle the grown-up disappointment of having noble and spiritually motivated hopes delayed and deferred?

In Hebrews 11 we find a hall of fame of faith. Some received what they were promised, while others didn't—at least not here on earth. And therein lies the secret of maintaining a positive and optimistic sense of hope and expectation when things don't appear to be working out. It's the realization that in eternity, all hope is realized.

Lord, I affirm a positive sense of expectation that
You will do all that You promised in my life! Amen.

Hope Changes Lives

*Through him you believe in God, who raised him from the dead
and glorified him, and so your faith and hope are in God.*
1 PETER 1:21

What oxygen is to the lungs, such is hope to the meaning of life.
EMIL BRUNNER

A self-made millionaire, Eugene Land, forever changed the lives of a sixth-grade class in East Harlem through a simple act of hope. Mr. Land had been asked to speak to a class of fifty-nine sixth-graders. Scrapping his prepared notes, he decided to speak to them from his heart.

"Stay in school," he admonished, "and I'll help pay the college tuition for every one of you." Now that's a speech! And it had an impact for years to come. In a time and place when few students graduated from high school, nearly 90 percent of that class went on to attend and graduate from college!

Hope is powerful. When we cultivate hope and share it with others, we create a brighter future for them and us. Hope truly changes lives.

Father, help me to give away what has been
given to me in abundance: hope. Amen.

The Rescue Boat

Now faith is being sure of what we hope for and certain of what we do not see.
HEBREWS 11:1

The object of hope is a future good which is arduous yet possible to obtain.
It is therefore necessary that the object of hope should be proposed to a man as
something which is possible, in order that he may hope.
THOMAS AQUINAS

Aboard a ship that was sinking, a woman stood with her blind husband as she grasped for the rescue boat. But an officer pushed the man toward the back of the line, yelling, "Women and children only in these boats!" The wife pleaded with him, explaining that he was blind and that she wouldn't get on the boat if her husband couldn't go with her. The officer then waved them both onto the rescue boat.

The man's hope was in his wife whom he could not see, but he trusted her in faith because he knew her and knew the love she had for him. In the same way, we cannot see God here on earth, but we can hope in what we cannot see because of the promises that He has made to us in His Word.

Lord, I can't see You, but I know You're real and at work in my life.
Thank You for the reassurance of Your presence and love. Amen.

A Renewed Strength

But those who hope in the LORD will renew their strength. They will soar on wings like eagles; they will run and not grow weary, they will walk and not be faint. ISAIAH 40:31

When God is our strength, it is strength indeed; when our strength is our own, it is only weakness. ST. AUGUSTINE

In a world that can wear us down mentally, physically, and spiritually, how do we renew our strength? What do we do in the face of too many projects, too many temptations, too many conflicts, and too many other soul- and energy-sapping dynamics at work in life?

The prophet Isaiah ministered to a nation on the verge of collapse. It wasn't just the acute threat from foreign powers—though that was an obvious stressor—but the once proud and righteous country was sinking in a mire created by its own cynicism and corruption. His antidote to spiritual fatigue was simple: Hope in the Lord.

Others might help you. Great. But don't put your hope in them. You might be able to muster some more determination to get the job done. Wonderful. But don't even place your hope in yourself. The only place to turn for a renewed spirit is the One who has given you every good and perfect gift, including any strength or talent you were born with. What a wonderful promise that we can run without growing weary!

So how is your day? How has your week been going? How does this month look to be shaping up for you? Are you hopeful and inspired? Or are you discouraged? Either way, place your hope in the Lord and let Him give you a supernatural strength.

Heavenly Father, You truly are the source of my hope for today, tomorrow, and all the days ahead of me. Thank You. Amen.

Right Desires

You do not have, because you do not ask God. When you ask, you do not receive, because you ask with wrong motives, that you may spend what you get on your pleasures. JAMES 4:2–3

Each time, before you Intercede, be quiet first, and worship God in His glory. Think of what He can do, and how He delights to hear the prayers of His redeemed people. Think of your place and privilege in Christ, and expect great things! ANDREW MURRAY

A Classic Devotional from C. H. Spurgeon

Man is a creature abounding in wants. He is ever restless. At the same time, there are desires in Christians also. To rob the saints of their desires would be to injure them greatly, for by their desires they rise out of their lower selves. Believers desire the best things: things that are pure and peaceful, admirable and elevating. They desire God's glory; therefore, their motives are higher than the motives that inflame the unrenewed mind. Such desires in Christians are frequently very fervent and forceful. Indeed, they should always be so. Desires from the Spirit of God stir the renewed nature, exciting and stimulating it. They make the believer groan in anguish until he can attain the things that God has taught him to long for.

If God will give for the asking but we remain poor, who is to blame? Is not our blame most grievous? Does it not look as if we are out of touch with God when we will not even ask a favor of Him?

God, thank You that You see and listen to my desires when I bring them to You. Thank You for Your goodness in hearing my prayers. I bring all my hopes, wishes, and disappointments to You today, God. Amen.

A Hopeless Hope

Against all hope, Abraham in hope believed and so became the father of
many nations, just as it had been said to him, "So shall your offspring be."
ROMANS 4:18

Hope against hope, and ask till ye receive.
JAMES MONTGOMERY

Abraham is known as the father of our faith. That title didn't come easily! First of all, he left his home in a sophisticated and affluent part of the world because he heard God calling him to a new land. Throughout his story in Genesis, the one constant is that he "picked up his tent stakes" and moved on.

But that was just the beginning of his challenges. When he got to the land, it was filled with warring tribes. Even harder to deal with, he and his wife seemingly could not have children. How do you become the father of a nation when you have no land and no child? But Abraham never gave up—and at an old age received his reward.

Will your faith persevere when you see no immediate results to feed your hope?

Lord, thank You for speaking to me and giving me a vision of my future. Keep my faith and sense of hope strong! Amen.

Hope Out Loud

*But in your hearts set apart Christ as Lord. Always be prepared
to give an answer to everyone who asks you to give the reason for the
hope that you have. But do this with gentleness and respect.*
1 PETER 3:15

Those who stand for nothing fall for anything.
ALEXANDER HAMILTON

"What's wrong with the world today?" is a perennial topic of discussion.
Wars, worldwide strife, death and sickness, natural disasters—ours is truly a
hurting world. Is it worse now than ever? That's another topic of conversation
and debate! But one thing for certain has not changed in the course of history:
the fallen human race needs God.

Perhaps that's why Peter instructed his fellow disciples to be ready to explain
the hope that they had. Knowing—and articulating—that it's God who saves us
and gives us hope for the future is good for our own spiritual life. Sharing—articulating—that reason for hope with others offers them what they need to hear
and is, again, good for our own souls. Are you able to verbally express the reason
you live with hope?

The hope that is in us is not passive; it must be active in order to be effective.
Nurture it within yourself, and be ready and able to proclaim it to everyone you know.

Lord, give me renewed hope in You and the words
to say to share that hope with others. Amen.

A Peek at What We Hope For

But the needy will not always be forgotten,
nor the hope of the afflicted ever perish.
Psalm 9:18

The best we can hope for in this life is a knothole peek at the
shining realities ahead. Yet a glimpse is enough. It's enough to convince
our hearts that whatever sufferings and sorrows currently assail us
aren't worthy of comparison to that which waits over the horizon.
Joni Eareckson Tada

Joni Eareckson Tada is one who understands the real meaning of hope when everything looks hopeless. She was an active young woman on a swimming trip with her sister and friends when she was injured diving into water she didn't know was shallow. The injury to her spinal column left her paralyzed and wheelchair bound for life.

Her story of tragedy and hope is described in her book simply titled *Joni*, one that has helped hundreds of thousands to look upward for a glimpse of hope that is to come. Her story has inspired many to look for that "knothole peek" of hope that we, no matter how challenging our circumstances, find in the living Christ. He does not allow suffering without hope.

Lord, thank You for sustaining me even in the most
difficult and painful circumstances. Teach me to look
to You for hope for the future. Amen.

Too Busy to Worry

Set your minds on things above, not on earthly things.
COLOSSIANS 3:2

It is of no use to say to men, "Let not your heart be troubled," unless you finish the verse and say, "Believe in God, believe also in Christ."
ALEXANDER MACLAREN

The act of hope is so much more enjoyable than the act of worrying. And yet it's often so much easier to mull over our worries than to think about the hope God offers us.

An anonymous quote declares: "Blessed is the person who is too busy to worry in the daytime, and too sleepy to worry at night."

Maybe if we busy our minds with meditating on the goodness of God and how we can serve Him, we'll have less mental energy to worry.

Reading the Psalms, making a list of God's works in our own lives, singing along to a favorite worship song, serving others as a volunteer—there are all kinds of ways to spend our time that cultivate faith in God's promises and keep us from brooding over what may or may not happen.

God, thank You for Your faithfulness.
Help me set my mind on You today. Amen.

Never Fear

So do not fear, for I am with you; do not be dismayed,
for I am your God. I will strengthen you and help you;
I will uphold you with my righteous right hand. ISAIAH 41:10

If the Lord be with us, we have no cause of fear.
His eye is upon us, His arm over us, His ear open to our prayer,
His grace sufficient, His promise unchangeable. JOHN NEWTON

The fear reaction is wired into our brains, a part of our physiology. It's what triggers our fight-or-flight reaction, which can save our lives during sudden life-threatening circumstances. But fear is also an emotion that can interrupt our spiritual progress—and our lives in general—when it slips out of our control.

John, Jesus' "beloved disciple," contrasts fear and love in 1 John 4:18—the two are complete opposites. And if God is love, He is the solution to out-of-control fear. Whatever you're afraid of, surrender that fear to a loving relationship with God. If you're afraid of the past, remember that He makes all things new. If you dread the future, meditate on His providence and plans for you. If you fear the loss of relationship, remember that He will never leave you and ask Him to help you nurture love and closeness with those around you. And if you fear dying or losing someone, remember that He has conquered death.

Fear can be a formidable foe. But God is truly able to help us expel it from our lives.

Father, I know that You can do anything. I ask for Your Spirit to fill me with Your love so that I might be free from fear. Amen.

God Never Sleeps

He will not let your foot slip—he who watches over you will not slumber;
indeed, he who watches over Israel will neither slumber nor sleep.
PSALM 121:3–4

I would rather walk with God in the dark than go alone in the light.
MARY GARDINER BRAINARD

A mother and her four-year-old daughter were preparing for bed one night. The child was afraid of the dark, and the mother, on this occasion, felt fearful also.

When the light was out, the child caught a glimpse of the moon outside the window. "Mother," she asked, "is the moon God's light?"

"Yes," answered the mother.

The next question was, "Will God put out His light and go to sleep?"

The mother replied, "No, my child, God never goes to sleep."

Then out of the simplicity of a child's faith, she said these words, which gave reassurance to the fearful mother: "Well, as long as God's light is on, He's awake, and we might as well go to sleep."

Be comforted today by the knowledge that God is always, always watching over you.

Lord, thank You that You will never leave me.
Help me to rest in Your love tonight as I sleep. Amen.

Today Is Your Day

Then they would put their trust in God
and would not forget his deeds
but would keep his commands.

PSALM 78:7

Living in the present means squarely accepting and responding
to it as God's moment for you now while it is called "today"
rather than wishing it were yesterday or tomorrow.

EVELYN UNDERHILL

A Classic Devotional from Alexander MacLaren

Memory and hope are meant to fit us for work in the flying moment. Both should impel us to the keeping of the commandments of God; for both yield motives which should incline us thereto. A past full of blessing demands the sacrifice of loving hearts and of earnest hands. A future so fair, so far, so certain, so sovereign, and a hope that grasps it, and brings some of its sweet fragrance into the else scentless air of the poor present, ought to impel to service, vigorous and continual. Both should yield motives which make such service a delight.

Heavenly Father, I thank You for my countless blessings.
Because of all You have done for me, give me a
heart to serve others in Your name.

The Miracle

God is our refuge and strength
an ever-present help in trouble.
PSALM 46:1

When God is involved, anything can happen.
CHARLES SWINDOLL

Herman Ostry's barn floor was under twenty-nine inches of water after a flood. He needed a miracle—and fast—to salvage his barn and be ready for winter. He needed to move his entire 17,000-pound barn to a new foundation more than 143 feet away. His son, Mike, devised a lattice work of steel tubing. He nailed, bolted, and welded the lattice on the inside and the outside of the barn, with hundreds of handles attached.

After one practice lift, 344 volunteers slowly walked the barn up a slight incline, each supporting less than fifty pounds. In just three minutes, the barn was on its new foundation. And Herman had his miracle.

If you're holding out for a miracle today, don't be surprised if the one God sends you comes at the hands of your friends and neighbors. We can always count on Him to come through, but He very often uses those nearest to us to see us through a difficult time.

Father, even though I sometimes feel like I'm hoping
against hope, I know You will come through for me.
Help me to see Your hand at work. Amen.

To the End

*God is not unjust; he will not forget your work and the love you
have shown him as you have helped his people and continue to help them.
We want each of you to show this same diligence to the very end,
in order to make your hope sure.* HEBREWS 6:10–11

*Consider the postage stamp: its usefulness consists in the
ability to stick to one thing till it gets there.* JOSH BILLINGS

You haven't run a marathon until you cross the finish line 26.2 miles from the start. You haven't really read a new novel until you turn the last page. You aren't actually married until you exchange vows and the minister declares you husband and wife. You aren't an inventor until you dust off the blueprints you sketched on the back of a napkin and build something.

Throughout the Bible, one of the key themes is finishing strong. Paul ran the race of life to win—even though it meant martyrdom. He was not alone. Of the original apostles, only John died of natural causes. But even he was exiled because of his faith.

Are you as good at finishing as you are at starting? Not every endeavor we start requires our follow-through. Some things don't matter that much. But faith is not one of them.

We may never face physical persecution for our Lord's sake, but each one of us has been called to walk with God, not just for a season, but for all our days. Look to God for hope and strength on your spiritual journey.

Lord, help me to stand firm till the end. Please give me
strength to stand up for You until the end of my days. Amen.

April

STORMS

Rumbling Sounds

I will both lie down in peace, and sleep;
For You alone, O Lord, make me dwell in safety.

PSALM 4:8

'Tis lasting calm, 'tis heavenly rest:
Come, Spirit of the Living God,
And in our spirits shed abroad
The peace that makes the troubled blest.

JOHN BROWNLIE

Even though we teach our children that thunder will not hurt them, the thunder of a violent storm does frighten them, especially during the night. Many a parent has woken in the middle of a stormy night to find a child squirming into the middle of the bed. Sure, it's a little bit of an inconvenience; a little sleep is lost. But there's an unmistakable joy in comforting a child, reassuring him or her that everything will be all right.

As our Heavenly Father, God finds the same joy in comforting us. He loves it when we need Him. He wants to reassure us that He will always provide for us and protect us. And He delights to hear our prayers.

Lord, thank You for being such a perfect, loving parent.
Thank You for Your love and comfort. Amen.

Walking With Peter

*Then Peter got down out of the boat, walked on the
water and came toward Jesus.* MATTHEW 14:30

*What is courage? It is the ability to be strong in trust,
in conviction, in obedience. To be courageous is to step out
in faith—to trust and obey, no matter what.* KAY ARTHUR

Okay, he ended up sinking like a rock, but for just a moment Peter did something amazing. He walked on water.

As amazing as that feat was, perhaps just as remarkable is that he left the boat not in shallow water, not on a beautiful, calm lake day, but in the midst of a storm.

Some argue that an act like that takes stupidity. But really it takes confidence. Not just a loud, self-aggrandizing, boastful kind of confidence, but the kind that truly believes a miracle is going to happen. For Peter, that belief was centered on Jesus. He had seen what He had done before and he trusted He would do it again in his life.

How is your sense of trust? Are you ready to walk on water when the next storm comes?

Heavenly Father, I do trust You and put myself in Your hands.
I know You can do amazing things in my life! Amen.

The Royal Way of Praying

Cast all your anxiety on him because he cares for you.
1 PETER 5:7

How often we look upon God as our last and feeblest resource!
We go to Him because we have nowhere else to go. And then we learn that the
storms of life have driven us, not upon the rocks, but into the desired haven.
GEORGE MACDONALD

A Classic Devotional from C. H. Spurgeon

We should have faith enough to believe that the present trouble, about which we are praying, is sent to us in love by God. We should pray concerning our trials in this way:

"Lord, I have this thorn in the flesh. I beseech You, deliver me from it, but meanwhile I bless You for it; for though I do not understand the why or the wherefore of it, I am persuaded there is love within it. Therefore, while I ask You to remove it, so far as it seems evil to me, yet wherein it may to Your better knowledge work for my good, I bless You for it, and I am content to endure it so long as You see fit."

Is not that a sweet way of praying? This is a royal way of praying. Such an amalgam of prayer and thanksgiving is more precious than the gold of Ophir.

Lord, I believe that You love me, no matter what's going wrong in my life. Help me to rest in Your love in the midst of difficulties. Amen.

God Hears Our Prayers

Be joyful always; pray continually; give thanks in all circumstances,
for this is God's will for you in Christ Jesus. 1 Thessalonians 5:16–18

If you want to see the rainbow, you must first put up with the rain.
Author Unknown

A farmer who lived near London during World War II wrote to the Scripture Gift Mission requesting prayer that no bombs would fall on his small farm. He enclosed a five-shilling offering. He explained that his harvest had been awful, and he didn't have enough money to bring in water for the parched crops. He could not afford another setback without losing his farm. The secretary of the mission wrote back and said he could not ask that his farm be spared but instead would pray that God's will would be done.

Soon afterward the largest bomb in the German arsenal hit the man's farm. The impact was so big that it unearthed a spring. The spring not only amply watered his farm, but also enabled him to share water with his neighbors. And the next year, he enjoyed an abundant harvest. He sent a fifty-pound check to the mission as a thanksgiving offering.

Thank God for unexpected blessings.

Lord, thank You for Your power to work for my good even in the worst of events. I trust You fully to take care of me. Amen.

I Love a Rainy Day

I have set my rainbow in the clouds, and it will be the sign of the covenant between me and the earth. GENESIS 9:13

Today you will encounter God's creation. When you see the beauty around you, let each detail remind you to lift your head in praise. MAX LUCADO

When you have an outdoor wedding or a big family-reunion picnic planned, a rainy day feels like a disaster. But most of the time, there are lots of reasons to love rainy days!

- No yard work, and you don't have to clean the car.
- Things like youth soccer games get cancelled, removing them from an already too-busy schedule.
- They make for a great time to stay inside and read a book.
- The grass is going to be thick and green before the onset of summer heat.
- Newly planted flowers need the water.
- They make us appreciate a bright, sunny day even more.
- We might get to see a rainbow—God's own sign that He will never destroy the earth by water again.

Rainy days. They may or may not be your favorite. But like all other days, they offer something positive. And since all days are God's days, a blessing can always be found in a storm cloud!

Father, thank You for both rain and sunshine in my life. I know that I need both experiences. And thank You that Your presence and blessings are found no matter the weather. Amen.

Peace in the Storm

I said, "Oh, that I had the wings of a dove!
I would fly away and be at rest—
I would hurry to my place of shelter,
far from the tempest and storm."
PSALM 55:6, 8

It is said that in some countries trees will grow,
but will bear no fruit because there is no winter there.
JOHN BUNYAN

Years ago several artists were asked to illustrate the calm in a storm. One that stood out depicted a raging storm at sea near some jagged mountainous rocks. Nestled in one of the rocks' crevasses was a bird resting peacefully, seemingly unaware of the storm's lashes from the tossing sea or the wind that caused the water to spray high above.

God wants us to know the same kind of peace: when the storms of life assail us, we can calmly watch as the crashing waters break and the wind blows spray all around us. He wants us to experience a perfect peace—His peace—trusting that the storm will move on by and that we will be safe in the arms of Jesus.

Dear Lord, I want to experience perfect peace in the middle of life's storms. Be my shelter and refuge, Father. Amen.

Game Day

For physical training is of some value, but godliness has value for all things, holding promise for both the present life and the life to come. 1 Timothy 4:8

True willpower and courage are not on the battlefield, but in everyday conquests over our inertia, laziness, and boredom. D. L. Moody

Athletes love to compete. Nothing beats game day: a brisk fall evening of football, a hot summer day of baseball, a basketball or volleyball game in a packed field house where the winds of winter are forgotten. Game days are what you work for, what you live for as an athlete.

Now practice is a different matter for many of these same athletes. Practice? That's tough! What enormous, beefy football lineman wants to run sprints—better known as "gassers"—on a sizzling August day? What basketball player wants to lift weights in May? What soccer player wants to do sit-ups and planks in December until his or her stomach muscles are quivering? And yet training provides the strength, speed, and agility for a successful game day.

Life is filled with challenges. Some are the training ground in life to build our strength and character so we can face whatever comes our way. Other storms are more like hurricanes: they are the game days of life. They represent the moments when all our training and knowledge is put to the test.

Are you ready for game day?

Dear God, thank You for all the challenges of life that help me grow stronger in spirit and faith. I pray that I will always be ready for whatever life throws my way. Amen.

Keep Going

The LORD our God said to us at Horeb, "You have stayed long enough at this mountain. Break camp and advance into the hill country of the Amorites."
DEUTERONOMY 1:6–7

Keep adding, keep walking, keep advancing; do not stop, do not turn back, do not turn from the straight road. ST. AUGUSTINE

A Classic Devotional from A. W. Tozer

When our Lord said, "One of you will betray Me," thank God those disciples had enough spirituality that nobody said, "Lord, is it he?" Every one of those disciples said, "Lord, is it I?" If they would not have so responded there could not have been a Pentecost. But because they were humble enough to point the finger in their own direction the Holy Spirit fell upon them.

Self-righteousness is terrible among God's people. If we feel that we are what we ought to be, then we will remain what we are. We will not look for any change or improvement in our lives. This will quite naturally lead us to judge everyone by what we are. This is the judgment of which we must be careful. To judge others by ourselves is to create havoc in the local assembly.

I hear the voice of Jesus saying to us, "You have stayed long enough where you are. Break camp and advance into the hill country." This would be a new spiritual experience that God has for us.

Lord, I don't want to stay where I am. Give me the courage and humility to see myself clearly, and thank You for Your unconditional love. Amen.

Nothing to Fear

I sought the Lord, and he answered me;
he delivered me from all my fears.
Those who look to him are radiant;
their faces are never covered with shame.

PSALM 34:4–5

God walks with us. He scoops us up in His arms or simply sits
with us in silent strength until we cannot avoid the awesome
recognition that yes, even now, He is here. GLORIA GAITHER

A little boy had been admitted to the hospital. When his parents briefly left him in the room alone for the first time, his nurse, who knew that he was alone, called his name over the intercom to ask him how he was doing. This was long before the wireless age and electronic gadgetry was new to him. The wide-eyed child sat up in his bed and responded, "Is that You, Lord?!"

Even when we feel all alone and afraid, we can know that God is speaking to us, wanting to know how we're doing, sometimes in mysterious ways. All that's required is the simple belief that God is always near and desires to speak to our hearts.

Lord, thank You for Your nearness. Thank You for
hearing my prayers. Give me an open heart to
hear You and see Your hand in my life. Amen.

God Our Security

For in the day of trouble
he will keep me safe in his dwelling;
he will hide me in the shelter of his tabernacle
and set me high upon a rock.
PSALM 27:5

Let nothing disturb you, let nothing frighten you:
everything passes away except God; God alone is sufficient.
ST. THERESA

The shepherd boy who wrote and played music that touched the hearts of many had grown into a mighty warrior. He was Saul's beloved champion in battle—and yet the disturbed king burned with jealousy and rage at David's exploits.

He needed and wanted David close, but uncontrollable fits would overcome Saul and he would strike out to slay him. David's life was not safe. He lived in a state of vigilant fear, wondering what mood the king would be in at a particular moment.

But even in these unreliable circumstances, David believed God's hand of mercy and protection was on his life—that God would "hide me" or "set me high upon a rock." Few of us live in such an insecure state as David did. But we have troubles of our own. How is your faith?

Lord, You do protect and provide for me in all circumstances of life.
Thank You for Your hand of mercy. Amen.

Pressed, But Not Crushed

We are hard pressed on every side, but not crushed; perplexed, but not in despair, persecuted, but not abandoned; struck down, but not destroyed. We always carry around in our body the death of Jesus, so that the life of Jesus may also be revealed in our body. 2 CORINTHIANS 4:8–10

It is misleading to imagine that we are developed in spite of our circumstances, for we are developed because of them. It is mastery in circumstances that is needed, not mastery over them. OSWALD CHAMBERS

A beloved husband and father died from cancer after years of chemotherapy and radiation, suffering in horrible ways from the effects of both. During that time, he clung to 2 Corinthians 4:8–10 as a source of hope. He prayed the passage constantly and found that it gave him courage to trust and endure.

He was perplexed, but not in despair. He was not forsaken and not destroyed, because he knew that come what may, the end result would be the same: he would be with Jesus and experience the glorious full manifestation of all His promises! His peace and poise under pressure became the touchstone for his family's faith after he was gone.

The good news is that we, too, can experience that hope. No matter what you are facing, God will preserve you and give you strength.

Dear God, with You on my side, nothing can destroy or crush me. Thank You for Your work in my life. Amen.

True Happiness

Is not the LORD your God with you? And has he not granted you rest on every side? . . . Now devote your heart and soul to seeking the LORD your God.

1 CHRONICLES 22:18–19

A life of obedience is not a life of following a list of do's and don'ts, but it is allowing God to be original in our lives. VONETTE Z. BRIGHT

A Classic Devotional from J. C. Ryle

It may be you are struggling hard for the rewards of this world. Perhaps you are straining every nerve to obtain money, or place, or power, or pleasure. If that be your case, take care. You are sowing a crop of bitter disappointment.

Thousands have trodden the path you are pursuing, and have awoke too late to find it end in misery and eternal ruin. They have fought hard for wealth, and honour, and office, and promotion, and turned their backs on God, and Christ, and heaven, and the world to come. And what has their end been? Often, far too often, they have found out that their whole life has been a grand mistake.

For your own happiness' sake resolve this day to join the Lord's side. Shake off your past carelessness and unbelief. Come out from the ways of a thoughtless, unreasoning world. Take up the cross, and become a good soldier of Christ. Fight the good fight of faith, that you may be happy as well as safe.

Lord, I want to run after You today—and every day.
Give me strength and wisdom to turn to You in all
things and make You my only goal. Amen.

When a Storm Isn't Really a Storm

Praise the LORD, O my soul, and forget not all his benefits. PSALM 103:2

God does not give us everything we want, but He does fulfill His promises.
DIETRICH BONHOEFFER

The following words may be upsetting to some. They may feel callous and insensitive. And they may not apply to your feelings and situations, but perhaps they are exactly what you—and all of us—need to read.

Here it is in a nutshell: not all the things that we think are problems are really problems.

We live in a prosperous time when even the "poor" are often wealthier than those who are considered wealthy in another culture. We've become so accustomed to having so much that what once felt like a special blessing now feels like a necessity. Again, this does not apply to all areas of discontent, and it does not mean that demands for fairness are selfish and indulgent. But many of us need to do a reality check on what we think we need to be happy.

How about you? Are you more demanding than giving? Have you turned blessings into necessities? Have you moaned and complained over things that really aren't that big of a deal in the grand scheme of life? Maybe the trouble is not God's goodness but our ability to receive the gifts He gives us.

Dear God, help me to cry for justice and fairness on
the same things that burden Your heart. And help me to
take in stride the petty annoyances of life! Amen.

Why Me?

He causes his sun to rise on the evil and the good, and sends rain on the righteous and the unrighteous. MATTHEW 5:45

Stand still and refuse to retreat. Look at it as God looks at it and draw upon His power to hold up under the blast. CHARLES SWINDOLL

I love God. I serve God. I help out at church. I'm nice to my neighbors. I volunteer in my community. I don't use bad language. I never kick the dog. I'm not greedy; I don't ask for much.

So why me? Why more problems? The car is making funny sounds; my interest rate went up so my mortgage payment is higher; no raises or bonuses at work; my kid needs braces; the doctor wants to run some tests; I think my mom is showing signs of Alzheimer's.

You get the idea. Life doesn't always seem fair. It would seem fair if bad things happened to bad people and good things to good people. But life comes fast. It is both wonderful and difficult—for all of us.

So does it matter that we are loving and serving God? Absolutely! Ultimately, there is a Day of Judgment. Those who live for God will receive an eternal reward and those who ignore God will then be ignored by God. Rain in someone's life is never a sign of God's disapproval. In fact, the storms of life become wonderful days when we display God's presence within us!

Lord, give me grace under pressure. Thank You for reassurance during difficult days. And thank You that they don't last. Amen.

Peace with Myself

We have different gifts, according to the grace given us.
ROMANS 12:6

Through my handicaps, I have found my self, my work, my God.
HELEN KELLER

Some people don't need to fight with anyone to be at war. Their battles are with themselves.

Maybe it was a tough upbringing. Maybe it was a traumatic event. Maybe it was a lost opportunity or relationship. Or maybe their battles within are the result of exalted opinions of themselves.

On this earth, few of us will ever be 100 percent satisfied with who we are and be totally at peace within. As we grow older, we should naturally experience that peace to a greater degree. But when self-warring is strong enough to hinder all other relationships, we need to take a good look inside.

Are you at peace with God? Do you believe He made you the way you are for a purpose? Your answers will lead you to how you need to pray!

God, thank You for making me who I am, with the people You put in my life, and with the plans You have for me. Amen.

Shipwrecked

In the day of my trouble I will call to you,
for you will answer me.
PSALM 86:7

It is the trial of our faith that is precious. If we go through the trial,
there is so much wealth laid up in our heavenly bank account
to draw upon when the next test comes. OSWALD CHAMBERS

Paul knew something about storms. A man of the world and accustomed to international travel before and after his conversion, he experienced plenty of rough waters and on one occasion was shipwrecked. (See Acts 27:39–44.)

On this occasion, Paul and his shipmates had a very specific message from God: obey and you will be saved. Every single person made shore alive—even if the ship itself was torn apart.

When the waters we are sailing on grow turbulent, it's easy to get our eyes off what matters and try some desperation moves. In financial storms, some have stolen and swindled; in relationship storms, some have been unfaithful; in storms at work, some have falsified reports and cheated on margins. The only sure way to get safely to shore is through simple obedience to God's will for our lives.

Lord, give me even greater resolve to do what is
right when storms rage around me. Amen.

With Help from the Holy Spirit

In the same way, the Spirit helps us in our weakness.
We do not know what we ought to pray for, but the Spirit
himself intercedes for us with groans that words cannot express.
ROMANS 8:26

O Holy Spirit of God, abide with us; inspire all our thoughts;
pervade our imaginations; suggest all our decisions; order all our doings.
JOHN BAILLIE

A Classic Devotional from Oswald Chambers

We realize that we are energized by the Holy Spirit for prayer; we know what it is to pray in the Spirit; but we do not so often realize that the Holy Spirit Himself prays in us prayers which we cannot utter. When we are born again of God and are indwelt by the Spirit of God, He expresses for us the unutterable.

Have we recognized that our body is the temple of the Holy Ghost? If so, we must be careful to keep it undefiled for Him. We have to remember that our conscious life, though it is only a tiny bit of our personality, is to be regarded by us as a shrine of the Holy Ghost. He will look after the unconscious part that we know nothing of; but we must see that we guard the conscious part for which we are responsible.

Lord, thank You that Your Spirit is within me,
helping me and drawing me closer to You. Amen.

Different Vantage Points

He who dwells in the shelter of the Most High
will rest in the shadow of the Almighty.
PSALM 91:1

If you want to hear God's voice clearly and you are uncertain,
then remain in His presence until He changes that uncertainty. Often, much
can happen during this waiting for the Lord. Sometimes, He changes pride
into humility, doubt into faith and peace. CORRIE TEN BOOM

After a long flight from the South Pacific, a family picked up their car and began a long drive from California to the East Coast, delighted to see America after several years away. As they neared Tombstone, Arizona, a huge storm reached the height of its intensity; thunder and lightning boomed and flashed ferociously. They were in awe and wanted to get closer to see the majestic beauty as lightning seemed to dance across the sky and around the buildings. It was a different kind of natural display than what they saw in the South Pacific, a display only Creator God could perform, with lightning and thunder in perfect unison.

From one vantage point, a storm poses danger and warrants fear. From another vantage point, storms provide us a beautiful display that entertains and excites the senses. The secret is to see God in the storm.

Father, give me patience and wisdom so that I might see Your
hand at work in my world, creating something beautiful. Amen.

Faithfulness in the Pit

*To the One who remembered us in our low estate
His love endures forever.
and freed us from our enemies,
His love endures forever.* PSALM 136:23–24

*Each of us may be sure that if God sends us on stony paths
He will provide us with strong shoes, and He will not send us out on any
journey for which He does not equip us well.* ALEXANDER MACLAREN

In Genesis 39:1–23 we read the fascinating story of Joseph. This handsome, proud, brilliant, favorite son—he had everything going for him—in an instant lost it all. He was unfairly sold into slavery by his own brothers and become a servant of Potiphar, an Egyptian army commander. Potiphar was so impressed with Joseph that he entrusted all that he had to Joseph's care. But just when things were looking up, Potiphar's wife made things much worse. When Joseph rejected her advances, she took revenge by accusing Joseph of trying to rape her. Predictably, Potiphar had Joseph thrown in jail.

But because Joseph was a man who loved the Lord faithfully, God blessed him even in the pit of prison, and Joseph was soon put in charge of all the other prisoners. Many years and events later, Joseph was made ruler over Egypt.

If there ever was a person who had reason to rage against life's unfairness, it was him. But he was a man with so much faith in God that he conducted himself with a sense of peace and purpose even while living in the pit.

Heavenly Father, You are with me and provide
everything I need—even in the pits of life. Amen.

All Things!

And we know that in all things God works for the good of those who
love him, who have been called according to his purpose.
Romans 8:28

I am mended by my sickness, enriched by my poverty,
and strengthened by my weakness.
Abraham Wright

Our culture craves comfort, the avoidance of pain, easy projects, nothing but success, leisure time, entertainment, fun hobbies, and anything else that can fit under the umbrella of "smooth sailing."

When things don't go right—a slip on ice, conflict with a loved one, a demanding and troublesome boss, a leaky roof, car trouble, financial setbacks—there is a prevailing attitude of surprised anger and resentment, a strong sense that life is unfair and cruel.

Paul, a survivor of every sort of calamity, challenges this mindset. Not only are difficulties inevitable, but they become opportunities to grow—and even become catalysts for great things to happen. Are you convinced that all things work together for good in your life?

Accept discipline. Ask God to help you get the most out of the difficulties you encounter. You might feel pain for a moment, but the long-term rewards will be great.

Heavenly Father, I don't understand why bad things
happen and especially don't understand how You can use
them for good in my life; but You do. Thank You! Amen.

Paid in Full

And God is able to make all grace abound to you, so that in all things at all times, having all that you need, you will abound in every good work. 2 CORINTHIANS 9:8

We are never more like God than when we give. CHARLES SWINDOLL

Along with many others, the Litt family suffered lean times during the Great Depression. In order to keep food on the table, Mr. Litt opened a charge account with the neighborhood grocer. Having an unpaid grocery bill pained and worried the proud father.

When she turned sixteen, Kathryn Litt went to work at the five and dime store to help with family expenses. And out of admiration for the many sacrifices he had made, she also wanted to give her dad a great birthday present, something he hadn't received in several years.

After receiving her first paycheck, she burst through the front door in excitement and handed her father a carefully wrapped present. He couldn't hide his tears when he found inside a neat stack of receipts from the grocery store, all marked "paid in full."

During times of trouble, it's tempting to draw inward in fearful selfishness. But when we react to difficulties with unselfish acts, we make life beautiful—for ourselves and for others, even in the worst of times.

Lord, help me to trust You so much that I am able to give freely to others even in the midst of my own troubles. Amen.

To Be Made Holy

Blessed is the man you discipline, O LORD,
the man you teach from your law.
PSALM 94:12

The vinedresser is never nearer the branches than when he is pruning them.
DAVID JEREMIAH

A Classic Devotional from Andrew Murray

Every child of God must at one time or another enter the school of trial. What the Scriptures teach us is confirmed by experience. They teach us further, that we are to count it a joy when God takes us into this school. It is a part of our heavenly blessedness to be educated and sanctified by the Father through chastisement.

Holiness is the highest glory of the Father, and also of the child. He "chastens us for our profit that we may be partakers of His Holiness." In trial the Christian would often have only comfort. Or he seeks to be quiet and contented under the special chastisement. This is indeed the beginning; but the Father desires something else, something higher. He would make him holy, holy, for his whole life.

Thank You for the challenges You allow in my life to
make me stronger and draw me closer to You. Amen.

The Burden Bearer

For my yoke is easy and my burden is light.
MATTHEW 11:30

Who best bear His mild yoke, they serve Him best.
JOHN MILTON

God tells us that He will bear our burdens, making our yoke easy. It is a promise to His children. But in order to experience His rest, we must first give our burdens over to Him. We do that through prayer, confessing that we cannot carry the weight of life without Him. He wants to bear our burdens for us and make our load light—but only with our permission.

There will be many people in our lives who will offer to carry our burdens. And while they can share in our pain and suffering—and while God often uses others as a means of His grace—people really cannot carry our heaviest burdens for us. They can help, but only Christ can lift the load.

Are you carrying a burden today that is best placed in God's hands?

Father, what a blessing it is to know that Your love for me is so great that You have promised not only to lighten my load, but to lift it, bearing it for me. Thank You for Your grace and compassion. Amen.

Self-Inflicted Storms

Before I was afflicted I went astray,
but now I obey your word.
It was good for me to be afflicted
so that I might learn your decrees.
PSALM 119:67, 71

He remembers our frame and knows that we are dust. He may sometimes chasten us,
it is true, but even this He does with a smile, the proud, tender smile of a Father who is
bursting with pleasure over an imperfect but promising son who is coming every day to
look more and more like the One whose child he is. A. W. TOZER

Life can feel very unfair—but it can feel very fair, too, even in the midst of storms. Not every calamity that comes our way is an accident of nature or a trial God has allowed to help us grow. Some storms are self-inflicted:

Health problems after years of bad eating habits.

Broken relationships after infidelity or a pattern of cruelty.

Financial woes after overspending for years.

Those are storms—but they aren't unfair. But there's still good news. God is a God of second chances. He won't eliminate every consequence of dumb behavior, but He will give us new meaning and purpose in life when we return to Him.

Is there someone in your life who needs to hear again that God gives second chances? If it's you, will you receive His mercy today?

Thank You for forgiveness and for
never giving up on me, God! Amen.

Why Worry?

But seek first his kingdom and his righteousness,
and all these things will be given to you as well.
MATTHEW 6:33

It is of no use to say to men, "Let not your heart be troubled,"
unless you finish the verse and say, "Believe in God, believe also in Christ."
ALEXANDER MACLAREN

In Matthew 6 Jesus told a parable expressing that the lilies of the field and the birds of the air are not concerned about where their food or clothing come from. They are clothed in beauty and eat plenty, even though they do not sow or reap; they have everything they need to live as flowers and birds.

We need to trust God so much that acquiring the daily necessities of life does not feel like a burden to us. If God is great enough to create all that we can see— as well as the vastness of what we cannot see, then He is surely able to provide, as He promised, all that we need to sustain us in life. Now, if you are stewing because you don't have as much as your neighbor, but have a full stomach, that is another matter to deal with on another day.

But be assured, God will provide you with everything you need. So why worry?

Lord, help me to trust You with the cares that sometimes
overwhelm me. Thank You for Your provision for me. Amen.

A Heavy Load, Not a Burden

Come to me, all you who are weary and burdened, and I will give you rest.
MATTHEW 11:28

No one is useless in this world who lightens the burden of it for anyone else.
CHARLES DICKENS

After the loss of her husband, a young widow received a call from a friend who said, "I have no idea what you are feeling now, but I want you to know that even though I don't understand, I am here for you. If all I can do is listen to you cry, or even cry with you, that is what I will do." Together they cried as the woman talked about her dear husband and how much she missed him. Then they laughed and talked about the good memories they both had of him.

You might pass by or sit beside people every day—in your office, in your home, in your church—who are crushed to the core and would love to have someone just listen to them or cry with them. What a great way to lift the burdens that weigh down those around us: to be a friend who reaches out and listens.

Father, You are the burden bearer. Thank You for inviting
me to cast my cares upon You. Help me to ease the
burden for someone else today, God. Amen.

The Master Potter at Work

"Go down to the potter's house, and there I will give you my message." So I went down to the potter's house, and I saw him working at the wheel. But the pot he was shaping from the clay was marred in his hands; so the potter formed it into another pot, shaping it as seemed best to him.

JEREMIAH 18:2–4

The Spirit brings order out of chaos and beauty out of ugliness. He can transform a sin-blistered man into a paragon of virtue. The Spirit changes people. The Author of life is also the Transformer of life. R. C. SPROUL

The potter must remake his vessels when there is a flaw in the clay that will cause it to crack later or when the color smears and he cannot get it to blend perfectly. He knows his craft and he knows when to take it down from his wheel and start all over to remake it into a fine vessel that will appeal to customers and serve the one who buys it.

In the same way, God knows us intimately—He did create us, after all—and knows how to shape us into who He created us to be. He uses different ways—often tests and trials—to make us more like Jesus. The process is lengthy and often painful, but we will be amazed by God's handiwork in the long run if we simply submit to His loving hand.

Lord, I believe that You can make me who You want me to be. Please use the events in my life to teach me to follow You more closely. Amen.

Worse Case Scenario

So he said to them, "Why are you afraid, O you of little faith?" After he got up, he rebuked the winds and the sea, and it became absolutely calm.

MATTHEW 8:26

The saints in heaven are happier but no more secure than are true believers here in this world. LORAINE BOETTNER

Many of Jesus' disciples were fisherman, and they knew from experience that the Sea of Galilee was notorious for its sudden storms. The squall recorded in Matthew 8:23–27 was especially furious. As the high winds whipped up the sea into vicious waves, the disciples grew frightened and frantic.

While all this was happening, Jesus was sleeping calmly in the back of the boat. The disciples finally had to wake Him because they were certain they were about to drown! Jesus woke up calmly and told the storm to be still. And it obeyed Him. He then looked at His disciples and asked why they had such little faith! They were simply speechless.

What did Jesus know that they didn't know? Ultimately, He understood the true worst case scenarios in life are death and an eternity without God. He also knew that His work on the cross would deliver us from these worst case scenarios. Anything else life throws at us is a snap compared to these. No wonder He was at peace. And that's exactly how we can experience peace in the midst of storms.

Lord, I pray that the knowledge of Your eternal love
and protection will so pervade my heart that I can walk
through life's storms with confidence in You. Amen.

Joy Comes in the Morning

Weeping may remain for a night,
but rejoicing comes in the morning.
PSALM 30:5

One thing we may be sure of, however: For the believer
all pain has meaning; all adversity is profitable.
JERRY BRIDGES

A Classic Devotional from C. H. Spurgeon

Christian! If thou art in a night of trial, think of the morrow; cheer up thy heart with the thought of the coming of thy Lord. Our trials will then seem light and momentary afflictions. Let us go on boldly; if the night be never so dark, the morning cometh, which is more than they can say who are shut up in the darkness of hell. Do you know what it is thus to live on the future—to live on expectation—to antedate heaven? Happy believer is to have so sure, so comforting a hope. It may be all dark now, but it will soon be light; it may be all trial now, but it will soon be all happiness. What matters it though "weeping may endure for a night," when "joy cometh in the morning?"

Father, thank You in advance for rolling away the clouds
in my life and bringing joy in the morning. Thank You, also,
for the strength You give in the middle of the darkest night. Amen.

A Whale of a Storm

*Whoever finds his life will lose it, and whoever loses
his life for my sake will find it.* Matthew 10:39

*We know that our reward depends not on the job itself
but on the faithfulness with which we serve God.* John Paul I

He was a faithful prophet of God, full of zeal and integrity. He knew right from wrong. That's why God's call for him to preach to the godless people of Nineveh caught him off guard. He may have had zeal and honor, but compassion and love weren't part of his spirit. So in a fit of anger and rebellion, he disobeyed God and went the opposite direction of Nineveh.

But God was intent that Jonah would follow His command, and He sent a storm and a fish to get him going in the right direction. (See Jonah 1:1–17.)

Amazingly, Jonah's preaching saved a people from destruction—though his preaching never did instill love in his own heart.

The next time a storm forms around you, it just may be an opportunity for you to do something bold for God on behalf of others. After all, those who have survived the storm can bless and help others who are in a storm of their own.

Father, help me to be obedient to Your calling on my life,
and give me eyes of mercy toward others. Amen.

May

PEACE

The Lion and the Lamb

"The wolf and the lamb will feed together, and the lion will eat straw like the ox, but dust will be the serpent's food. They will neither harm nor destroy on all my holy mountain," says the LORD. ISAIAH 65:25

Christ alone can bring lasting peace—peace with God—peace among men and nations—and peace within our hearts. BILLY GRAHAM

Maybe you remember the story of Koko, the female gorilla that raised several kittens as her own, a rare example of an animal—other than a human—caring for babies of a different species. As amazing as that story seems, the Bible describes an era to come when lions and lambs will lie down together. Another image that's completely contrary to nature—or what we expect from nature.

But that's just a highlight of the glorious future when God redeems the earth: there will be peace so perfect that it defies everything we currently know and believe could be possible.

Today, as has been the case throughout human history, we experience discord and enmity. But we have the promise of God's Holy Spirit working within us now, and we have the promise of a glorious peace in the future. That is something that should motivate us to be peacemakers—and something for which to praise God.

Thank You, Lord, for Your promises and for Your redeeming power. I pray that You would transform my heart and make me a peacemaker. Amen.

One Hug to Go, Please

Always try to be kind to each other and to everyone else.
1 THESSALONIANS 5:15

Let us be kind to one another, for most of us are fighting a hard battle.
IAN MACLAREN

The restaurant was crowded. A handful of waitresses tried to serve the many guests. A family of four made rude remarks regarding the service, and the father spoke harshly to his server. She rushed to the back and returned with a tray filled with food. On her return trip, a plate fell from her tray and shattered. After a stunned half-second, the waitress broke down and cried.

From the next table, a woman stood up without a word and gave the waitress a hug. The waitress cried on her shoulder for a few seconds before cleaning up the dish. When the waitress returned to the family's table, the father apologized to her, and a smile returned to her face.

It's funny how the kind actions of others can bring out the best in people, even during difficult circumstances. Whom can you encourage today?

Lord, help me sow the seeds of peace and kindness in my life. Amen.

Hold Yourself Accountable

Great peace have they who love your law,
and nothing can make them stumble.
PSALM 119:165

Do with your hearts as you do with your watches, wind them up
every morning by prayer, and at night examine whether your hearts
have gone true all that day, whether the wheels of your affections have
moved swiftly towards heaven. Oh, call yourselves to account!
Keep your reckonings even, for that is the way to keep your peace.
THOMAS WATSON

When you think of experiencing peace in your life, you probably don't think of words like "discipline" and "accountability." But think again. When you lack discipline in your life, when you don't hold yourself accountable, what results? Usually chaos and problems. In other words, the opposite characteristics of peace.

If you want to experience peace in all its forms, it always begins with God's grace. But on that foundation, God has laid out a framework of plans and decisions within which we can live according to His will. They always require effort in the form of discipline and accountability. But what sounds like it could be a burden becomes a source of great satisfaction and reward.

Heavenly Father, help me to walk in
Your will and ways each step of my life. Amen.

Pursuing Peace

The kingdom of God is not eating and drinking, but righteousness and peace and joy in the Holy Spirit. For he who serves Christ in these things is acceptable to God and approved by men. Therefore let us pursue the things which make for peace and the things by which one may edify another.

ROMANS 14:17–19

One day we must come to see that peace is not merely a distant goal we seek, but that it is a means by which we arrive at that goal. We must pursue peaceful ends through peaceful means.

MARTIN LUTHER KING, JR.

What does a peacemaker look like?
Not self-absorbed and insistent on one's own way;
Generous and happy to share;
Doesn't hold grudges;
Not envious of others' success and blessings;
Doesn't criticize harshly;
More focused on solutions than problems;
Self-confident—doesn't get feelings hurt easily;
Sees the big picture of life, not petty quarrels.
When others see you—and when you look in the mirror—do you see a peacemaker?

Lord, help me to bring peace into all my
relationships and all areas of my own life. Amen.

Spiritual Understanding

*The man without the Spirit does not accept the things that come
from the Spirit of God, for they are foolishness to him, and he cannot
understand them, because they are spiritually discerned.*

1 CORINTHIANS 2:14

*The point of having an open mind, like having an
open mouth, is to close it on something solid.*

G. K. CHESTERTON

A Classic Devotional from A. B. Simpson

This is the special work of the Holy Ghost, to give to us a new spiritual vision
and organ of apprehension; so that the soul directly perceives divine things
and realities. Perhaps the first effect of this divine illumination is that the
things of God become intensely real, and stand out with vividness and distinct-
ness, like figures cut in relief on the wall. The person of Christ, the light of His
countenance, the distinct sweetness of His Spirit, the "peace that passeth all
understanding," the joy of the Lord, the heavenly world, all become to the heart
more actual and intensely vivid than the things we see with our outward eyes,
and touch with our human hands; so that we can say of Christ with the apostle,
"That which we have seen with our eyes, which we have looked upon, and our
hands have handled of the Word of Life."

Lord, I pray that You would enlighten my understanding
and help me see You more clearly. Amen.

Walking in Peace

*Therefore, having been justified by faith, we have peace with
God through our Lord Jesus Christ.* ROMANS 5:1

*A spiritual secret is to learn contentment with the things
God doesn't explain to us.* AMY CARMICHAEL

We are blessed to have two types of peace: the peace of God and peace with God. When Christ shed His blood at Calvary, He paid the price for our peace and reconciliation with God. But in addition to no longer being separated from our Creator, when we walk with Christ in faith, we can experience the peace of God—no matter what is swirling around us.

It's an incredible privilege, knowing that God never forsakes us and being in His presence continuously. We cannot see Him, but we can still know with certainty that He is near as we enjoy His fellowship through prayer and Bible meditation.

God's peace is available to all who will receive Him and allow Him to be an intimate part of their lives. He wants to teach us how to walk in perfect peace. He longs to spend time with us and to be all we need in every situation. He can handle all of our cares and pressures. Have you drawn near to God? Have you leaned on Him with all your needs and concerns? Are you ready to enjoy His peace?

Lord, thank You for the peace of knowing You.
Give me grace to walk more closely with You today
and enjoy Your peace more deeply. Amen.

First Things First

Seek first his kingdom and his righteousness, and all these things will be given to you as well. MATTHEW 6:33

When you put God first, you are establishing order for everything else in your life. ANDREA GARNEY

A Classic Devotional from Oswald Chambers

Immediately we look at these words of Jesus, we find them the most revolutionary statement human ears ever listened to. "Seek ye first the kingdom of God." We argue in exactly the opposite way, even the most spiritually-minded of us—"But I must live; I must make so much money; I must be clothed; I must be fed." The great concern of our lives is not the kingdom of God, but how we are to fit ourselves to live. Jesus reverses the order: Get rightly related to God first, maintain that as the great care of your life, and never put the concern of your care on the other things.

Jesus is not saying that the man who takes thought for nothing is blessed—that man is a fool. Jesus taught that a disciple has to make his relationship to God the dominating concentration of his life, and to be carefully careless about every thing else in comparison to that. It is one of the severest disciplines of the Christian life to allow the Holy Spirit to bring us into harmony with the teaching of Jesus in these verses.

Lord, I want to reorder my thoughts today and
preoccupy myself with knowing and following You.
Thank You for taking care of me as I do so. Amen.

You Are Forgiven and I Love You

*"Come now, let us reason together," says the LORD. "Though your
sins are like scarlet, they shall be as white as snow; though they
are red as crimson, they shall be like wool."* ISAIAH 1:18

*Forgiveness is the answer to the child's dream of a miracle by which what
is broken is made whole again, what is soiled is again made clean.*
DAG HAMMARSKJOLD

Several years ago in Spain, a father named Juan had become estranged from
his son, Paco. After more than a year spent apart, Juan set off to find his son. He
searched for months to no avail.

In a last, desperate effort to find him, the father put a full-page ad in a Madrid
newspaper. It read: *Dear Paco, meet me in front of this newspaper office at noon on
Saturday. You are forgiven. I love you, Your father.*

On Saturday, eight hundred different young men named Paco showed up, all
seeking forgiveness and love from their fathers.

Our world is hungry for reconciliation. The good news is that a message of
acceptance and forgiveness, an offer of peace, can go a long way. With whom can
you share God's acceptance today?

God, thank You that You reach out to us. I pray that You would
use me to create reconciliation and peace in my world. Amen.

The Author of Peace

LORD, you establish peace for us;
all that we have accomplished you have done for us.
ISAIAH 26:12

How completely satisfying to turn from our limitations to a God who has none.
Eternal years lie in His heart. For Him time does not pass, it remains; and
those who are in Christ share with Him all the riches of limitless time and
endless years. God never hurries. There are no deadlines against which He
must work. Only to know this is to quiet our spirit and relax our nerves.
A. W. TOZER

In a study on "peace of mind" performed by Duke University, several factors were found to contribute greatly to emotional and mental stability. Among common-sense indicators like avoiding self-pity and accepting challenges as a part of life, researchers identified other factors of peace of mind, including the ability to forgive and avoid living in the past, and a belief in something larger than oneself. Not surprisingly, these findings support God's recipe for personal peace: accept His will; believe in His love for you and His plan for you; forgive and receive forgiveness; look forward to the future.

No matter what circumstances or habits are waging war on your inner peace right now, God can give you the grace to live in peace in His presence.

Dear God, I need to trust You more to experience Your peace.
I do affirm my absolute faith in You. Amen.

Just Another Night

For to me, to live is Christ and to die is gain.
PHILIPPIANS 1:21

No matter what may be the test, God will take care of you.
C. D. MARTIN

On the night before Nicholas Ridley's execution in 1555, just hours before he was to become a martyr for his faith, his brother offered to remain with him in the prison chamber to help comfort him. But Nicholas declined the offer and replied that he intended to go to bed and sleep the same as he would on any other night of his life. Even his accusers were amazed at his peace and calm.

Ridley was undoubtedly well versed on the life of Paul. The man who took Christianity to the world wrote a letter to the Philippian church that became known as the "epistle of joy"—even though it was written from a prison cell as he was en route to Rome to face his death.

Our lives may not be threatened for the faith we hold dear, but we are still promised a supernatural peace when we lay down our heads at night, resting in the everlasting arms of God.

Father, Your gifts of grace amaze me. Help me to steep
myself so deeply in the knowledge of Your promises and
goodness that nothing disturbs my peace. Amen.

Be Thankful

Let the peace of Christ rule in your hearts, since as members
of one body you were called to peace. And be thankful.
COLOSSIANS 3:15

We should spend as much time in thanking God for
His benefits as we do asking Him for them.
ST. VINCENT DE PAUL

Which comes first—the gift, or the spirit of thanksgiving? Common wisdom says that we get the gift first, then we say thank you for receiving it. While that is true, some gifts will never be recognized or received without a spirit of thanksgiving.

How many people sabotage the blessings in their life because of a crummy attitude? They are dissatisfied and disappointed—and let the world know it—despite a plethora of gifts from God and others all around them.

All of us can be thankful for the many things God has done for us. But there may be deeper levels of spirituality—even more of His nature and goodness—that we can experience through the attitude of gratitude. Have you said thank you to God today?

Lord, thank You for the gifts and blessings
You have lavished on my life. Amen.

The Door of Hope

Never be lacking in zeal, but keep your spiritual fervor, serving the Lord. Be joyful in hope, patient in affliction, faithful in prayer. ROMANS 12:11–12

God is the only one who can make the valley of trouble a door of hope.
CATHERINE MARSHALL

Think about it. If you had everything you wanted, if there were no challenges in your life, if you didn't have any questions about why things are the way they are, and if you didn't feel there was something for you to accomplish that is bigger than your abilities; what would you have to hope for? Nothing, of course. You would already have everything.

We know that's not the way the world works—but sometimes we act and feel as though that's exactly what we believe. We seem surprised by problems and challenges.

We live in a fallen world with fallen people. That accounts for so many of the trials we face. But beyond that, God wants us to live in reliance on Him. For that reason, He doesn't grant our every wish and give us everything our heart desires exactly when we want it. He wants us to grow in the ways that really matter— patience, kindness, self-control, and other fruits of the spirit (see Galatians 5:22–23 for a list).

Don't have everything you want right now? Well, that gives you something to hope for!

Lord, as I work and wait for various blessings in my life,
help me to grow in character and maturity. Amen.

An Invitation to Peace

I will listen to what God the LORD will say;
he promises peace to his people, his saints.
PSALM 85:8

Consider Jesus. Know Jesus. Learn what kind of Person it is you say you
trust and love and worship. Soak in the shadow of Jesus. Saturate your soul
with the ways of Jesus. Let Him overwhelm you with the way He is.
JOHN PIPER

Peace is one of those elusive states of mind that run from us when we chase them. We can't get peace because it is our chief goal. Peace is almost always the result of other decisions we make in life: kindness, forgiveness, sober judgment, and many others.

If we want to experience peace, then there is no better place to start than pursuing the One who is the giver of peace, the Prince of Peace, the One whose sacrifice made peace between God and man—as well as man and man—possible in the first place. If you would pursue peace pursue Jesus. Talk to Him. Listen to Him. Worship Him. Thank Him. Realize He is right beside you, and within you, closer than any human being could ever be to you. Experience peace by experiencing Jesus every day of your life!

Dear God, thank You for sending Jesus to this world to bring
us peace. Thank You that He is in my life now. Amen.

Be of Good Cheer

I have told you these things, so that in me you may have peace. In this
world you will have trouble. But take heart! I have overcome the world.
JOHN 16:33

If our hearts have been attuned to God through an abiding faith
in Christ, the result will be joyous optimism and good cheer.
BILLY GRAHAM

"Don't worry, be happy" may be too simplistic of a formula for life, but the
"be happy" part is definitely a principle from God's Word.

David said: "You have filled my heart with greater joy than when their grain
and new wine abound" (Psalm 4:7). Solomon said: "A cheerful heart is good
medicine, but a crushed spirit dries up the bones" (Proverbs 17:22). Jesus said:
"In the world you will have tribulation; but be of good cheer, I have overcome
the world" (John 16:33 NKJV).

Even if you have some problems and worries that are gnawing at you today,
all the more reason to make a conscious decision to shake off the blues and
embrace a cheerful disposition.

Dear God, thank You for the gift of joy.
I choose happiness in You today. Amen.

Restored Peace

Restore to me the joy of your salvation
and grant me a willing spirit, to sustain me.
PSALM 51:12

Our Savior kneels down and gazes upon the darkest acts of our lives.
But rather than recoil in horror, he reaches out in kindness and says,
"I can clean that if you want." And from the basin of his grace,
he scoops a palm full of mercy and washes our sin.
MAX LUCADO

Nothing erodes personal peace more quickly and profoundly than guilt. Could the fact that our no-fault culture has persistently tried to eliminate guilt as an appropriate response and feeling contributed to the amount of unhappiness there is—in a nation filled with blessings? Certainly we can have feelings of guilt that we don't really need to bear, but the true purpose of guilt is to remind us to make things right, when that we've done wrong, with God and others.

Have guilt feelings robbed you of peace? Is the guilt based on a wrongdoing in your life? If so, all you need to do is ask God—and perhaps another person—for forgiveness to experience His peace again.

Lord, forgive me for any wrongs I've committed.
Restore peace in my life. Amen.

Pursue Unity

Aim for perfection, listen to my appeal, be of one mind,
live in peace. And the God of love and peace will be with you.
2 Corinthians 13:11

All the gifts of prayer, and of preaching; all the zeal, the ardor, the love, the
self-denial in the church, are produced by the same Spirit. There should be,
therefore, unity. The church is united in the agency by which it is saved; it
should be united in the feelings which influence its members.
Albert Barnes

Churches, companies, families, charities, and other groups of people have split apart over the simplest and deepest disagreements. Something as crazy as the color of new carpet in the sanctuary has led some people to leave a church fellowship. To a church situated in the diverse and contentious city of ancient Corinth, Paul writes with instructions to the believers to be of one mind and live in peace. If they will pursue unity, he preaches, they will experience God's peace.

We, too, live in a diverse and discordant culture. Civility has become the exception, not the rule. Rudeness is not only tolerated, it is sometimes applauded. This condition permeates politics, news, and entertainment—and encroaches into every area of community, including church and family.

Are you a peacemaker? Do your words and actions pursue a path of peace? If not, today is a new day to get started.

Heavenly Father, give me the wisdom and
poise to build unity in my world. Amen.

The Paths of Wisdom

Blessed is the man who finds wisdom, the man who gains understanding, for she is more profitable than silver and yields better returns than gold. . . . Her ways are pleasant ways, and all her paths are peace. PROVERBS 3:13–14, 17

Knowledge is horizontal. Wisdom is vertical; it comes down from above.
BILLY GRAHAM

If asked, how wise are you, most of us wouldn't know exactly how to answer. We talk a lot about intelligence, but not very much about wisdom, so we don't always know what wisdom looks like. Solomon gives one sign that helps us recognize wisdom in our own life and the lives of others when he writes of wisdom: "Her ways are pleasant ways, and all her paths are peace" (Proverbs 3:17).

Nobody's life is always and only pleasant. No one walks exclusively on paths of peace. Not even our Lord, Jesus Christ, experienced such a life, and He was the wisest man who ever lived.

But there can still be great insight gained by asking ourselves the question, do my decisions, attitudes, words, and lifestyle create peace or discord? How we answer might suggest something about our current state of wisdom—and how we can become wiser in this world with God's help.

Lord, give me the gift of wisdom that
I may walk in paths of peace. Amen.

The Truce of 1914

Glory to God in the highest, and on earth peace
to men on whom his favor rests. Luke 2:14

To cherish peace and goodwill, to be plenteous in mercy,
is to have the real spirit of Christmas. Calvin Coolidge

It happened in the midst of the fiercest fighting of World War I. The story most remembered was that a German soldier began singing "Stille Nacht" and his solo soon became a chorus as he was joined by English voices singing "Silent Night." A British regiment serenaded the Germans with "The First Noel" and the Germans sang back to them, "O Tannenbaum."

Men from both armies laid down their weapons and crept cautiously and then quickly into No Man's Land to share food, cigars, drinks—and even play a game of soccer together.

Funny how a song about the Savior's birth became a rallying point for peace—right in the middle of a war. But that's exactly why the Baby was born: to bring "peace on earth."

Does your attitude proclaim that you are a person of peace and good will? Is there a person with whom you need to call a truce and be reconciled? Not just for a day but from this point forward?

Lord, thank You for coming to bring us peace. I pray that
You would fill my heart and make me a peacemaker. Amen.

Our Inheritance

I do not give to you as the world gives.
Do not let your hearts be troubled and do not be afraid.
JOHN 14:27

This blessed friend is Jesus; it is his will and plan that we hang
on to him, and hold tight always, in whatever circumstances.
JULIAN OF NORWICH

A Classic Devotional from Dwight L. Moody

Did you ever think that when Christ was dying on the cross, He made a will? Perhaps you have thought that no one ever remembered you in a will. You have been remembered, if you are in the kingdom. Christ remembered you in His will. He willed His body to Joseph of Arimathea, He willed His mother to John, the son of Zebedee—and what a legacy it was! Better than bonds and stocks—and He willed his Spirit back to His Father. But to His disciples He said, "My peace, I leave that with you; that is my legacy. My joy, I give that to you." "My joy," think of it! "My peace give I unto you"—not our peace, but His peace!

Christ rose to execute His own will. If He had left us a lot of gold, thieves would have stolen it in the first century; we never would have got it; but He left His peace and His joy for every true believer.

God, thank You for Your many blessings,
including the inheritance of peace. Amen.

The Promise of Peace

If it is possible, as much as depends on you, live peaceably with all men.
ROMANS 12:18

Anger is an acid that can do more harm to the vessel
in which it stands than to anything on which it is poured.
ANONYMOUS

Jesus' own life was anything but peaceful. He was born in a stable after an arduous journey. His family was forced to flee to Egypt when he was an infant because a madman was murdering baby boys. His father died. He became the most celebrated teacher of his country, drawing the wrath of the religious and political establishment. Ultimately, He died on the cross.

But Jesus brought peace: between God and man; between estranged family members; and even between enemies.

Why don't we see more evidence of it? As long as humans have the freedom to live for or against God, we will not see peace in full bloom. But the seed is planted. Sprigs and shoots can be seen in the most unlikely places. The promise of what is to fully be!

God of peace, thank You for sending the Prince of
Peace to bring hope and promise to the world. Amen.

Every Moment

In repentance and rest is your salvation,
in quietness and trust is your strength. Isaiah 30:15

Let this be your chief object in prayer, to realize the presence of your Heavenly
Father. Let your watchword be: Alone with God. Andrew Murray

A Classic Devotional from Brother Lawrence

[Brother Lawrence] told me, that all consists in one hearty renunciation of everything which we are sensible does not lead to God; that we might accustom ourselves to a continual conversation with Him, with freedom and in simplicity. That we need only to recognize God intimately present with us, to address ourselves to Him every moment, that we may beg His assistance for knowing His will in things doubtful, and for rightly performing those which we plainly see He requires of us, offering them to Him before we do them, and giving Him thanks when we have done.

That, without being discouraged on account of our sins, we should pray for His grace with a perfect confidence, as relying upon the infinite merits of our Lord. That God never failed offering us His grace at each action; that he distinctly perceived it, and never failed of it, unless when his thoughts had wandered from a sense of God's Presence, or he had forgot to ask His assistance.

That God always gave us light in our doubts, when we had no other design but to please Him.

God, thank You for always being near me, for always providing grace.
I know that walking with You will lead me to peace. Amen.

New Shoes

*As a father has compassion on his children, so the L*ORD *has compassion on those who fear him.* PSALM 103:13

God's goodness is the root of all goodness; and our goodness, if we have any, springs out of His goodness.
WILLIAM TYNDALE

In New York City during the Depression years, a little boy of ten was standing before a shoe store, barefoot, peering through the window, and shivering with cold. A lady approached the boy and said, "My little fellow, why are you looking so earnestly in that window?"

"I was asking God to give me a pair of shoes," was his answer.

The lady took the boy by the hand and went into the store. After washing and drying his feet, she tucked them into a pair of socks and bought him a pair of shoes. As she turned to go, the incredulous boy caught her by the hand, and looking up at her with tears in his eyes, he asked: "Are you God's Wife?"

No question, life is hard. But sometimes we lose sight of the truth that God is good, that it is in His nature to give. We can experience His goodness by thanking Him for it, and by reflecting His giving nature to others.

God, You have made my life so good. Help me to bring some of Your goodness into the lives of others. Amen.

The God of All Comfort

[He] comforts us in all our troubles, so that we can comfort those in any trouble with the comfort we ourselves have received from God.
2 CORINTHIANS 1:4

In Christ the heart of the Father is revealed, the higher comfort there cannot be than to rest in the Father's heart.
ANDREW MURRAY

Too much comfort can be a problem, obviously. Too much convenience, too little discipline can cause us to grow complacent, ineffective, unready for challenges that come our way. But there's a different, more necessary type of comfort—the kind of loving care that makes life not only bearable, but joyful. And the Bible tells us that God offers us that kind of comfort in abundance. Paul calls God the "Father of compassion and the God of all comfort" (2 Corinthians 1:3), and David says of the Good Shepherd, "your rod and your staff, they comfort me" (Psalm 23:4).

It's not that God is cushiony and coddling. It's that He has entered our world and taken on our pain. Even if He doesn't take away our hard times, He promises to stay beside us, loving us every step of the way.

And that is a very comforting thought.

Lord, thank You for the comfort of knowing You.
Help me experience Your loving care today. Amen.

Forgive to Live

*Therefore, as God's chosen people, holy and dearly loved,
clothe yourselves with compassion, kindness, humility, gentleness and
patience. Bear with each other and forgive whatever grievances you may
have against one another. Forgive as the Lord forgave you.*

COLOSSIANS 3:12–13

*Learning how to forgive and forget is one of
the secrets of a happy Christian life.*

WARREN WIERSBE

Grudges and grievances. We feel them; we welcome them; we ponder them; they grow; they make themselves at home in our lives. It's almost as if we enjoy them and the drama they bring—but ultimately they sap energy, joy, peace, and spiritual vitality. In fact, we end up being judged in the same way we judge others (see Matthew 7:2). What we think is going to protect our very self is the thing that gnaws at it.

The antidote is simple. Not easy. But simple. Forgiveness. Not holding someone's wrongs against them. Considering their slights and disregard for naught; as if they were never done against us. *I forgive you.* A simple phrase. A different task. But a task empowered and rewarded by God!

Lord, I forgive others as You have forgiven me. Amen.

Peace Within

Be anxious for nothing, but in everything by prayer and supplication,
with thanksgiving, let your requests be made known to God.
PHILIPPIANS 4:6

Where there is peace, God is.
GEORGE HERBERT

A Classic Devotional from T. M. Anderson

Paul would have us understand that Christ imparts a measure of His own peace to our worshipping hearts when we make everything pertaining to life a matter of prayer. We can readily comprehend the possibilities of prayer when we perceive that mortal man can obtain a measure of the peace which the God of Peace possesses in His divine nature. It is not necessary for the children of God to enter heaven in order to enjoy the priceless possession of peace. Christ wills to give the heavenly heritage of His Peace to all the sons of God. He revealed this truth when He said in John 14:27, "Peace I leave with you; My peace I give to you; not as the world gives do I give to you. Do not let your heart be troubled, nor let it be fearful."

Lord, thank You for the gift of peace. Teach me to be still
before You and lay my worries at Your feet. Amen.

Bold Peace

Make every effort to keep the unity of the Spirit through the bond of peace.
EPHESIANS 4:3

Courage is almost a contradiction in terms. It means a strong desire to live taking the form of readiness to die.
G. K. CHESTERTON

Being a peacemaker doesn't make a person a doormat or a pushover; it doesn't mean the person has no backbone or is weak; it doesn't even mean that person will never fight.

Men and women of peace, in fact, have a special strength. They are self-confident and don't create strife by having to try and prove their superiority to others. They are self-sufficient and don't start battles by grasping and grabbing. That means they are able to be generous. They have a strong sense of self-worth and don't feel slighted at every turn of life. They are self-disciplined and don't make messes for others to clean up.

No, creating peace is not for the weak or lazy. It is a bold endeavor of those who are strong in spirit. Are you ready to take the peace challenge?

Dear God, give me the strength that brings peace to my world. Amen.

Changing Names

Then Saul, who was also called Paul, filled with the Holy Spirit . . .
ACTS 13:9

Prayer is the risen Jesus coming in with His resurrection power,
given free rein in our lives, and then using His authority to enter
any situation and change things. OLE KRISTIAN O. HALLESBY

He was educated at the highest levels in both law and theology. He was an international traveler, aware and sophisticated in the ways of the world. A young leader with all the right connections, he was climbing the career ladder at a rapid pace. Devout. Respected. Even feared. But he was a man at war with himself. He was Saul.

On his way to Damascus, a trip where he planned to strike a violent blow against this new branch of the Jewish faith that was spreading like wildfire, he encountered the risen Christ. He was struck blind and Jesus spoke to him in an audible voice: "Saul! Saul! Why do you persecute me?" (Acts 22:7).

From that moment, the persecutor became a preacher; the man who was roiling inside with turmoil came to inner peace. Saul was renamed by God Himself and became Paul. Meeting the risen Lord changes everything!

Thank You for giving me a new life and new
heart when I met You, God. Amen.

It Is Well With My Soul

The Lord gives strength to his people;
the Lord blesses his people with peace.
PSALM 29:11

It is not too much to say that all real growth in the spiritual life—all victory
over temptation, all confidence and peace in the presence of difficulties and
dangers, all repose of spirit in times of great disappointment or loss, all
habitual communion with God—depend upon the practice of secret prayer.
AUTHOR UNKNOWN

In 1873 Horacio Spafford sent his family ahead of him to Europe, planning to join them later. But the ship carrying his wife and four daughters never made it to the U.K. After a collision with another ship, it sank, and Spafford's four daughters with it. His wife survived. Spafford took a ship to France to meet his wife, and when they passed over the site of the shipwreck, the captain showed him the spot where his daughters lost their lives. As he stood, weeping, on the bridge of the ship, God led him to write the words to the classic hymn, "It Is Well with My Soul." The opening lines still provide comfort today: "When peace like a river attendeth my way, when sorrow like sea billows roll, whatever my lot Thou hast taught me to say, it is well, it is well with my soul."

Grief and heartache are real. But even in the middle of tragedy, when we accept God's will and loving care, we can experience perfect peace.

God, please strengthen my trust in You so that I
can rest in Your peace during times of tragedy. Amen.

A Prayer for Peace

The mind controlled by the Spirit is life and peace. ROMANS 8:6

First keep the peace within yourself, then you can also bring peace to others.
THOMAS À KEMPIS

A Classic Devotional from Reinhold Niebuhr

God grant me the serenity
to accept the things I cannot change;
courage to change the things I can;
and wisdom to know the difference.
Living one day at a time;
enjoying one moment at a time;
accepting hardships as the pathway to peace;
taking, as He did, this sinful world
as it is, not as I would have it;
trusting that He will make all things right
if I surrender to His Will;
that I may be reasonably happy in this life
and supremely happy with Him
forever in the next.
Amen.

Lord, I want to live in Your presence at all times, finding my
peace in You. Teach me to live the way You want me to. Amen.

Peace in My Heart

Let us draw near to God with a sincere heart in full assurance of faith, having our hearts sprinkled to cleanse us from a guilty conscience and having our bodies washed with pure water. Hebrews 10:22

God will not lightly or easily lose His people. He has provided well for us: blood to wash us in; a Priest to pray for us, that we may be made to persevere; and, in case we foully fall, an Advocate to plead our cause. John Bunyan

You can do everything right and still not feel at peace in your heart about your relationship with God. Eighteenth-century giant, John Wesley, came to America as a missionary, ministered to prisoners, and preached throughout the English countryside in open-air revival services. He read his Bible and prayed every day. But despite all those efforts, he still felt insecure and unsure of his salvation.

If Wesley had a troubled heart, what hope is there for us? What he discovered was that peace of heart, assurance of our relationship with God, can only come from God Himself, not our efforts. While someone read from Luther's Preface to the Epistle to Romans at a prayer meeting in Aldersgate, he had an experience that changed his life forever: "While he was describing the change which God works in the heart through faith in Christ, I felt my heart strangely warmed. I felt I did trust in Christ, Christ alone for salvation; and an assurance was given me that He had taken away my sins, even mine, and saved me from the law of sin and death." If you're lacking assurance, turn to Christ alone, and your heart, too, can be "strangely warmed."

Lord, I need peace and assurance of Your presence.
Help me to trust in You and not my own efforts. Amen.

Undisturbed

Peace I leave with you; my peace I give you. John 14:27

Peace rules the day when Christ rules the mind. Author Unknown

A Classic Devotional from Oswald Chambers

Are you painfully disturbed just now, distracted by the waves and billows of God's providential permission, and having, as it were, turned over the boulders of your belief, are you still finding no well of peace or joy or comfort; is all barren? Then look up and receive the undisturbedness of the Lord Jesus. If you allow anything to hide the face of Jesus Christ from you, you are either disturbed or you have a false security.

Are you looking unto Jesus now, in the immediate matter that is pressing and receiving from Him peace? If so, He will be a gracious benediction of peace in and through you. But if you try to worry it out, you obliterate Him and deserve all you get. We get disturbed because we have not been considering Him. When one confers with Jesus Christ the perplexity goes, because He has no perplexity, and our only concern is to abide in Him. Lay it all out before Him, and in the face of difficulty, bereavement and sorrow, hear Him say, "Let not your heart be troubled."

Lord, I know that You offer perfect peace.
Help me bring my entire mind to You today. Amen.

June

GOD'S WORD

Book of Books

For the word of the LORD is right and true; he is faithful in all he does.
PSALM 33:4

God has placed the work of His Son in the Word and has communicated this Word to us. When we believe in His Word, we are believing in Him.
WATCHMAN NEE

A Classic Devotional from C. H. Spurgeon

My friends, stand over this volume (the Bible), and admire its authority. This is no common book. It is not the sayings of the sages of Greece; here are not the utterances of philosophers of past ages. If these words were written by a man, we might reject them; but O let me think the solemn thought, that this book is God's handwriting—that these words are God's! Oh, book of books! And wast thou written by my God? Then will I bow before thee. Oh! if you could ever remember that this Bible was actually and really written by God. Oh! if ye had been let into the secret chambers of heaven, if ye had beheld God grasping his pen and writing down these letters—then surely ye would respect them; but they are just as much God's handwriting as if you had seen God write them.

Lord, thank You for speaking to me through Your Word.
Help me to grow in knowledge of it this month. Amen.

The Written Word of God

*So we have the prophetic word made more sure, to which you do
well to pay attention as to a lamp shining in a dark place, until the
day dawns and the morning star arises in your hearts. But know this
first of all, that no prophecy of Scripture is a matter of one's own
interpretation, for no prophecy was ever made by an act of human will,
but men moved by the Holy Spirit spoke from God.* 2 PETER 1:19–21

*God's word in the Bible can have power only because it corresponds to God's
word in the universe. It is the present Voice which makes the written Word all-
powerful.* A. W. TOZER

Some Bible teachers have suggested that we should read the Bible each time as
if we have never read from its pages before. Easier said than done. Passages from
Scripture are entrenched in our culture and have been infused with certain imagery
and emotions, an effect compounded if you grew up in church. But the point is,
behind the words of the Bible beats the heart of God, and we should strive to
encounter His message and meaning in a fresh way every time we open our Bibles.

Maybe a good first step is to slow down. Emphasize small chunks of Scripture
rather than long passages. Go over the words more than once, even out loud if
you'd like. And let their meaning penetrate your heart. The important thing is
that if you've not established the regular practice of reading God's Word, get
started! As you read, realize that God is speaking directly to you.

God, thank You for Your inspired Word. Give me grace
and understanding to allow it deep into my life. Amen.

A Sure Foundation

Therefore everyone who hears these words of Mine and acts on them, may be compared to a wise man who built his house on the rock. Matthew 7:24

When you have read the Bible, you will know it is the word of God, because you will have found it the key to your own heart, your own happiness and your duty. Woodrow Wilson

When the late Queen Victoria was asked the secret of England's greatness, she took down a copy of the Scriptures, and pointing to the Bible, she said, "That Book explains the power of Great Britain." Daniel Webster once affirmed: "If we abide by the principles taught in the Bible, our country will go on prospering and to prosper." These great leaders truly believed that the only sure foundation of a nation's belief and practice was God's Word.

There are plenty of wise books on history's shelf, some of which offer unintentional wisdom and examples of what not to do. But the wisdom of the Bible teaches us not only how to order our earthly lives for maximum gains, but how to align our hearts and spirit with the Almighty God. And that's wisdom of eternal value.

The words of God are truly a firm foundation for nations. And for our lives.

Thank You, God for the solid foundation of Your Word.
Help me to know it well enough to build my life upon it. Amen.

Direct Communication

How sweet are your words to my taste,
sweeter than honey to my mouth!
PSALM 119:103

The Bible is a letter from God with our personal address on it.
SØREN KIERKEGAARD

A Classic Devotional from A. W. Pink

If it were announced upon reliable authority that on a certain date in the near future an angel from heaven would visit New York and would deliver a sermon upon the invisible world, the future destiny of man, or the secret of deliverance from the power of sin, what an audience he would command! There is no building in that city large enough to accommodate the crowd which would throng to hear him. If upon the next day, the newspapers were to give a verbatim report of his discourse, how eagerly it would be read! And yet, we have between the covers of the Bible not merely an angelic communication but a Divine revelation. How great then is our wickedness if we undervalue and despise it! And yet we do.

Lord, thank You that You communicate with us through Your Word.
I want to know Your will, Lord. Amen.

The Creeping Wilderness

He who heeds discipline shows the way to life. Proverbs 10:17

The neglected heart will soon be a heart overrun with worldly thoughts; the neglected life will soon become a moral chaos; the church that is not jealously protected by mighty intercession and sacrificial labors will before long become the abode of every evil bird and the hiding place for unsuspected corruption. The creeping wilderness will soon take over that church that trusts in its own strength and forgets to watch and pray. A. W. Tozer

No great company sets a goal to slide into mediocrity. No in-love newlyweds plan to divorce down the road. No fit, muscular athlete figures how to put on a hundred pounds and get totally out of shape in the next few years. No neighborhood holds a meeting to outline steps toward a rundown community. No committed, vibrant Christian dreams of a day when he or she will walk far from God, living a life of joyless compromise.

The common denominator in all the above too-often-true scenarios is neglect. The wilderness does not swallow up a great city in a day, it creeps closer and closer—through neglect.

Prayer. A community of believers. God's Word. These are neglected at great risk to our souls!

Lord, give me diligence to take care of my soul
and walk ever more closely with You. Amen.

Seek Understanding

All Scripture is God-breathed and is useful for teaching, rebuking, correcting and training in righteousness, so that the man of God may be thoroughly equipped for every good work. 2 TIMOTHY 3:16–17

When you are reading a book in a dark room, and come to a difficult part, you take it to a window to get more light. So take your Bibles to Christ.
ROBERT MURRAY M'CHEYNE

Much of the Bible is easy to understand. Some parts are difficult. Don't let them throw you off. As Mark Twain, not known as a saint or churchman, once said, "It ain't those parts of the Bible that I can't understand that bother me, it is the parts that I do understand."

Still, it's normal to think about and really want to understand harder passages. Here are a few references available:

1. Bible dictionaries: Some words are not part of our modern vocabulary, so knowing their classic meaning helps.
2. Bible handbooks: Some passages are difficult because they are written about and to a culture much different from our own. Knowing about those cultures helps.
3. Bible commentaries: There are scores of verse-by-verse reference books written by biblical scholars to explain nuances and difficult passages.
4. God's Word: Look up passages with similar themes. They will help explain a question you have on a hard passage.

As you read and study, don't forget to pray for understanding. Be patient with yourself and with your questions. Your study is not in vain.

Dear Lord, there are some parts of the Bible I just don't understand. I pray for Your wisdom to hear and heed Your Word. Amen.

Friendship and Fear

The LORD confides in those who fear him;
he makes his covenant known to them. PSALM 25:14

A proper fear of God is that indefinable mixture of reverence and pleasure, joy
and awe which fills our hearts when we realize who God is and what He has
done for us. It is a love for God which is so great that we would be ashamed
to do anything which would displease or grieve Him, and makes us happiest
when we are doing what pleases Him. SINCLAIR B. FERGUSON

Friendship and fear don't naturally go together. You're probably not too scared of the people you call friends. And yet our relationship with God is characterized by both familiarity and formality, closeness and reverence.

Friendship with God is a miraculous gift. In the Old Testament, only a few were said to enjoy friendship with God; in the New Testament, Jesus tells His disciples, "Today I have called you friends." The necessary attitude for anyone who wants to be friends with God is to "fear" Him. This doesn't mean we regard Him as someone who might unpredictably harm us. But it does mean recognizing how much we need Him, how we would be lost without Him, and that He is the center of all life and deserves our respect.

When we fear God—hold Him in reverence and respect—we get to enjoy His company and guidance through prayer and His Word. And that is truly a friendship to celebrate.

Dear God, thank You for reaching out to me. Please cultivate in my heart a healthy fear of You and help me to walk in Your ways. Amen.

Make a Plan

All his laws are before me; I have not turned away from his decrees. Psalm 18:22

For some years now I have read through the Bible twice every year.
If you picture the Bible to be a mighty tree and every word a little branch,
I have shaken every one of these branches because I wanted to know
what it was and what it meant. Martin Luther

Every Bible reader has a favorite verse or book, one he or she returns to often for comfort and wisdom. But as wonderful as those familiar favorites can be, there are countless other precious gems in Scripture waiting to be discovered. The only way to find them is to read what we've never read before. That's why a Bible reading plan can be such a valuable tool for spiritual growth.

Your Bible may have a reading plan near the front that will direct you to finish the whole Bible in one year. If not, there are plenty of other ways to read a wider range of Scripture than you ever have before. Do an Internet search for reading plans; some sites offer plans you can even check off as you go along. Consider Bible software or even a program for your smart phone that can provide you with a passage of Scripture every day. Select an unfamiliar book of the Bible each month and read through it with a friend. Whatever method or plan you use, ask God to help you grow in love for His Word.

God, thank You for speaking to me through the Bible.
Help me to grow more and more familiar with it. Amen.

Soaking in the Word

I lift up my hands to your commands, which I love,
and I meditate on your decrees. PSALM 119:48

Meditation is the activity of calling to mind, and thinking over,
and dwelling on, and applying to oneself, the various things that one knows
about the works and ways and purposes and promises of God. J. I. PACKER

One of the benefits of God's Word is a cleansing and renewing of our minds. How does that happen? Our minds and hearts are pulled away from problems, disappointments, challenges, temptations, failures, resentments, and other negative thoughts and emotions and are redirected to God's thoughts, God's feelings, God's promises, God's principles. But this isn't just an exercise in self-help and guided thoughts. We are told in Hebrews that the Word of God is "living and active" (4:12). God's words aren't just ink on a page or bytes on an electronic device. Because they have been spoken by God Himself, they have a special way of touching us and renewing us in our inner core.

Are you worried, angry, tempted, distracted, resentful? Why not bathe in God's Word right now? It's good to read through the full range of writings from the Bible, but for this activity, pick a short passage from the Psalms or New Testament. Read it slowly a couple of times. Ask God to speak to you while you read each time. Memorize a key phrase or two. Repeat those phrases throughout your day. Truly bask and soak in the heart of God as you savor His words to you.

God, today I choose to ignore all distractions and focus my mind on truths from Your Word. Let Your words sink deep into my spirit. Amen.

Whatever Is Noble

Finally, brothers, whatever is true, whatever is noble, whatever is right, whatever is pure, whatever is lovely, whatever is admirable—if anything is excellent or praiseworthy—think about such things. PHILIPPIANS 4:8

We scoff at honor and are shocked to find traitors among us. C. S. LEWIS

To say that our culture is coarse and profane is an understatement. The entertainment industry fills media outlets with a constant barrage of words and images that do little or nothing to edify the soul—if not damage it. Paul provides a checklist of virtues we would be wise to dwell on:

- Whatever is noble
- Whatever is true
- Whatever is right
- Whatever is pure
- Whatever is lovely
- Whatever is admirable
- Whatever is excellent or praiseworthy

Is it time for a personal audit of your thought life? Is it perhaps time to take a "fast" from popular entertainment in order to focus on what is ennobling? There's no better place to start than God's Word.

Lord, thank You for checking my spirit on what I choose to fill my mind with. I turn to thoughts of You and Your Word today. Amen.

False Interpretation

But false prophets also arose among the people, just as there
will also be false teachers among you, who will secretly introduce
destructive heresies, even denying the Master who bought them,
bringing swift destruction upon themselves. 2 PETER 2:1

A false interpretation of Scripture causes that the gospel of the Lord becomes
the gospel of man, or, which is worse, of the devil. JEROME

When Martin Luther made the proclamation of "sola scriptura" as the only authority for the Christian's life, part of the phrase has been commonly ignored. He actually said, "Scripture rightly divided," which simply means, "interpreted correctly."

One of the most important reasons to read God's Word and know it ourselves is that it protects us from false prophets. In every age of the church there have been men and women who use the Bible for their own purposes, not to build God's kingdom.

We don't need to live in a posture of skepticism and overanalyze every word from a Bible teacher's lips. But we do need to know God's Word well enough to know when someone has an agenda that is not God's.

Lord, protect us from false prophets and false teachings.
Help me be true to You and Your Word. Amen.

The Word and Prayer

*If you remain in me and my words remain in you,
ask whatever you wish, and it will be given you.* JOHN 15:7

*Have you noticed this? Whatever need or trouble you are in, there is
always something to help you in your Bible, if only you go on reading till
you come to the word God specially has for you.* AMY CARMICHAEL

A Classic Devotional from Andrew Murray

The vital connection between the Word and prayer is one of the simplest and earliest lessons of the Christian life. Before prayer, God's Word strengthens me by giving my faith its justification and its petition. And after prayer, God's Word prepares me by revealing what the Father wants me to ask. In prayer, God's Word brings me the answer, for in it the Spirit allows me to hear the Father's voice.

Prayer is not monologue, but dialogue. Its most essential part is God's voice in response to mine. Listening to God's voice is the secret of the assurance that He will listen to mine. When God reveals Himself in His words, He does indeed give Himself—His love and His life, His will and His power—to those who receive these words, in a reality passing comprehension. In every promise, He gives us the power to grasp and possess Himself. In every command, He allows us to share His will, His holiness, and His perfection. God's Word gives us God Himself.

God, teach me to hear Your voice through Your Word. Amen.

A Healing Word

This is my comfort in my affliction, That Your word has revived me.
PSALM 119:50

*Nothing ranks higher for mental discipline than a
planned and systematic study of God's Word, from whence
life's parameters and values are planted in the mind.*
RAVI ZACHARIAS

Mental illness is a difficult thing for any individual or family to deal with. With it comes a host of issues—painful emotions, financial difficulties due to medical bills and missed work, alienation from loved ones, and a harsh and persistent stigma, to name just a few. But even though it might seem a simplistic solution, many people dealing with mental illness have found great value in memorizing Scripture. They find that God does speak to them through His Word and that comforting words from Scripture—verses that speak of God's faithfulness and love in particular—help to calm their thinking processes, making them better able to deal with what life throws at them.

The truth is that the Bible offers all of us hope, and memorizing Bible passages can give us strength for all our day-to-day difficulties. When we mull over the truths of God's Word, we are better equipped for life.

Lord, thank You for the comfort of Your Word. Direct me
to truths in the Bible that will help me to love You better. Amen.

Finding Truth

For the word of God is living and active. Sharper than any double-edged sword, it penetrates even to dividing soul and spirit, joints and marrow; it judges the thoughts and attitudes of the heart. Hebrews 4:12

Our claim is that God has revealed Himself by speaking; that this divine (or God-breathed) speech has been written down and preserved in Scripture; and that Scripture is, in fact, God's Word written, which therefore is true and reliable and has divine authority over men. John Stott

One of the prevailing temptations of our pluralistic, highly educated culture is to see truth as relative. Right and wrong, the attributes of God, the need and nature of salvation; essential beliefs and practices are not considered absolute, but merely suggestive.

Throughout Scripture, we are told that some issues are a matter of personal conscience, so there is plenty of room for debate and personal conviction.

But that doesn't mean all matters—or even most matters—of faith have an element of personal decision. For example, Paul declares that if there is no resurrection of Christ, there is no salvation or promise of heaven available. (See 1 Corinthians 15:12–19.) How do we know what is absolute and what involves choice? There is only one sure source of revelation: God's Word. Listen to good preachers and teachers, but never let them take the place of getting to know God's Word for yourself.

Father in heaven, thank You for speaking
directly to me through Your Word. Amen.

God's Promises

*For by these He has granted to us His precious and magnificent promises,
so that by them you may become partakers of the divine nature, having
escaped the corruption that is in the world by lust.* 2 PETER 1:4

*You never know how much you really believe anything until its truth or
falsehood becomes a matter of life and death to you.* C. S. LEWIS

A Classic Devotional from C. H. Spurgeon

If you would know experimentally the preciousness of the promises, and enjoy
them in your own heart, meditate much upon them. There are promises which
are like grapes in the wine-press: if you will tread them the juice will flow. Thinking over the hallowed words will often be the prelude to their fulfillment. Many a
Christian who has thirsted for the promise has found the favor which it ensured
gently distilling into his soul even while he has been considering the divine
record; and he has rejoiced that ever he was led to lay the promise near his heart.

But besides meditating upon the promises, seek in thy soul to receive them as
being the very words of God. Speak to thy soul thus, "My soul, it is God, even
thy God, God that cannot lie, who speaks to thee. Therefore, seeing that it is
the word of a God so true, so immutable, so powerful, so wise, I will and must
believe the promise."

Lord, I know that You are faithful. Today I praise
You for Your promises and Your goodness to me. Amen.

The Battle Suit

Take the helmet of salvation and the sword of the Spirit,
which is the word of God. EPHESIANS 6:17

In opposition to all the suggestions of the devil, the sole, simple, and sufficient
answer is the word of God. This puts to flight all the powers of darkness.
The Christian finds this to be true in his individual experience. It dissipates
his doubts; it drives away his fears; it delivers him from the power of Satan.

CHARLES HODGE

The Bible is referred to as a sword because we use the strength of the Word of God in spiritual battles. The Bible is effective because truth cuts into the falsehood of sin; it causes the sinner to return to God; it wards off the attacks of Satan. The Word fights on.

As we learn the truths of God's Word, we then have possession of the battle gear necessary to fight the enemy of our souls. We have what will cause him to flee: the sword of God's truth. Jesus said, "If you hold to my teaching, you are really my disciples. Then you will know the truth, and the truth will set you free" (John 8:31–32).

God has given us the power on earth we need to live for Him, but we must be willing to call upon Him and ask Him for help. That begins with a commitment to His Word. God will deliver His children as His Word has promised.

Lord, may I ever be ready for battle by learning Your Word. Amen.

The Blessing of Obedience

Get yourself ready! Stand up and say to them whatever I command you.

JEREMIAH 1:17

The gospel alone is sufficient to rule the lives of Christians everywhere. Any additional rules made to govern men's conduct added nothing to the perfection already found in the Gospel of Jesus Christ. JOHN WYCLIFFE

Eric Liddell, known as the "Flying Scotsman," was an Olympic runner—and a minister of the gospel. He took a strong stand when he refused to compete in a race because the meet was held on a Sunday. Rather than running, Eric was at church preaching as the games continued without him. He was faithful to what he knew was God's will in his life. Since that day in 1924 his testimony has ministered to thousands of people, young and old, as they have struggled to determine the right thing to do in similar circumstances to those Eric faced. Eric later went on to be the winner of the 400 meter race at the 1924 Summer Olympics held in Paris—he chose to honor God with his decisions, and he was blessed with success. His passion for running was evident, but his love and commitment to Christ, who gave him the ability to run, was foremost in his heart and mind.

When you know God's will in a specific area of your life, do you obey? Do you receive the blessing He has for you?

Father, I am not always quick to obey. Help me to see the wisdom and experience the riches of living for You! Amen.

The Milk of Life

Like newborn babies, long for the pure milk of the word,
so that by it you may grow in respect to salvation. 1 PETER 2:2

The precepts of the Lord are right, rejoicing the heart;
The commandment of the Lord is pure, enlightening the eyes. KING DAVID

When new parents-to-be begin learning all they need to know about raising a baby, the subject of feeding usually takes up plenty of their time. Those early feedings are so important. The baby needs the nourishment that only Mommy can give within the first few days of birth—the milk provides antibodies that will contribute vitally to the overall well-being of the baby.

Just as newborn babies need their mothers' milk, new Christians need the rich milk of the Word of God to prepare them for life as God's child. Studying the Bible, learning from Christ in prayer, and receiving mentorship from stronger, more seasoned Christians are all vital to help a newfound faith grow strong and resilient.

But the Word of God is vital no matter when you became a Christian. It's what establishes those early steps, and also what keeps you going in the middle.

Lord, I pray that Your Word would nurture my spirit and
give me faith and confidence in You, come what may. Amen.

Every Jot and Tittle

Every word of God is flawless; he is a shield to those who take refuge in him.
Do not add to his words, or he will rebuke you and prove you a liar.
PROVERBS 30:5–6

We must allow the Word of God to confront us, to disturb
our security, to undermine our complacency and to overthrow
our patterns of thought and behavior. JOHN STOTT

A Classic Devotional from John Wesley

If, then, we have spoken the word of God, the genuine unmixed word of God, and that only; if we have put no unnatural interpretation upon it, but have taken the known phrases in their common, obvious sense—and when they were less known, explained scripture by scripture; if we have spoken the whole word, as occasion offered, though rather the parts which seemed most proper to give a check to some fashionable vice, or to encourage the practice of some unfashionable virtue; and if we have done this plainly and boldly, though with all the mildness and gentleness that the nature of the subject will bear; then, believe ye our works, if not our words; or rather, believe them both together. Here is all a Preacher can do; all the evidence that he either can or need give of his good intentions. There is no way but this to show he speaks as of sincerity, as commissioned by the Lord, and as in his sight.

Lord, help me share Your Word with others
in a way that leads them to You. Amen.

Tips for Reading and Studying Scripture

For they received the message with great eagerness and examined the Scriptures every day to see if what Paul said was true. ACTS 17:11

As you read, pause frequently to meditate on the meaning of what you are reading. Absorb the Word into your system by dwelling on it, pondering it, going over it again and again in your mind, considering it from many different angles, until it becomes part of you. NANCY LEIGH DEMOSS

A Classic Devotional from Thomas Boston

- Follow a regular plan in reading of them, that you may be acquainted with the whole; and make this reading a part of your private devotions.
- Set a special mark, however you find convenient, on those passages you read, which you find most suitable to your case, condition, or temptations; or such as you have found to move your hearts more than other passages. And it will be profitable often to review these.
- Read with a holy attention, arising from the consideration of the majesty of God, and the reverence due to him. This must be done with attention, first, to the words; second, to the sense; and, third, to the divine authority of the Scripture
- Let your main purpose in reading the Scriptures be practice, and not bare knowledge. Read that you may learn and do, and that without any limitation or distinction, but that whatever you see God requires, you may study to practice.

Lord, I want Your Word to make a difference in my life.
Teach to me to read and study it so that I might grow in You. Amen.

Hope in Your Word

How sweet are your words to my taste, sweeter than honey to my mouth! PSALM 119:103

*The longer you read the Bible, the more you will like it;
it will grow sweeter and sweeter; and the more you get into the spirit of it,
the more you will get into the spirit of Christ.* WILLIAM ROMAINE

A Classic Devotional from King David

Your word is a lamp to my feet
   and a light for my path.
I have taken an oath and confirmed it,
   that I will follow your righteous laws.
I have suffered much;
   preserve my life, O LORD, according to your word.
Accept, O LORD, the willing praise of my mouth,
   and teach me your laws.
Though I constantly take my life in my hands,
   I will not forget your law.
The wicked have set a snare for me,
   but I have not strayed from your precepts.
Your statutes are my heritage forever;
   they are the joy of my heart. PSALM 119:105–111

Lord, I come to Your Word today, wanting to make it
part of me and to delight in it my whole life. Help me to
follow You by following Your Word. Amen.

Blessed Is the One Who Reads

Blessed is the one who reads the words of this prophecy, and blessed are those
who hear it and take to heart what is written in it, because the time is near.

REVELATION 1:3

Down through the centuries in times of trouble and trial God has brought
courage to the hearts of those who love Him. The Bible is filled with assurances
of God's help and comfort in every kind of trouble which might cause fears to
arise in the human heart. You can look ahead with promise, hope, and joy.

BILLY GRAHAM

Peter and John were with Jesus shortly before His return to His Father's right
side. In a poignant conversation Jesus foretold Peter's violent death as a martyr and
John's long life. (See John 21:18–24.) All the other apostles died at the hands of
those who persecuted the Christian faith, but John died of old age as an exile on the
island of Patmos. It was there that he received a vision that came directly from God,
which is known as the Book of Revelation, the final entry in the New Testament.

This is not just a book a prophecy, but a hard look at how believers—now and
then—live in the present. In John's preface he provides a word of wisdom all of us
of faith are wise to heed: "Blessed is the one who reads the words of this prophecy,
and blessed are those who hear it and take to heart what is written in it, because
the time is near" (1:3). We are reminded that the "Day" is near, that true strength
in times of judgment and difficulty is found in a faithful reading of God's Word.

Lord, thank You for the blessings that follow when I read Your Word.
Today I choose to make reading Scripture a priority in my life. Amen.

Overcoming Distortion

He writes the same way in all his letters, speaking in them of
these matters. His letters contain some things that are hard to understand
which ignorant and unstable people distort, as they do the other
Scriptures, to their own destruction. 2 PETER 3:16

We should not interpret Scripture in the light of our experiences,
but we should examine our experiences in the light of the teaching of Scripture.
MARTYN LLOYD-JONES

Read through the book of Acts in a single setting and you will discover a major transition at chapter 11. In the first ten chapters, the leading man, the hero of the faith is Peter. But in chapter 11, it is Paul who becomes the leading figure. This makes sense on the basis of 1:8, where we find the outline of the book—and the marching orders for the early believers—to share the gospel in Jerusalem, Samaria, and the ends of the earth. Paul, the great missionary, is the one who took Jesus to the Roman Empire—the ends of the earth.

Peter was obviously acquainted with Paul's writings (his thirteen letters) and admits they can be tough to understand. But his warning about our responsibility in handling God's Word is crystal clear. We are to be careful in how we interpret and teach the words of the Bible. Those who are careless or, worse, deliberately distort God's Word will be held accountable.

Be bold in sharing God's Word with others—but always with respect and reverence.

God, I never want to go astray in reading Your Word—or cause
anyone else to do so either. I pray for wisdom and a spirit of
reverence as I spend time with Your Word. Amen.

Beautiful Music to Share

*Let your light shine before men, that they may see your good deeds
and praise your Father in heaven.* MATTHEW 5:16

Our faith grows by expression. If we want to keep our faith, we must share it.
BILLY GRAHAM

Concert violinist Fritz Kreisler earned a fortune with his concerts and compositions, but he generously gave most of it away. So when he discovered an exquisite violin on one of his trips, he wasn't able to buy it. Later, having raised enough money to meet the asking price, he returned to the seller, hoping to purchase the beautiful instrument. But to his great dismay, it had been sold to a collector. Kreisler made his way to the new owner's home and offered to buy the violin. The collector said it had become his prized possession and he would not sell it.

Keenly disappointed, Kreisler was about to leave when he had an idea. "Could I play the instrument once more before it is consigned to silence?" he asked. Permission was granted, and the great virtuoso filled the room with such moving music that the collector's emotions were deeply stirred. "I have no right to keep that to myself," he exclaimed. "It's yours, Mr. Kreisler. Take it into the world, and let people hear it."

We are to take the gospel, the Word of God, to the masses and not lock it away in silence. Sharing the good news and proclaiming the truths of the Bible is not the work only of overseas missionaries, but also of every believer.

Lord, it amazes me that You have entrusted me with sharing the gospel message with the world. Give me diligence to follow Your calling. Amen.

Pass It On

These commandments that I give you today are to be upon your hearts.
Impress them on your children. Talk about them when you sit at home and
when you walk along the road, when you lie down and when you get up.
DEUTERONOMY 6:6–7

Your top-priority job as a parent, then, is to be an evangelist in your home.
You need to teach your children the law of God; teach them the gospel
of divine grace; show them their need for a Savior; and point them to Jesus
Christ as the only One who can save them. JOHN MACARTHUR

King David knew the importance of God's Word for his personal life. He said, "I have hidden your word in my heart that I might not sin against you" (Psalm 119:11). But he was also committed to passing on a love and reverence for God's Word to the next generation. According to his son Solomon, David said to him: "My son, pay attention to what I say; listen closely to my words. Do not let them out of your sight, keep them within your heart; for they are life to those who find them and health to a man's whole body" (Proverbs 4:20–22).

Do you share God's Word with your children? If they are still in the home, do you take them to church and Bible class? Do you ever sit down and read aloud from a Bible story book or a Bible passage? One of the greatest privileges and responsibilities of parenting is to pass on our faith to the next generation.

Father in heaven, thank You for the gift of children.
I pray that you would help me to share with them a love for
Your Word that will guide their steps all of their days.

A Royal Priesthood

Therefore he is able to save completely those who come to God through him, because he always lives to intercede for them. Such a high priest meets our need—one who is holy, blameless, pure, set apart from sinners, exalted above the heavens. HEBREWS 7:25–26

The priest is not made. He must be born a priest; must inherit his office. I refer to the new birth—the birth of water and the Spirit. Thus all Christians must become priests, children of God and co-heirs with Christ the Most High Priest.
MARTIN LUTHER

In all religions and all ages, a priest is an intermediary who ushers common people into the presence of divinity. This has usually involved special rituals, including, for some faiths, a sacrifice that would remove sin or any other barriers separating man from God. In the person of Jesus, something amazing happens. The "divine"—the one to be worshiped—becomes His own priest, His own sacrifice, and the One who brings us directly into the presence of God. The writer of Hebrews says, "We should approach the throne of grace boldly" (4:16). No one need usher us before God.

We need not go through any intermediary for salvation, and in the same way, God has spoken clearly and plainly to us through His Word so that each of us can hear His voice. Thank God that there are those who will help us understand and experience Scripture, but ultimately, we can go directly to God's Word to receive the encouragement and challenge He has for us.

Lord, the privilege of interacting with You through Your Word is amazing. Help me to honor that privilege in my life today. Amen.

Things That Corrupt

Be self-controlled and alert. Your enemy the devil prowls around like a roaring lion looking for someone to devour. 1 PETER 5:8

Keep your thoughts right, for as you think, so are you. HENRY H. BUCKLEY

A Classic Devotional from Richard Baxter

Be thoroughly acquainted with your temptations and the things that may corrupt you—and watch against them all day long. You should watch especially the most dangerous of the things that corrupt, and those temptations that either your company or business will unavoidably lay before you.

Watch against the master sins of unbelief: hypocrisy, selfishness, pride, flesh pleasing and the excessive love of earthly things. Take care against being drawn into earthly mindedness and excessive cares, or covetous designs for rising in the world, under the pretence of diligence in your calling.

At first these things will be very difficult, while sin has any strength in you, but once you have grasped a continual awareness of the poisonous danger of any one of these sins, your heart will readily and easily avoid them.

Lord, temptations surround me all day. Give me strength to direct my attention to You and Your Word in order to avoid temptation. Amen.

Clothed in Humility

He guides the humble in what is right and teaches them his way.
All the ways of the LORD are loving and faithful for those
who keep the demands of his covenant. PSALM 25:9–10

For those who would learn God's ways, humility is the first thing,
humility is the second, humility is the third. ST. AUGUSTINE

In the classic children's story of the emperor's new clothes, the emperor was visited by two swindlers who promised that if he provided them with gold thread, they would produce for him the finest clothes in the world. But not just any clothes; magical clothes: only those who were smart and fit for their position could see the clothes they made, they promised. That really appealed to his pride.

You know the rest of the story. The emperor paraded through the streets naked, unwilling to admit that he couldn't see the clothes he was wearing (or not wearing). A simple child pointed out that he was wearing nothing, and the emperor was humiliated in front of the whole town. And so were those who pretended to see his clothes.

You will never accidentally leave the house in the buff believing you're wearing fine clothes, and hopefully you will never fall victim to a shady swindler. But all of us are vulnerable to the sin of pride. Even foolish pride. It makes smart people do dumb things.

Wisdom comes from a proper respect for God and a humble walk before Him.

Lord, I ask You for wisdom and a humble heart. Amen.

A Fresh Word

Open my eyes that I may see wonderful things in your law. Psalm 119:18

When you read God's Word, you must constantly be saying to yourself,
"It is talking to me, and about me." Soren Kierkegaard

You've heard the joke in regard to marriage: A wife asks her husband if he loves her. He answers her, "Of course." She then asks why he never tells her he loves her. He answers, "I told you I loved you twenty years ago and I never changed my mind."

Good marriages need words of affection repeated. Often. Similarly, we need to hear from God every day. The Bible is filled with insights, so when we sit down to read it, often we encounter something brand new for our spiritual life. But sometimes the very same words, containing the very same truth, speak to us in a new and fresh way. A Bible verse as well known as John 3:16 can be a brand new reality we hear for the very first time—even though we've heard it hundreds of times before. As you open the pages of God's Word, do so with an open heart and a sense of anticipation. God has something fresh and new to say to you.

Lord, I want to hear You speak through Your Word.
Please show me what You want me to know today. Amen.

Through the Ages

The statutes of the LORD are trustworthy, making wise the simple.
The precepts of the LORD are right, giving joy to the heart. PSALM 19:7–8

It is not at all incredible, that a book which has been so long in the possession
of mankind should contain many truths as yet undiscovered. BISHOP BUTLER

No other book has had a greater influence on the course of history than God's Word. Consider the testimony of greats from previous generations:

- George Washington: It is impossible to rightly govern the world without God and the Bible.
- Abraham Lincoln: I am profitably engaged in reading the Bible. Take all of this Book that you can by reason and the balance by faith, and you will live and die a better man. It is the best Book which God has given to man.
- Thomas Jefferson: I have always said that a studious perusal of the sacred volume will make better citizens, better fathers, and better husbands.
- John Quincy Adams: So great is my veneration for the Bible that the earlier my children begin to read it the more confident will be my hope that they will prove useful citizens of their country and respectable members of society. I have for many years made it a practice to read through the Bible once every year.
- Daniel Webster: If there is anything in my thoughts or style to commend, the credit is due to my parents for instilling in me an early love of the Scriptures.

What is your testimony on the importance of God's Word?

Lord, help me to place the kind of priority on Your Word that reflects my trust in You—and that sows seeds of greatness in me. Amen.

July

SERVICE

Serving the Poor

*There will always be poor people in the land. Therefore I
command you to be openhanded toward your brothers and toward
the poor and needy in your land.* DEUTERONOMY 15:11

We cannot do great things on this earth, only small things with great love.
MOTHER TERESA

The motto "Give a man a fish and he will eat for a day; teach a man to fish and
he will eat for a lifetime," forms a foundation for the work of many charities
and ministries as they strive to help the people they serve grow progressively
self-sufficient. So many of the poor in our midst need not just food for today, but
encouragement, compassion, and a mentor to help them meet their challenges
for a brighter tomorrow. So, as we try to follow the Bible's command to look
after the poor, it might be a good idea to pray for wisdom about how we might
best help someone move to a new level in life.

There's nothing wrong with giving money. Most service agencies rely on dona-
tions. But don't be afraid to get a little dirty, to get creative with your giving. Pick
up a few extra groceries for a food pantry while you're at the store. Serve a few
hours a week at a homeless shelter. Give your time to mentor a child at risk. Whatever you do, ask God to help you meet the deepest needs of those around you.

Father, I'm in awe of Your compassion for the poor.
Show me how to reach out to others with Your
compassion and love this month. Amen.

Always Enough

*Taking the five loaves and the two fish and looking up to heaven, he gave thanks
and broke the loaves. Then he gave them to the disciples, and the disciples gave
them to the people. They all ate and were satisfied, and the disciples picked up
twelve basketfuls of broken pieces that were left over.* MATTHEW 14:19–20

*We can be certain that God will give us the strength and resources we need to
live through any situation in life that he ordains. The will of God will never
take us where the grace of God cannot sustain us.* BILLY GRAHAM

In the nineteenth century, evangelist George Mueller founded many homes for
children throughout England to care for kids orphaned by war. With so many
mouths to feed, he daily prayed for provision for even the most basic needs of
the children. One particular day, when supplies were especially low, Mueller
prayed, "Lord, You are the God who knows our every need. I know we will have
enough food today." Not long after he prayed, his wife came in and announced,
"A man I'd never seen before came to the back door. He said, 'I know you're
trying to feed some orphans. God bless you for it. This is to help you in that good
work.' And George, he gave me a huge bag of oats, and look—molasses!"

"Praise God!" said Mueller. "Today I will tell the story of how Jesus fed the
five thousand."

Maybe you're feeling a little low on resources today, unsure of how to help
those around you. Remember that for every great need, there is a great God.

Father, thank You for always providing for me.
Help me share from my abundance. Amen.

Prayers for a Nation

If my people, who are called by my name, will humble themselves and pray and seek my face and turn from their wicked ways, then will I hear from heaven and will forgive their sin and will heal their land. 2 CHRONICLES 7:14

Our prayers lay the track down on which God's power can come. Like a mighty locomotive, his power is irresistible, but it cannot reach us without rails. WATCHMAN NEE

Most reading these words are from the United States, but even if you are from another country, you will appreciate prayers of leaders for the spiritual life of a nation.

George Washington: "Preserve and defend our rulers in church and state. Bless the people of this land, be a father to the fatherless, a comforter to the comfortless, a deliverer to the captives, and a physician to the sick. Let thy blessings guide this day and forever through Jesus Christ."

Thomas Jefferson: "Almighty God, Who has given us this good land for our heritage; We humbly beseech Thee that we may always prove ourselves a people mindful of Thy favor and glad to do Thy will."

Abraham Lincoln: "With malice toward none, with charity for all, with firmness in the right as God gives us to see the right, let us finish the work we are in ... to do all which may achieve and cherish a just and a lasting peace among ourselves and with all nations."

God, thank You for my country, for its rich land and
heritage and its wonderful freedoms. I pray for
Your hand on us as a nation today. Amen.

The Soul of a Nation

I urge, then, first of all, that requests, prayers, intercession and thanksgiving be made for everyone— for kings and all those in authority, that we may live peaceful and quiet lives in all godliness and holiness. 1 TIMOTHY 2:1–2

For my own part, I sincerely esteem [the Constitution] a system which without the finger of God, never could have been suggested and agreed upon by such a diversity of interests. ALEXANDER HAMILTON

What makes a country great? No question, it is tied to its spiritual quality.

Is America a Christian nation? That can't be answered by history, but the past can encourage the right spirituality for the future:

Samuel Adams: "Let divines and philosophers, statesmen and patriots, unite their endeavors to renovate the age by impressing the minds of men with the importance of educating their little boys and girls, inculcating in the minds of youth the fear and love of the Deity."

Patrick Henry: "It cannot be emphasized too clearly and too often that this nation was founded, not by religionists, but by Christians; not on religion, but on the gospel of Jesus Christ. For this very reason, peoples of other faiths have been afforded asylum, prosperity, and freedom of worship here."

John Jay: "We've staked the future of all our political institutions upon our capacity to sustain ourselves according to the Ten Commandments of God."

Our earliest leaders committed their work to God. We can't make that same choice for all our fellow citizens, but we can make it for ourselves.

Lord, I want to follow You in everything I do. Amen.

Stay Connected

*I am the vine; you are the branches. If a man remains in me and I in him,
he will bear much fruit; apart from me you can do nothing.*

JOHN 15:5

*God is not in the business of helping the humanly strong become stronger;
rather he takes the weak and makes them strong in himself.*

ERWIN W. LUTZER

Movement, growth, work, force, life itself—all require energy. The power
source for the Christian life is connection to Jesus Christ. Jesus paints a picture
of a vineyard. It may spread over acres, but every living branch that bears fruit is
connected to the vine.

Often, when we don't feel like we are effective in our service—as a spouse,
a parent, a minister, a volunteer—we focus on techniques. We think of better
methods and programs for making a difference. Maybe we need to first take a
step backwards and ask ourselves a few simple questions: How connected am I
to Jesus Christ? Am I close to Him? Does He have my faith and love? It's amazing
how everything else falls into place when that question is answered positively.

Are you bearing fruit? Are you connected to the vine?

Heavenly Father, I love You and want nothing
more than to be close to You. Amen.

We Must Pray

Devote yourselves to prayer, being watchful and thankful. Colossians 4:2

*Pray often, for prayer is a shield to the soul, a sacrifice to God,
and a scourge for Satan.* John Bunyan

A Classic Devotional from E. M. Bounds

No insistence in the Scriptures is more pressing than that we must pray. No exhortation is more often reiterated, none is more hearty, none is more solemn and stirring, than to pray. No principal is more strongly and broadly declared than that which urges us to pray. There is no duty to which we are more strongly obliged than that of praying. There is no command more imperative and insistent than that of praying. Are you praying in everything without ceasing (1 Thessalonians 5:17)? Are you praying in your prayer closet, hidden from the eyes of others? Are you praying always and everywhere? These are personal, pertinent, and all-important questions for every soul.

God's Word shows us, through many examples, that God intervenes in this world in answer to prayer. How clear it is, when the Bible is consulted, that the almighty God is brought directly into the things of this world by the prayers of His people.

Lord, I know that I can't do Your will without praying.
Draw me close to You today. Amen.

God's Plans

"For I know the plans I have for you," declares the LORD, "plans to prosper you and not to harm you, plans to give you hope and a future." JEREMIAH 29:11

If we do not lay out ourselves in the service of mankind whom should we serve?
JOHN ADAMS

As a young man, William Carey worked as a shoemaker living in London. He was fascinated by explorers and missionaries, anyone who traveled to foreign lands. And his interest in other cultures soon became a deeply felt compassion for the lost and needy of the whole world. Some reported that on the walls of his shop, he hung hand-drawn maps of other countries, annotated with information he found about the climate, diet, and religions of various areas of the world. He built a globe from scraps of leather left over from the shoes he made, and he regularly prayed over it for the people of each country that he thought had never heard the gospel message. And later in life, he became a missionary to India and served many with the message and love of Christ.

Whether or not you serve on an overseas mission field, God has given all of us a calling. How do you find out what yours is? You can probably find it in your areas of interest. You might not think your passions in life are very useful; but in God's hands, they can be used to help and serve others.

Lord, show me what I can do to serve You by
serving others, and give me joy in doing it. Amen.

Blessed to Be a Blessing

And do not forget to do good and to share with others,
for with such sacrifices God is pleased. HEBREWS 13:16

Nothing is really ours until we share it. C. S. LEWIS

As a Christmas present, Michael received a brand new car from a close friend who had just inherited a large sum of money. Several weeks later, after the holidays, as Michael left the office to go home, a shabbily dressed man stood near his parking spot, admiring his new wheels. "Hey man, is this your car?" the man asked.

Michael nodded with a gulp. "My friend gave it to me for Christmas."

The man was astonished. "You mean, your friend gave it to you, and it cost you nothing? Man, I wish . . ." Michael anticipated what the wish would be—that the man, too, would love to have such a generous friend.

"I wish," the man continued to Michael's amazement, "that I could be a friend like that."

Jesus said, "It is more blessed to give than to receive" (Acts 20:35). When we pray for blessings, we ought also to pray that we might use those gifts to bless someone else. What can you bless someone with today, even if it's something small?

Dear Lord, whether I have a lot or a little, You have given me something I can share. Show me someone I can bless today. Amen.

By Grace Alone

*But by the grace of God I am what I am, and his grace to me was
not without effect. No, I worked harder than all of them—yet not I,
but the grace of God that was with me.* 1 CORINTHIANS 15:10

*Yes, God's grace is always sufficient, and His arms are always
open to give it. But, will our arms be open to receive it?* BETH MOORE

A Classic Devotional from Andrew Murray

I reminded him of the difference, the absolute contrast between law and
grace. Law demands; grace bestows. Law commands, but gives no strength to
obey. Grace promises and performs, doing everything for us. Law burdens, casts
down, and condemns. Grace comforts, makes strong and glad. Law appeals to
self to do its utmost; grace points to Christ to do all. Law requires effort and
strain, urging us toward a goal we can never reach. Grace works all of God's
blessed will in us. I pointed out to him how his first step should be to completely
accept his failure and his inability, as God had been trying to show him, instead
of striving against it. With this acceptance and confession, he could sink down
before God in utter helplessness. There he would learn that, unless grace gave
him deliverance and strength, he could never do better than he had done, and
that grace would, indeed, work all for him. He must come out from under law,
self, and effort, taking his place under grace and allowing God to do all.

Lord, I know that when I am weak, I am strong in You.
Thank You for the grace that makes serving You a joy. Amen.

Serving and Communion

But Martha was distracted by all the preparations that had to be made. She came to him and asked, "Lord, don't you care that my sister has left me to do the work by myself? Tell her to help me!" LUKE 10:40

In the service of the Lord, it is not where but how you serve. J. REUBEN CLARK

Martha was just doing what she knew to do, what seemed natural to her: preparing the house and a meal for her dinner guests. Her sister, Mary, chose to sit at the feet of Jesus and listen to Him teach. At some point, it must have become too much for Martha, and she burst out angrily, asking Jesus to tell Mary to help her. But instead, He told her, "Martha, Martha . . . you are worried and upset about many things, but only one thing is needed. Mary has chosen what is better, and it will not be taken away from her" (Luke 10:41–42).

God does not discourage us from serving others with hospitality and seemingly mundane chores. But like Martha, we must guard against the tendency to get preoccupied and bogged down in our responsibilities, forgetting the One we are ultimately serving. When our service becomes a burden or a distraction from communion with God, we know we need to realign our priorities.

God, thank You for the privilege of serving You, but thank You even more for the joy of simply being in Your presence. Help me keep my eyes on You even as I serve. Amen.

Led by the Spirit

*Paul and his companions traveled throughout the region of
Phrygia and Galatia, having been kept by the Holy Spirit
from preaching the word in the province of Asia.*

ACTS 16:6

*The teacher of teachers gives his guidance noiselessly. I have never heard
him speak, and yet I know that he is within me.* THERESE OF LISIEUX

Don't know where God wants you to serve? Just ask Him to show you and then
keep your eyes open to the opportunities all around you. Many will come as a
complete surprise:
- A missed flight connection puts you in a seat next to someone dealing with
  spiritual issues;
- A wrong turn takes you by an outreach center you had never heard of;
- A waitress opens up and shares some difficulties she is experiencing;
- A conflict with a neighbor becomes the open door for a new relationship.

Paul had plans to minister in Bithynia. God had plans for him to minister in
Macedonia—and introduce the Good News to a whole new continent (see Acts
16:6–10). He was led by the Spirit. And the same Spirit of God will lead you too.

God, thank You for Your Spirit to guide
and direct my steps and work. Amen.

Pass It On

Teach me to do your will, for you are my God; may your good Spirit lead me on level ground. PSALM 143:10

If we have the true love of God in our hearts, we will show it in our lives.
DWIGHT L. MOODY

A Classic Devotional from A. B. Simpson

Some of us are shivering and wondering why the Holy Spirit does not fill us. We have plenty coming in, but we do not give it out. Give out the blessing that you have, start larger plans for service and blessing, and you will soon find that the Holy Ghost is before you, and He will present you with blessings for service, and give you all that He can trust you to give away to others.

There is a beautiful fact in nature which has its spiritual parallels. There is no music so heavenly as an Aeolian harp, and the Aeolian harp is nothing but a set of musical chords arranged in harmony, and then left to be touched by the unseen fingers of the wandering winds. And as the breath of heaven floats over the chords, it is said that notes almost Divine float out upon the air, as if a choir of angels were wandering around and touching the strings.

And so it is possible to keep our hearts so open to the touch of the Holy Spirit that He can play upon them at will, as we quietly wait in the pathway of His service.

Lord, I want to be used by You to bless others.
Help me attune myself to Your song today. Amen.

Bear One Another's Burdens

Carry each other's burdens, and in this way you will fulfill the law of Christ.
GALATIANS 6:2

*Give me a stout heart to bear my own burdens. Give me a willing
heart to bear the burdens of others. Give me a believing heart
to cast all burdens upon Thee, O Lord.* JOHN BAILLIE

We are not responsible to carry certain burdens of others. In Galatians 6:5, Paul says that "each one should carry his own load." Another translation for the word in that verse would be a "backpack." All of us are able to carry a certain amount of weight in life. In fact, doing things for others that they should do for themselves can lead to a cycle of co-dependence that is unhealthy for the one not pulling his own weight—and for the one carrying multiple backpacks.

But there are some burdens that are excessive. They are too heavy for one person to lift alone. Physical disabilities, emotional trauma, and other burdens can crush one's spirit through sheer magnitude. In cases like this, Paul says we can fulfill the law of Christ by helping someone carry the load. Is there someone in your life who needs you to share the love of Christ with him or her? Are you willing to help someone carry that weight?

Lord, I pray for eyes to see the needs around me.
Help me be a burden-bearer, Father God. Amen.

God's Gift of Rest

*By the seventh day God had finished the work he had been doing;
so on the seventh day he rested from all his work.* Genesis 2:2

*Jesus knows we must come apart and rest a while,
or else we may just plain come apart.* Vance Havner

According to Genesis 2:2, even God rested after creating the universe. And unlike God, we get tired. When our bodies and brains are tired, they don't function like they were created to and need renewal. But just as much as physical rest, we need to recharge our spirits as well. We need to take a moment at the end of the day to simply breathe slowly and say a short prayer in order to take care of our souls.

Few men lived as intense a life as King David. Kingdom builder and warrior, he faced strife and danger—some of it self-induced—his entire adult life. An emotional man who was subject to the same laws of fatigue and exhaustion as the rest of us, is it any wonder he described the blessed man as one who meditates on God in the morning and at night (Psalm 1:2)?

Sometimes we run the risk of burning ourselves out even in serving God. Don't wait until the point of exhaustion to take time to slow down, thank God, and ask Him for His help and grace.

Dear Lord, I need Your refreshing,
renewing grace to keep me going. Amen.

The Lion's Den

God has said, "Never will I leave you; never will I forsake you." HEBREWS 13:5

Do not let Satan deceive you into being afraid of God's plans for your life.
R. A. TORREY

When you follow God's call on your life, you might find yourself in some unfamiliar places. A seedy part of town. On stage, speaking in front of a large group. A completely different country. You might get a little scared. And that's okay. What's important to remember is that God is always with you.

Remember Daniel in the lion's den? He was kept overnight in a sealed pit with hungry lions, but when morning came, he shouted from the bottom, "My God sent his angel, and he shut the mouths of the lions. They have not hurt me, because I was found innocent in his sight" (Daniel 6:22). You probably won't be thrown into a literal pit of lions, but you might find yourself under pressure as you serve God. Whatever happens—whether God delivers you miraculously or simply gives you strength to cope—know that He is near you, pleased with you, helping you, turning a lion's den into a sanctuary of praise.

Lord, sometimes I get scared. I feel unable to meet the
challenges in front of me. Help me remember that
You are working in and through me. Amen.

Heeding God's Call

The harvest is plentiful, but the workers are few. Ask the Lord
of the harvest, therefore, to send out workers into his harvest field.
Go! I am sending you out like lambs among wolves. Luke 10:2–3

God always gives us strength enough, and sense enough,
for everything He wants us to do. John Ruskin

A Classic Devotional from William Booth

A young Christian once came to me, and told me that for some time she had been giving the Lord her profession and prayers and money, but now she wanted to give Him her life. She wanted to go right into the fight. In other words, she wanted to go to His assistance in the sea. As when a man from the shore, seeing another struggling in the water, takes off those outer garments that would hinder his efforts and leaps to the rescue, so will you who still linger on the bank, thinking and singing and praying about the poor perishing souls, rush to the rescue of this multitude of dying men and women.

Does the surging sea look dark and dangerous? Unquestionably it is so. He who beckons you from the sea however, knows what it will mean, and knowing, He still calls to you and bids to you to come. You must do it! You cannot hold back.

Now what will you do?

Lord, I know that You have given me a job to do.
I ask You to show me what it is and strengthen my
resolve to serve You with my whole being. Amen.

Spiritual Gifts

His master replied, "Well done, good and faithful servant!
You have been faithful with a few things; I will put you in charge of many
things. Come and share your master's happiness!" MATTHEW 25:23

In the great orchestra we call life, you have an instrument and a song,
and you owe it to God to play them both sublimely. MAX LUCADO

Albert Schweitzer, winner of the Nobel Peace Prize in 1952, was a biblical scholar (often a controversial one), a medical doctor and missionary, and a celebrated musician. Few people achieve his success in even one arena, let alone three. In the eyes of God, however, it would seem that Schweitzer was not greater than anyone else who uses their talents to their utmost in the service of others, whether those talents are musical gifts, physical strength, or a compassionate heart.

Jesus' parable of the talents gives us some perspective. The master gave his servants a number of talents, "each according to his ability" (Matthew 25:15). The ones who multiplied their talents were rewarded; but the servant who simply buried his talent faced punishment. It's a sobering thought: we will be judged on how well we use our abilities. Even if we have fewer than someone else, we must always put what we have to use.

The gifts and abilities God gives us are to be used for God's kingdom, in service to Him and others. Each time we serve in this way, we increase the potential of our gift.

Lord, help me to know what my gifts are,
and show me how to use them for You. Amen.

When Service Hurts

*But even if I am being poured out like a drink offering on the sacrifice
and service coming from your faith, I am glad and rejoice with all of you.*
PHILIPPIANS 2:17

The cost of true greatness is humble, selfless, sacrificial service.
JOHN MACARTHUR

In the New Testament, Paul stands as an icon of sacrificial service. He endured beatings and floggings (2 Corinthians 11:25), he wept over wayward and hurtful congregations (2 Corinthians 2:4), and he frequently went without (Philippians 4:12). Yet he affirmed, "I can do everything through him who gives me strength" (Philippians 4:13).

God does not give all of us the same gifts, and He does not call us all to the same vocation. But all of us are called to humility. Paul told the Philippian church, "Your attitude should be the same as that of Christ Jesus: Who, being in very nature God, did not consider equality with God something to be grasped, but made himself nothing" (Philippians 2:5–7). It can be painful to serve God and others to the point of sacrifice. But as Paul discovered, God supplies our every need along the way.

Thank You, God, for so many examples in
Scripture and in my life of people who serve You faithfully.
Create in me a heart that beats to do Your will. Amen.

God at Work

It is God who works in you to will and to act according to his good purpose.
PHILIPPIANS 2:13

The Lord doesn't promise to give us something to take so we can handle our weary moments. He promises us himself. That is all. And that is enough.
CHARLES SWINDOLL

A father and his young son returned home after a trip to the grocery store. The son loved being with his dad and wanted to help him finish the chore. In fact, he wanted to carry the largest bag—which was much too heavy for him—inside. The father had a simple solution. He put the bag in his son's arms and then picked him up and carried both inside.

What a lovely picture of how our Heavenly Father works within us. He loves our willingness to take on any assignment. But He knows what we can and cannot do in our strength. When the load is too heavy, the assignment too big, He honors our willing spirit by lifting us up and allowing us to do His work. He empowers us to accomplish more than we can in our own strength.

Do all you can—but realize it is God's power working through you that makes the difference.

Dear God, I can accomplish great things
with You working in and through me. Amen.

Bigger Than You

*If anyone serves, he should do it with the strength God provides,
so that in all things God may be praised through Jesus Christ. To him
be the glory and the power for ever and ever. Amen.* 1 PETER 4:11

*The smallest things become great when God requires them of us; they are small
only in themselves; they are always great when they are done for God, and
when they serve to unite us with Him eternally.* FRANÇOIS FÉNELON

It was only a couple of pennies, but her gift continues to give through the centuries as a model of humble and generous sharing. She was a widow who didn't give with fanfare or from a surplus overflow. But she gave from her heart and God made something tiny grow into something large and beautiful. (See Mark 12:41–43.)

A young boy shared a little bread and a few fish and it fed thousands. God knows how to multiply! It doesn't matter what size your gift is. You might not have much money or influence; you may not have tremendous talents or gifts; you might feel like you're out of energy right now. But if you give out of a loving heart, a humble heart, a compassionate heart, God can take something small and turn it into something great.

Dear God, thank You for taking what I bring to
the table and making something great out of it. Amen.

Gifts to Give

A generous man will himself be blessed.
PROVERBS 22:9

You cannot out-give God.
BILLY GRAHAM

Go ahead and try. You can't do it. It's impossible to give and not get something in return. Oh, there will be times you extend love and don't have it reciprocated; you might give sacrificially from limited funds—and still be short on cash; it is possible to help others get their lives in order only to be left completely alone in a moment of need. None of those things are likely, but they are possible.

But you still can't come up empty handed. It's not possible. Because God, your Heavenly Father, sees your gifts of love and is pleased. Even if no one else thanks you, know that He will reward your kindness.

Maybe you won't receive a return on your investment of service in this lifetime. You probably will, but maybe you won't—but be assured that the very best rewards are eternal.

Dear God, thank You that You return my acts of kindness to me in greater measure than I could ever give. Amen.

Your Little Secret

When you give to the needy, do not let your left hand know what your right hand is doing, so that your giving may be in secret. Then your Father, who sees what is done in secret, will reward you. MATTHEW 6:3–4

If you serve others for the reward of gaining their admiration and gratitude, then your reward will be fleeting and ultimately dissatisfying. If you serve others for the reward of bringing pleasure to your Father God's heart as you work side by side with him, then you will gain eternal rewards. AUTHOR UNKNOWN

The art of self-promotion is alive and well. We have photographers, publicists, and brand specialists to shape a wonderful impression of the good things we do. We blog and Twitter and update Facebook on our every act of kindness.

Well, there are causes, organizations, needs, and ministries that need to be promoted so that some people will be inspired to participate in and help with worthy acts of service. But all of us need to check our own hearts and motives on why we do what we do. Is it for the praise and admiration of others, or is it out of love for people and the desire to honor God? Some acts of service need to be a well-kept secret between you and God.

Lord, I want to love others and honor
You in my words and deeds. Amen.

Serve Where You Are

He appointed the priests to their duties and encouraged them in the service of the LORD's temple. 2 CHRONICLES 35:2

In the Kingdom of God, service is not a stepping-stone to nobility: it is nobility, the only kind of nobility that is recognized. T. W. MANSON

A Classic Devotional from C. H. Spurgeon

Dear friends, do you not think we frequently limit our estimate of serving God to the public exercises of the sanctuary, and forget the strong claims that our Lord has upon our private fidelity and obedience? You say, "I cannot serve God," when you cannot teach in the school or preach in the pulpit, when you are unable to sit on a committee or speak on a platform: as if these were the only forms of service to be taken into account. Do you not think that a mother nursing her baby is serving God? Do you not think that men and women going about their daily toil with patient industry discharging the duties of domestic life are serving God? If you think rightly you will understand that they are. The servant sweeping the room, the mistress preparing the meal, the workman driving a nail, the merchant casting up his ledger, ought to do all in the service of God.

Lord, I want to do everything I do to the best of my abilities and serve You even in the small things. Amen.

Pass It On

In the same way, let your light shine before men, that they may see your good deeds and praise your Father in heaven. MATTHEW 5:16

One drop of water helps to swell the ocean; a spark of fire helps to give light to the world. None are too small, too feeble, too poor to be of service. Think of this and act. HANNAH MORE

The concept of "pay it forward" is built on the idea that people have done good things for you that you can't repay directly back to them—but for which you can show gratitude by doing something good for someone who can't repay you. You simply pay forward.

The ultimate expression of paying it forward is what Jesus Christ did for each of us. Even when we were sinners, even when we were enemies with God, He died for us so we could experience eternal life.

How do we pay that gift forward? Simple. We can never repay Him for His sacrificial love toward us, so we share His love with others who need the gift of life. When was the last time you paid it forward?

Dear God, help me to pass on to others the love
you so freely gave to me through Your Son. Amen.

You Have a Purpose

For we are God's workmanship, created in Christ Jesus to do good works, which God prepared in advance for us to do. EPHESIANS 2:10

Set yourself earnestly to discover what you are made to do, and then give yourself passionately to the doing of it. MARTIN LUTHER KING JR.

I'm not sure I have a purpose in life. I don't know what I am supposed to do to make the world better.

You might be right. You might not personally have a purpose in life. But there's good news. *God* has a purpose for you. When He created you, He fashioned you in such a way that you could accomplish things that build His kingdom. But that's not all. There's more good news. Not only did He create you with the ability to accomplish great things, He also prepared specific tasks that would utilize your gifts.

Maybe it's a person only you can reach. Maybe it's a ministry you are supposed to start. Maybe it's a gift of encouragement you are to lavish on hundreds and thousands of people. Look in your heart. Look around you. Ask God to open your eyes. And get busy!

Heavenly Father, open my eyes to the tasks and opportunities You have set before me. Amen.

Charity

*Suppose a brother or sister is without clothes and daily food. If one of
you says to him, "Go, I wish you well; keep warm and well fed," but does
nothing about his physical needs, what good is it? In the same way, faith by
itself, if it is not accompanied by action, is dead.* JAMES 2:15–17

*Without charity external work is of no value, but anything done in charity, be
it ever so small and trivial, is entirely fruitful inasmuch as God weighs the love
with which a man acts rather than the deed itself.* THOMAS À KEMPIS

Is it possible to do good things for the wrong reasons? Absolutely. Does that
mean these good deeds are worthless and achieve no good ends? Not necessarily.
Your good deeds, done for the wrong reasons, may very well bless others tremen-
dously. However, the benefit to you and your soul is negated.

Faith without actions is a dead faith, but conversely, actions without love are
rarely as effective in making a lasting difference in the world—and are spiritually
dead for the one who is doing them.

We experience peace and joy when there is agreement between our internal
beliefs and external actions. Is it time for you to ask God to kindle within you a
love for others? Is it time to express your love and faith in tangible acts?

Heavenly Father, change me from the inside
so I change the world through my service. Amen.

On the Front Lines

Be ready to do whatever is good. Titus 3:1

The man or woman who is compelled by Jesus' love and empowered by His Spirit does the will of God from the heart. F.F. Bruce

The life of first responders—EMTs, firefighters, police officers, and others—is undeniably stressful and challenging when emergencies strike. They go through extensive and continual training to be ready for such moments. And they must always be ready for whatever comes their way, whether it's the grisly scene of an accident or the duty of informing a stranger that their loved one won't be coming home tonight. Some days, nothing big happens. Other days, something huge happens.

God calls us to be ever vigilant, always ready to explain our hope in God to someone who doesn't believe in Him, always alert to spiritual attacks, quick with love and kindness to those in need. We never know when someone around us might need God to work through us.

Are you ready to spring into action?

Lord, help me be alert to Your plans, ready to do Your will. Amen.

This Is My Song

*He restores my soul. He guides me in paths
of righteousness for his name's sake.* PSALM 23:3

*It seemed intended by the blessed providence of God that I
should be blind all my life, and I thank him for the dispensation.
If perfect earthly sight were offered me tomorrow I would not accept it.
I might not have sung hymns to the praise of God if I had been distracted
by the beautiful and interesting things about me.* FANNY CROSBY

Fanny Crosby, blinded at six weeks old in 1820, was raised by her mother and grandmother after her father's death when she was a baby. But as she moved through her childhood, adolescence, and into her adult years, she always maintained her faith in God's goodness. She never believed that He was punishing her, and she believed that if she kept her heart open to Him, He would lead her.

As a seven-year resident of a school for the blind, she learned to play the piano and guitar and how to sing. And she went on to spend her whole life serving the Lord through her poetry and music, writing such beloved hymns as "Blessed Assurance" and "Jesus Is Tenderly Calling You Home," which are still sung by millions today.

Even when we find ourselves hindered by circumstances or even handicaps, if we keep trusting God, He can use us where we are. If we will just keep trusting Him, we will have many reasons to proclaim, "This is my story, this is my song, praising my Savior all the day long."

God, I trust that You can use me, and I pray that
You would make me ready to serve You. Amen.

Sacramental Service

Now I rejoice in what was suffered for you, and I fill up in my flesh what is still lacking in regard to Christ's afflictions, for the sake of his body, which is the church. Colossians 1:24

You and I are human post offices. We are daily giving out messages of some sort to the world. They do not come from us, but through us; we do not create, we convey. Vance Havner

A Classic Devotional from Oswald Chambers

The Christian worker has to be a sacramental "go-between," to be so identified with his Lord and the reality of His Redemption that He can continually bring His creating life through him. It is not the strength of one man's personality being superimposed on another, but the real presence of Christ coming through the elements of the worker's life. When we preach the historic facts of the life and death of Our Lord as they are conveyed in the New Testament, our words are made sacramental, God uses them on the ground of His Redemption to create in those who listen that which is not created otherwise.

We have to see that we are in such living sympathy with God that as we proclaim His truth He can create in souls the things which He alone can do.

Lord, I ask for Your presence in me so that everyone I meet has a chance to see You. Amen.

Love in Deed

If anyone has material possessions and sees his brother in need but has no pity on him, how can the love of God be in him? 1 JOHN 3:17

If you can't feed a hundred people, then feed just one. MOTHER TERESA

Actions speak louder than words. We all know the common bit of wisdom and few would disagree with the statement. But how many of us still struggle to implement this principle in our lifestyles? How many of us rationalize our lack of love in action on the basis of our fine intentions and words?

Maybe the needs around us are so great that we simply don't know where to start. But perhaps the biggest reason we don't help others in love is that we are too focused on our own needs, wants, and comforts.

Is God's love in you being choked off because it is bottled up? We stem the input when we put a dam in front of the output. How do you reactivate the flow of God's love in your life? He will do it for you. Your job is simply to meet a need right in front of your eyes.

Dear God, thank You for the opportunities
You put before me to share Your love. Amen.

Hospitality

Do not forget to entertain strangers, for by so doing some people have entertained angels without knowing it. HEBREWS 13:2

When there is room in the heart, there is room in the house. DANISH PROVERB

When was the last time you visited someone and felt truly welcome and comfortable? What made you feel that way? In all likelihood, it wasn't just fancy sheets or top-shelf meals. It was the effort your friend put into making you feel at home.

Throughout Scripture, an act of hospitality becomes the scene for a holy moment. Abraham serves a meal for three strangers—who turn out to be God, delivering His prophecy about Abraham and Sarah's future (Genesis 18:1–15). The widow at Zarephath makes a cake of bread for Elijah out of the very last of her flour and oil, and miraculously she never runs out of food (1 Kings 17:7–24). Peter's mother serves Jesus and the disciples after He heals her from a fever (Matthew 8:14–15).

In our modern day, hospitality can turn into something no less holy. God blesses us for receiving others into our homes. And when we take the time to demonstrate care for someone else, we realize that we are merely returning the love God gives to us.

Thank You for the people You've given me to love. Be with me as I plan to show them hospitality this week. Amen.

August

Joy

A Walk in the Woods

Burst into song, you mountains, you forests and all your trees,
for the LORD has redeemed Jacob, he displays his glory in Israel.
ISAIAH 44:23

The creation is quite like a spacious and splendid house, provided and filled with the
most exquisite and the most abundant furnishings. Everything in it tells us of God.
JOHN CALVIN

God brings joy to our lives in various ways: a kind word from a friend, an accomplishment at work, the gentle whisper of His Spirit. But throughout the ages, God has brought joy to us through the wonder of His creation. Feeling down? Maybe all you need is a walk in the woods.

Consider the reaction of Carl Boberg when he looked at the world God made:

"When I look down From lofty mountain grandeur
And hear the brook And feel the gentle breeze; Then sings my soul,
My Saviour God, to Thee, How great Thou art!"

Take time to notice and celebrate God's greatness and gifts, and you'll suddenly find many reasons to be joyful.

Thank You, God, for the beauty of creation. Help me
to see You in the world around me today. Amen.

Joyfully Asking

Delight yourself in the Lord
and he will give you the desires of your heart.
Psalm 37:4

They who love God with all their hearts, find that His ways are ways of
pleasantness, and all His paths are peace. Such joys, such brimful delights,
such overflowing blessednesses, do the saints discover in their Lord.
C. H. Spurgeon

If you're a parent, you're familiar with the innate desire to give gifts to your children, things that will make them happy. In fact, you may even have to check your impulse to spoil them. As our Heavenly Father, God too enjoys giving His children gifts. In Matthew 7:11, Jesus says, "If you, then, though you are evil, know how to give good gifts to your children, how much more will your Father in heaven give good gifts to those who ask him!"

Of course not every prayer will be answered the way we expect or want. God won't give us what is not in our ultimate best interest, and He won't give us what would distract us from Him. But He does desire us to live joyfully. And that knowledge should inspire us to pray boldly—and to rejoice that we have such a wonderful God.

Lord, please work in my heart so that I delight in You.
And thank You for the gifts You give. Amen.

Joyfully Working

Blessed is the man who fears the LORD,
who finds great delight in his commands.

PSALM 112:1

Joy, not grit, is the hallmark of holy obedience. We need to be light-hearted in
what we do to avoid taking ourselves too seriously. It is a cheerful revolt against
self and pride. Or work is jubilant, carefree, merry. Utter abandonment to
God is done freely and with celebration.

RICHARD J. FOSTER

The motivational adage tells us: if you enjoy what you do for a living, you'll never work a day in your life. There is a parallel in the Christian life: if you find joy in God and doing the things that bring God joy, your service to Him will never feel like drudgery and an unwelcome burden.

We worry a lot about taking time for ourselves so that we don't burn out and become weary in doing good. But perhaps it is a sense of self-preoccupation that saps us of energy, and the act of giving and serving that reenergizes us.

Does service energize you and bring you joy? If not, turn your attention to the heart of God and what brings Him joy. You will find God's joy to be contagious!

Dear God, show me the things that
I can do that will bring joy to You. Amen.

Happy Thoughts

Be transformed by the renewing of your mind.
ROMANS 12:2

*Seek to cultivate a buoyant, joyous sense
of the crowded kindnesses of God in your daily life.*
ALEXANDER MACLAREN

Between personnel problems and cranky patients, Amy experienced consider-able stress on her job as a nurse. Some of her frustration went home with her. Although she tried to spare her kids from her moods, four-year-old Brad took notice when her nerves were ragged. One evening, before she left for the night shift at the hospital, the child seemed sad as he hugged her goodbye. But sudden-ly his face seemed to brighten with an idea and he said: "Mom, while you're at work, think happy thoughts."

With a smile, she said, "Thanks, Brad, I will." And that night she did just that—for Brad. But that night's shift went so much better than usual that she soon found herself thinking happy thoughts for herself.

All of us have reasons for joy—an activity we love, a fun-loving friend, or in Amy's case, a tenderhearted young child waiting for her at home. When we choose to dwell on those delightful things in life, we find that joy fills us a little more easily, even during tough days.

God, today I choose, with Your help, to think about the good things in my life. Thank You for the joy You have given me. Amen.

Joy Multiplied

But thanks be to God, who always leads us in triumphal procession in Christ and through us spreads everywhere the fragrance of the knowledge of him.

<small>2 CORINTHIANS 2:14</small>

It is no use walking anywhere to preach unless we preach as we walk.

<small>ST. FRANCIS OF ASSISI</small>

A Classic Devotional from F. B. Meyer

Ours must be the joy of the Lord. It begins with the assurance of forgiveness and acceptance in the Beloved. It is nourished in trial and tribulation, which veil outward sources of consolation, and lead us to rejoice in God through our Lord Jesus. It is independent of circumstances, so that its possessors can sing in the stocks. It lives not in the gifts of God, but in God Himself. It is the fruit of the Spirit, who begets in us love, joy, peace, long-suffering. Get the Lord Himself to fill your soul, and joy will be as natural as the murmur of a brook to its flow.

And such joy will always reveal itself to others. You will desire to send portions to those for whom nothing is prepared. Your joy will be contagious; it will shed its kindly light on sad and weary hearts.

Father in heaven, help me to show a joy
that is irresistible and contagious to those around me.
Thank You for placing that joy in my heart. Amen.

A Joy No One Can Steal

Now is your time of grief, but I will see you again and you will rejoice, and no
one will take away your joy.

JOHN 16:22

God made you. He knows how you operate best. And He knows
what makes you happy. The happiness He gives doesn't stop
when the party's over. It lasts because it comes from deep within.

JOHN MACARTHUR

Even with the most expensive and sophisticated security system in the world,
you can never make your home fail-safe from burglars. But there is something
you have that can't be stolen from you. You don't even have to hide it but can
keep it right out in the open. It's your joy in Christ.

Oh, there are some who will try to rob it from you through using hurtful words
or slighting you in some other way. But they do not have the power to seize it.
You can decide to let them take it—but that's your choice, not their cunning.

There are some people who are so committed to killing joy wherever it is
found that we might be wiser just to steer clear of them. But even in circumstances where there is no escape from the thief who wants to rob joy so that
gloom can take root, you can still keep your joy by simply putting your eyes on
the Author and Giver of joy, Jesus Christ.

Dear God, Your gift of joy makes life wonderful. Help me
experience it and share it, no matter who would try to bring
depression and gloom to my life and world. Amen.

A Joyless Faith

But I tell you: Love your enemies and pray for those who persecute you,
that you may be sons of your Father in heaven.

MATTHEW 5:44–45

Nothing graces the Christian soul as much as mercy.

SAINT AMBROSE

Is someone making your life miserable? Driving you crazy? Keeping you from some simple goals and plans you have for your life? If so, what is your response to that person? Do you complain to others about that person's unfairness? Or do you pray for him or her?

But we can maintain and restore joy by loving the unlovable person through intercessory prayer. Don't just ask God to make that person start treating you better; ask God to change him or her on the inside—and to use you to minister in that person's life. That's not an easy prayer to pray. But the reward for truly loving as Christ loves is incredible. It may not be a physical or monetary reward, but what greater gift can we receive than the gift of joy?

Lord, I lay aside my legitimate complaints and frustrations right
now in order to bless and pray for those who act against me.
Thank You for allowing me to experience You more fully
in my life as I intercede for others. Amen.

The Joy of Knowing Jesus

*I have told you this so that my joy may be in you
and that your joy may be complete.*
JOHN 15:11

According to Jesus, it is God's will that His children be filled with the joy of life.
CATHERINE MARSHALL

A Classic Devotional from Andrew Murray

Abiding fully in Christ is a life of exquisite and overflowing happiness. As Christ gets more complete possession of the soul, it enters into the joy of its Lord. His own joy, the joy of heaven, becomes its own, and that in full measure, and as an ever-abiding portion.

We all know the value of joy. It alone is the proof that what we have really satisfies the heart. Just this makes gladness such a mighty element in the Christian character: there is no proof of the reality of God's love and the blessing He bestows, which men so soon feel the force of, as when the joy of God overcomes all the trials of life. And for the Christian's own welfare, joy is no less indispensable: the joy of the Lord is his strength; confidence, and courage, and patience find their inspiration in joy. With a heart full of joy no work can weary, and no burden can depress; God Himself is strength and song.

Lord Jesus, I want to be more connected to You
and to know Your joy more deeply. Amen.

Joyful Acceptance

*I have learned the secret of being content in any and every situation,
whether well fed or hungry, whether living in plenty or in want.*
PHILIPPIANS 4:12

*Lord grant me the serenity to accept the things I cannot change, the courage
to change the things I can, and the wisdom to know the difference.*
REINHOLD NIEBUHR

We all have things in our lives that we can't change. They run a broad spectrum between minor annoyances, like a family member's persistent, annoying behavior, and real tragedies, like the loss of someone close to us.

But even in situations that are beyond our control, we can choose how we respond. The wisdom of Niebuhr's "Serenity Prayer" reminds us that we can't change some situations and we can't change other people, but we can change ourselves. We can modify our own response to that annoying family member. We can adopt a positive attitude in sticky circumstances. In other words, we can choose joy.

And even during those moments when we can't change our emotions, when grief overwhelms us, we can still choose God. When we do, we are accepting His promise to bring joy into our lives.

Lord, I want to choose joy today. Fill me with Your Holy Spirit and give me wisdom to respond rightly to everything in my life. Amen.

Go with Joy

You will go out in joy
and be led forth in peace;
the mountains and hills
will burst into song before you,
and all the trees of the field
will clap their hands.

ISAIAH 55:12

Attitude is a little thing that makes a big difference.

WINSTON CHURCHILL

Bad habits are easier to form than good habits. It's easier to wallow in a bad attitude than to change the way we look at life in a positive way. Those principles are true of both groups and individuals.

What is the attitude of the various groups you belong to? Your neighborhood friends? Your work department? Your family? Your church? Is there a spirit of negativity and complaining—or a spirit of joy? Most importantly, what attitude do you bring to the table?

Are you positive or negative? Do you go forth into the world with a contagious joy—where even mountains and hills begin to shout—or do you succumb to a prevailing negativity? The choice is yours!

Dear God, help me to take joy into every situation
and every meeting I have today. Amen.

His Joy and Our Joy

I am coming to you now, but I say these things while I am still in the world,
so that they may have the full measure of my joy within them.
JOHN 17:13

Joy is a net of love by which you can catch souls.
MOTHER TERESA

A Classic Devotional from Oswald Chambers

What was the joy that Jesus had? It is an insult to use the word happiness in connection with Jesus Christ. The joy of Jesus was the absolute self-surrender and self-sacrifice of Himself to His Father, the joy of doing that which the Father sent Him to do. Jesus prayed that our joy might go on fulfilling itself until it was the same joy as His. Have I allowed Jesus Christ to introduce His joy to me?

The full flood of my life is not in bodily health, not in external happenings, not in seeing God's work succeed, but in the perfect understanding of God, and in the communion with Him that Jesus Himself had. Be rightly related to God, find your joy there, and out of you will flow rivers of living water. Be a centre for Jesus Christ to pour living water through. The life that is rightly related to God is as natural as breathing wherever it goes. The lives that have been of most blessing to you are those who were unconscious of it.

Lord, please fill me with Your joy, and pour it
into the lives of others through me. Amen.

Unbeatable Joy

*He chose us in him before the creation of the world to be holy
and blameless in his sight. In love he predestined us to be adopted
as his sons through Jesus Christ, in accordance with his pleasure and will.*

EPHESIANS 1:4–5

*Resolve to keep happy and your joy and you shall form
an invincible host against difficulties.*

HELEN KELLER

Someone may think he or she can put you in your place with a sarcastic slam in your direction, a joke at your expense, an unfair criticism, or some other form of putdown. But no one can make you feel bad about yourself if you march into life with an unconquerable joy; a joy that looks in the face of hardship and opposition and smiles.

Where does that joy come from? How can you develop that inner peace and confidence that doesn't allow the pettiness of life to rob you of joy? Simple. It's coming to the point in life that you know beyond a shadow of a doubt that the one opinion that really matters—the only opinion that really matters—is what your Heavenly Father thinks of you. Since He loves you so much, you have much to be joyful for!

God, I walk in joy today, knowing You
know me best and love me most. Amen.

Time to Party

Rejoice in the Lord always. I will say it again: Rejoice!
PHILIPPIANS 4:4

*Whence comes this idea that if what we are doing is fun,
it can't be God's will? The God who made giraffes, a baby's fingernails,
a puppy's tail, a crook necked squash, the bobwhite's call, and a young
girl's giggle, has a sense of humor. Make no mistake about that.*
CATHERINE MARSHALL

Do you think of parties as wholly unspiritual? Do you think of time spent enjoying the company of friends as "wasted" or idle?

Jesus Himself was criticized sharply for attending parties. One of His most famous Bible stories was of a son who wandered far from home, squandering all his father had given him. But when he did finally come to his senses and return to his family, the father's immediate response was to throw a huge party to celebrate having his son back home. (See Luke 15:11–32.)

God has created a rhythm to life that involves work and worship, yes, but also play. Sure, some people need to rein themselves in and play a little less. But God has given us reasons to celebrate, and we should devote time to rejoicing as an act of worship. So go ahead and throw that party sooner than later. It could be just what you—and your friends—need to draw closer to God.

Dear Lord, You have given me much to celebrate.
Thank You for the chance to do so. Amen.

Rejoice in the Success of Others

Rejoice with those who rejoice; mourn with those who mourn.
ROMANS 12:15

If God accepts me as I am, then I had better do the same.
HUGH MONTEFIORE

We live in a competitive world where it is difficult for many people to find joy in the success of others. How do you feel when a friend gets a promotion? When someone else in the company wins the award? When a classmate gets the top score on a test? When a sibling gets an incredible return on an investment? Do you feel instant joy or pangs of resentment and jealousy?

We are often much better at comforting someone in their times of sorrow than sincerely celebrating their moments of triumph.

The answer is simple but difficult: we must first realize our own success is measured in the eyes of God—not in comparison with others. When that sinks into our hearts and minds, it is so much easier to rejoice in the success of others. Sincerely.

Thank You, Heavenly Father, for defining success in my life. Thank You for blessing me and for blessing those around me. Amen.

Because He Loves

*If you have any encouragement from being united with Christ,
if any comfort from his love, if any fellowship with the Spirit, if any
tenderness and compassion, then make my joy complete by being
like-minded, having the same love, being one in spirit and purpose.*

PHILIPPIANS 2:1–2

*This is the secret of joy. We shall no longer strive for our own way;
but commit ourselves, easily and simply, to God's way,
acquiesce in His will, and in so doing find our peace.*

EVELYN UNDERHILL

A Classic Devotional from Alexander Maclaren

We may think of the joy that belongs to the Divine Nature as coming from the completeness of His being, which is raised far above all that makes of sorrow. But it is not in Himself alone that He is glad; but it is because He loves. The exercise of love is ever blessedness. His joy is in self impartation; His delights are in the sons of men. His gladness is in His children when they let Him love them, and do not throw back His love on itself. He is glad when His face is mirrored in ours, and the rays from Him are reflected from us.

God, it's amazing to me that You delight in us, Your children.
Help me to understand Your love and rejoice in You today. Amen.

True Joy

In all my prayers for all of you, I always pray with joy.
PHILIPPIANS 1:4

Joy is not the absence of trouble but the presence of Christ.
WILLIAM VAN DER HOVEN

Paul's letter to the Philippians is considered the book of joy in the New Testament. Written from a prison in Rome, Paul gave these characteristics of true joy:

True joy is found in bonds of fellowship: "I thank my God every time I remember you. In all my prayers for all of you, I always pray with joy because of your partnership in the gospel from the first day until now" (1:3–5).

True joy finds its confidence in the work of God: "Being confident of this, that he who began a good work in you will carry it on to completion until the day of Christ Jesus" (1:6).

True joy grows proportionally with love: "And this is my prayer: that your love may abound more and more in knowledge and depth of insight" (1:9).

True joy is based on righteous living: "So that you may be able to discern what is best and may be pure and blameless until the day of Christ, filled with the fruit of righteousness that comes through Jesus Christ" (1:10–11).

True joy brings glory to God: "To the glory and praise of God" (1:11).

Are you experiencing God's joy today?

Lord, I want to exhibit the qualities of true joy in my life.
Thank You that You have started and will finish
a good work in and through my life. Amen.

The Mark of a Hero

The LORD is my strength and my shield;
my heart trusts in him, and I am helped.
My heart leaps for joy
and I will give thanks to him in song.

PSALM 28:7

I am of the opinion that we should not be concerned about working for God
until we have learned the meaning and delight of worshiping Him.

A. W. TOZER

What makes a hero a hero? Great deeds are usually what sets a hero apart from others. But what makes one hero-eligible before the great deeds are accomplished? A biblical hero is always characterized by great faith. And that faith is marked by a sense of joy. Not joy in circumstances; it's hard to feel joyful when facing a giant named Goliath. But joy that is focused on God.

Mary's heart leapt with joy toward God at the foretelling of the birth of Jesus (Luke 1:46–55); the apostle Paul rejoiced in God even when facing certain death (Philippians 4:4); David could not contain his joy in God and danced through the streets (2 Samuel 6:14–15).

The list goes on and on. Does your heart leap for joy at the thought of God?

Heavenly Father, You are my source of joy in life;
I rejoice in You. Amen.

I Choose Joy

Be joyful always.
1 THESSALONIANS 5:16

I choose joy. I will invite my God to be the God of circumstance. I will refuse the temptation to be cynical, the tool of the lazy thinker. I will refuse to see people as anything less than human beings, created by God. I will refuse to see any problem as anything less than an opportunity to see God.

MAX LUCADO

What will your attitude be today? Positive or negative? Dissatisfied or grateful? Optimistic or cynical? Unhappy or joyful?

All good gifts come from God, including joy. But God still invites us to participate in receiving His gifts and blessings through our own free will. We can't save ourselves, but we must say yes to salvation. We can't walk worthy of His calling on our own, but we can say yes to His strength through simple obedience. And we can't force ourselves to be joyful. But we can say yes to God's kind and delightful offering by saying yes through our attitudes.

Have you chosen joy for your life? For today?

Heavenly Father, I say yes to You and Your gift of joy today. Amen.

How to Be Happy

Though you have not seen him, you love him;
and even though you do not see him now, you believe in him
and are filled with an inexpressible and glorious joy.
1 PETER 1:8

Happy is the person who not only sings, but feels God's eye is on the sparrow,
and knows He watches over me. To be simply ensconced in God is true joy.
C. C. COLTON

A Classic Devotional from R. A. Torrey

The text tells us that the way to obtain this "inexpressible and glorious joy," the way to be inexpressibly happy at all times and under all circumstances, is just by believing on the unseen Christ Jesus. What does it mean to believe on Jesus Christ? There is no mystery at all about that. It simply means to put confidence in Jesus Christ to be what He claims to be and what He offers Himself to be to us, to put confidence in Him as the One who died in our place; to put confidence in Him as the One who was raised from the dead and who now has "all power in heaven and on earth," and therefore is able to keep us day by day, and give us victory, over sin and worship and adore Him. It is wonderful the joy that comes to him who thus believes on Jesus Christ. But one must really believe on Jesus Christ to have this joy.

Lord, I know that trusting You completely will bring
me fullness of joy. Teach me to rely on You. Amen.

Say Cheese!

On the third day a wedding took place at Cana in Galilee. Jesus' mother was there, and Jesus and his disciples had also been invited to the wedding.

JOHN 2:2

The religion that makes a man look sick certainly won't cure the world!

PHILLIPS BROOKS

The great Bible teacher William Barclay said: "A gloomy Christian is a contradiction of terms, and nothing in all religious history has done Christianity more harm than its connection with black clothes and long faces." When people who are without faith look at your face, what do they see? A twinkle in the eye and a smile teasing at the corners of your mouth? Or a dark, sullen anger or unhappiness? Maybe if we wanted to learn to share our faith with the world more effectively, we wouldn't attend another class on personal evangelism at church, but would spend time in front of the mirror practicing our smile!

If your feelings are characterized more by gloom than glee today, don't chase after happiness or psychoanalyze yourself. Instead turn your heart toward God. One of the fruits of the Spirit that He gives to believers is joy (Galatians 5:22). Take a deep breath and pause until the emotions that are swirling around inside you are stilled. Simply set your eyes on Jesus and ask Him to restore your joy. He is more than able to do so. And that's something to smile about.

Father, You are the Source of joy in my life. My eyes
are on You. My heart is set on You. I love and adore You.
Thank You for the blessing of your joy. Amen.

Where Joy Won't Be Found

Why spend money on what is not bread,
and your labor on what does not satisfy?
ISAIAH 55:2

Joy is the most infallible sign of the presence of God.
LEON BLOY

Someone has observed that men have pursued joy in every avenue imaginable; some have successfully found it, while others have not. But we can know for sure that joy cannot be found in these places—

Not in Unbelief: Voltaire remains one of the greatest cynics and skeptics in literature. He wrote: "I wish I had never been born."

Not in Pleasure: Lord Byron lived a life of pleasure if anyone did. He wrote: "The worm, the canker, and grief are mine alone."

Not in Money: millionaire Jay Gould had plenty of that. When dying, he said: "I suppose I am the most miserable man on earth."

Not in Position and Fame: Lord Beaconsfield enjoyed more than his share of both. Yet he wrote: "Youth is a mistake; manhood a struggle; old age a regret."

Not in Military Glory: Alexander the Great conquered the known world in his day. Having done so, he wept in his tent and said, "There are no more worlds to conquer."

Lord, I know that the real joy in life is in Christ alone. Thank You for sending Your Son that I might know joy in Him. Amen.

A Sudden Change

But the fruit of the Spirit is love, joy, peace, patience, kindness, goodness, faithfulness, gentleness, self-control; against such things there is no law.
GALATIANS 5:22–23

Joy is the echo of God's life in us.
JOSEPH MARMION

A Classic Devotional from Thomas Watson

Spiritual joy is a sweet and delightful passion, arising from the apprehension and feeling of some good, whereby the soul is supported under present troubles, and fenced against future fear. Joy is not a fancy, or conceit; but is rational, and arises from the feeling of some good, as the sense of God's love and favour. Joy is so real a thing that it makes a sudden change in a person; and turns mourning into melody. As in the spring-time, when the sun comes to our horizon, it makes a sudden alteration in the face of the universe: the birds sing, the flowers appear, the fig-tree puts forth her green figs; every thing seems to rejoice and put off its mourning, as being revived with the sweet influence of the sun; so when the Sun of Righteousness arises on the soul, it makes a sudden alteration, and the soul is infinitely rejoiced with the golden beams of God's love.

Father, may Your comforts delight my soul with Your great joy. Amen.

A Testimony to Joy

Who can proclaim the mighty acts of the Lord
or fully declare his praise?
PSALM 106:2

How many people have you made homesick for God?
OSWALD CHAMBERS

On the news reports that followed the infamous Hurricane Katrina hurricane, viewers sadly shook their heads or just looked on in horror as they saw images of the New Orleans streets underwater, waterlogged homes, and stranded survivors. But even amidst all the shock and horror at the destruction, some interviewees gave testimony of God's protection and provision during the storm. They praised Him with gratitude for the whole nation to hear. Other tragedies have generated similar displays of amazing joy.

One of the reasons we are to rejoice in God is so that others will know of His goodness. Yes, it's good for our own soul, but it also blesses others. Our testimony of God's joy—even in the midst of difficulties—can be a life-changing witness to those around us. And in the process, we stir and reinforce our own faith.

Lord, help me to shout for joy as I seek
to share Your goodness with others. Amen.

Enduring Joy

Let us fix our eyes on Jesus, the author and perfecter of our faith,
who for the joy set before him endured the cross, scorning its shame,
and sat down at the right hand of the throne of God.

HEBREWS 12:2

Christ came to take away our sins, to roll off our curse, to unbind our chains,
to open our prison house, to cancel our debt; in a word, to give us the oil of joy
for mourning, the garment of praise for the spirit of heaviness. Is not this joy?

OCTAVIUS WINSLOW

The perfect picture of joy is found in the life of Jesus. And what an amazing, active, buoyant, effective, fulfilling life He lived. But we don't see the full measure of His joy in the miracle of turning water to wine at a wedding, nor in the feeding the five thousand. Amazingly, we don't see Jesus' joy in full bloom until the darkest moment of his life: "for the joy set before him [he] endured the cross" (Hebrews 12:2).

In John 15:11 we read that Jesus spoke to His disciples, "I have told you this so that my joy may be in you and that your joy may be complete." In His final instructions He was teaching those He loved how to have the same joy He had through closeness to God the Father. But it was on the cross that He paid the price that made this joy possible.

Next time you struggle with a sense of joy, simply consider Jesus.

Lord, thank You for the cross that saves me and brings
me to You, for the joy of knowing You. I love You. Amen.

Joy for Eternity

Then I saw a new heaven and a new earth, for the first heaven and the first earth had passed away, and there was no longer any sea. REVELATION 21:1

The enjoyment of God is the only happiness with which our souls can be satisfied. To go to heaven, fully to enjoy God, is infinitely better than the most pleasant accommodations here. Fathers and mothers, husbands, wives, or children, or the company of earthly friends, are but shadows, but God is the substance. These are but scattered beams, but God is the sun. These are but streams. But God is the ocean.

JONATHAN EDWARDS

It's been said that those who let their minds dwell on heaven are of no earthly good. But is it possible that the opposite is true? The history of the Christian church is filled with accounts that those who thought most of heaven did the most good here on earth.

The realization that this present life is not all there is does give one a perspective that every moment here on earth counts. It challenges us to walk closely with God so as to not miss an eternity in heaven with Him—and to put our hands to the task of bringing friends, family members, and loved ones along with us.

Do you live your life today with the understanding that the much greater portion of your existence will be spent after your death? Are you making your life count in eternity? And are you inviting others to enjoy the presence of God for eternity with you?

Lord, thank You for the gift of eternal life and for inviting me to spend eternity with You. I pray that my loved ones will join me in heaven. Amen.

The Joy of God's Presence

Light is shed upon the righteous
and joy on the upright in heart.
Rejoice in the LORD, you who are righteous,
and praise his holy name.
PSALM 97:11–12

The more we enjoy of God, the more we are ravished with delight.
THOMAS WATSON

There's a popular legend told in the Middle East of a wise and good king who loved his people. He deeply wanted to know how they lived, to know about their hardships. So he often dressed as a working man or a beggar and visited the homes of the poor. None of them suspected that he was their ruler. On one occasion, he visited a very poor man who lived in a cellar. He ate the poor-quality food the man ate and spoke kind, comforting words to him. Later he visited the poor man again. This time, he decided to reveal his true identity and told him, "I am your king." He thought the man would surely ask for a gift or favor. But instead, the man said, "You left your palace to visit me. You ate my food and sat with me in this dreary place. You were kind to me. To others you have given your rich gifts. But to me you have given yourself!"

God has done everything good and kind and generous to have fellowship with us; even becoming a human. When we recognize His presence, we experience gladness of heart. We have a King who is with us always.

Lord God, I praise You today. Thank You for coming into my life. Amen.

The Choice to Be Happy

We proclaim to you what we have seen and heard, so that you also may have fellowship with us. And our fellowship is with the Father and with his Son, Jesus Christ. We write this to make our joy complete.

1 JOHN 1:3–4

We all desire to be happy. That is something that is innate in human nature; nobody wants to be miserable, though I am aware of the fact that there are people who seem to enjoy being miserable and some who seem to find their happiness in being unhappy!

MARTYN LLOYD-JONES

Do we have a choice when it comes to joy?

The Apostle James says: "Consider it pure joy, my brothers, whenever you face trials of many kinds" (James 1:2). Paul says, "Rejoice in the Lord always. I will say it again: Rejoice!" (Philippians 4:4). Jesus said to His disciples, "Do not let your hearts be troubled and do not be afraid" (John 14:27).

Is joy a choice? The biblical answer is clearly yes. But throughout Scripture there is a strong recognition that it is not always an easy choice. Life can be tough. We get hurt. There are disappointments. Sometimes circumstances seem to conspire against us. And yet as an act of worship, as a matter of prayer, as a declaration of faith, as an act of love for Jesus, we can choose joy. Just the fact that God has given us a choice to experience joy is a reason to rejoice.

Heavenly Father, I choose to walk in the joy
You have so graciously given to me. Thank You! Amen.

Harvest Time

He makes grass grow for the cattle,
and plants for man to cultivate—
bringing forth food from the earth:
wine that gladdens the heart of man,
oil to make his face shine,
and bread that sustains his heart.

PSALM 104:14–15

We know that our reward depends not on the job itself
but on the faithfulness with which we serve God.

JOHN PAUL I

Every year, farmers go into a flurry of activity when harvest time arrives. The memory of the long hours of hard labor necessary to guarantee a good crop seems to fade in the distance. They feel pride at seeing the finished results of all their work—grain, vegetables, and livestock that will feed many people.

We all experience harvest times in our lives, whether we own a farm or can't keep a houseplant alive. We must work hard toward our goals, whether they're professional, personal, or spiritual. But if we're persistent and diligent, we'll experience a harvest; we'll reap rewards from our labors. And that's a very special kind of joy, the thrill of hard work paying off.

God, give me diligence to keep working so that I might see
fruit in my life and in the lives of others. Amen.

Too Easily Pleased

For where your treasure is, there your heart will be also.
MATTHEW 6:21

Where your pleasure is, there is your treasure; Where your treasure is,
there is your heart; Where your heart is, there is your happiness.
AUGUSTINE

Could it be that so many in our modern culture are unhappy because they have mistaken fleeting pleasures for a deep abiding joy, and in so doing, have treasured unworthy ends? C. S. Lewis probed this thought when he said: "Indeed, if we consider the unblushing promises of reward and the staggering nature of the rewards promised in the Gospels, it would seem that our Lord finds our desires not too strong, but too weak. We are half-hearted creatures, fooling around with drink and sex and ambition when infinite joy is offered us, like an ignorant child who wants to go on making mud pies in the slum because he cannot imagine what is meant by the offer of a holiday at the sea. We are far too easily pleased."

All of us need a spiritual checkup from time to time to make sure our hearts and our desires are in line with God's will for our lives. Where do you find your pleasure? What do you consider your treasure? Have you given your heart to something of infinite worth?

O God, my pleasure is in you. I give You my heart.
I treasure my relationship with You! Amen.

Thank God for Happiness

Is any one of you in trouble? He should pray.
Is anyone happy? Let him sing songs of praise.
JAMES 5:13

All our life is a celebration for us; we are convinced, in fact,
that God is always everywhere. We sing while we work . . .
we pray while we carry out all life's other occupations.
ST. CLEMENT OF ALEXANDRIA

Into every life a little rain must fall. Sometimes things go wrong. But sometimes things go right. And when they do, James says, we should praise God.

What's going right in your life today—what is making you happy? Is there a relationship in your life that's thriving? Do you have the simple blessings of a job and reliable transportation to work? Have you found an activity or service opportunity that brings you joy? You might have to do a little looking around and count your blessings; sometimes those little reasons for joy and gratitude get overlooked. But when you find something to be happy about, be happy.

When we find ourselves in trouble, we need to turn to God for help and strength. But when things are going well, we—again—need to turn to God. He deserves our thanksgiving for the good things He gives us.

Lord, You have given me so many reasons to be happy.
Today I want to express my joy as praise to You. Amen.

A Fountain of Joy

*Though you have not seen him, you love him; and even though you do not see him
now, you believe in him and are filled with an inexpressible and glorious joy.*
1 PETER 1:8

When I met Christ, I felt that I had swallowed sunshine.
E. STANLEY JONES

A Classic Devotional from Dwight L. Moody

Happiness is caused by things that happen around me, and circumstances will mar it; but joy flows right on through trouble; joy flows on through the dark; joy flows in the night as well as in the day; joy flows all through persecution and opposition. It is an unceasing fountain bubbling up in the heart; a secret spring the world can't see and doesn't know anything about. The Lord gives his people perpetual joy when they walk in obedience to him.

Joy is love exalted; peace is love in repose; long-suffering is love enduring; gentleness is love in society; goodness is love in action; faith is love on the battlefield; meekness is love in school; and temperance is love in training. The world does not understand theology or dogma, but it understands love and sympathy.

God, thank You for the joy You offer me, a joy that transcends
all circumstances. Help me walk closely with You. Amen.

September

Obedience

Keep in Step

Since we live by the Spirit, let us keep in step with the Spirit.
GALATIANS 5:25

*God is God. Because He is God, He is worthy of my trust and obedience.
I will find rest nowhere but in His holy will, a will that is
unspeakably beyond my largest notions of what He is up to.*
ELISABETH ELLIOT

What goes into living the Christian life? Many traditions of the faith have answered that question with certain emphases and nuances, but three common traits have always been part of the Christian walk: faith, trust, and obedience.

Faith is a belief in the reality of God, the goodness and love of God, and the relationship God desires to have with us. "Now faith is being sure of what we hope for and certain of what we do not see" (Hebrews 11:1). Trust is an ongoing expression of faith; it is placing our confidence in God and depending on Him every step of the way. It is our basis for assurance that God is with us in all circumstances of life. "Though he slay me, yet will I hope in him" (Job 13:15).

Obedience is when we acknowledge that Jesus is not only our Savior—but our Lord. It is the full expression of faith, where we trust God so much we submit to His commands, His ways, His will. "But if we walk in the light, as he is in the light, we have fellowship with one another, and the blood of Jesus, his Son, purifies us from all sin" (1 John 1:7).

Lord, I want to keep in step with the Spirit. Give me the faith and trust to obey Your commands and will in all my steps. Amen.

The Protection of Obedience

The wise are cautious and avoid danger;
fools plunge ahead with reckless confidence.
PROVERBS 14:16

Danger and delight grow on one stalk.
SCOTTISH PROVERB

A family visited with friends in a tropical country. In the midst of a seemingly peaceful moment, the kids playing and the adults conversing casually, the father who called this exotic island his home suddenly stood up and shouted to his son, "Hit the ground!" The son did so immediately, crouching under the large tree nearby. The visiting family was shocked at the father's tone and the son's instant obedience. Then they learned that the father saw a poisonous snake hanging from the tree that was close to striking him. The father's quick reaction and the boy's quick obedience saved him.

The child obviously sensed the urgency in his father's voice and facial expression. But he also had an implicit trust in his dad's judgment and instructions. We ought always to have the same trust in our Heavenly Father's commandments. They are always for our good and protection.

Lord God, help me to know Your commandments
and obey them without question. Amen.

Carry Your Cross

*If anyone would come after me, he must deny
himself and take up his cross and follow me.*
MARK 8:34

The only lasting treasure is spiritual; the only perfect freedom is serving God.
MALCOLM MUGGERIDGE

A Classic Devotional from Alexander Smellie

The cross which my Lord bids me take up and carry may assume different shapes. I may have to content myself with a lowly and narrow sphere, when I feel that I have capacities for much higher work. I may have to go on cultivating year after year, a field which seems to yield me no harvests whatsoever. There are many crosses, and every one of them is sore and heavy. None of them is likely to be sought out by me of my own accord. But never is Jesus so near me as when I lift my cross, and lay it submissively on my shoulder, and give it the welcome of a patient and unmurmuring spirit.

He draws close, to ripen my wisdom, to deepen my peace, to increase my courage, to augment my power to be of use to others, through the very experience which is so grievous and distressing, and then I grow under the load.

Lord, I choose to take up my cross and follow You.
Thank You for being close to me when I do so. Amen.

The Free Obedience of Christ

The reason my Father loves me is that I lay down my life—only to take it up again. No one takes it from me, but I lay it down of my own accord.

JOHN 10:17–18

Obey God one step at a time, then the next step will come into view.

CATHERINE MARSHALL

A Classic Devotional from R. Murray McCheyne

There is nothing more certain than that no man can lay down his life for another. Two things that made it right in Christ to lay down His life: He is the Lord of all and the Father gave Him a commandment to lay it down. "I have power to lay it down, and I have power to take it again. This commandment have I received of my Father." He was not forced to lay His life down though men bound Him, but He laid down His life Himself. At Nazareth, they tried to cast Him over the hill on which the city was built, but He passed through the midst of them and escaped. He could have done this to the very end. When He saw them at a distance, coming down the hill with their torches, He could have fled; but He would not. The Father said, "Go into the world, and lay down your life for sinners." . . . It is true, it pleased the Lord to bruise Him, but He put Himself into the hands of divine justice.

Jesus, thank You, for the living example of laying my life down for You. Help me to do so out of obedience to Your commands. Amen.

In View of God's Mercy

Therefore, I urge you, brothers, in view of God's mercy, to offer your bodies as living sacrifices, holy and pleasing to God—this is your spiritual act of worship.
ROMANS 12:1

Worship is our response to the overtures of love from the heart of the Father. Its central reality is found "in spirit and truth." It is kindled within us only when the Spirit of God touches our human spirit.
RICHARD J. FOSTER

Paul spends the first eleven chapters of Romans establishing the truth that salvation is a gift from God; there is no justification before Him on the basis of our works. He was fighting hard against the idea that legalism is the basis for our faith.

But in chapter 12 of Romans, he shows that good works, obedience, sacrifice, commitment, discipline, and lifestyle are a huge part of what it means to be a Christian. They don't make us children of God, but we do them because we are children of God. Because of God's mercy—His gift of new life through the blood of Jesus—Paul urges us to offer ourselves as living sacrifices.

Have you offered yourself completely to God for His use and purposes in the world?

Heavenly Father, thank You for Your mercy
that gave me new life. I give that life to You. Amen.

Use Your Talents

Each one should use whatever gift he has received to serve others,
faithfully administering God's grace in its various forms.
1 PETER 4:10

One thing taught large in the Holy Scriptures is that while God gives
His gifts freely, He will require a strict accounting of them at the end of the road.
A. W. TOZER

There is a familiar story of three men who were given varying talents by their master. (See Matthew 25:14–30.) The man with the most talents did the most. *Not surprising.* The man with the second most talents came in second place. *Not unexpected.* The third man did absolutely nothing. *Of course. He didn't have enough to make a difference.* When the master saw that he had buried what was given to him, he took it away.

Is that fair? What if he had lost the meager amount on a bad investment? Wouldn't he have been in bigger trouble? Jesus' story doesn't seem to indicate that. He says nothing about being judged on the basis of failing. Judgment is based on doing nothing, burying the talents God has given us.

What resources has God given you to work with in life? Has He given you a lot or a little or something in between? Your answer isn't important. All that matters is what you're going to do with what you've got. What investment do you need to make in your world?

Lord, help me to conquer fear and use my talents
for good—for You. Thank You for blessing me. Amen.

Two Brothers

*For whoever does the will of my Father in heaven
is my brother and sister and mother.*
MATTHEW 12:50

*Give God an inch, and He'll take a mile, encouraging
and strengthening you each step of the way.*
JONI EARECKSON TADA

The Bible is filled with famous brothers. Cain and Abel. Jacob and Esau. Peter and Andrew. The prodigal and his older brother. But there are two unnamed brothers that Jesus introduced in a parable. (See Matthew 21:28–31.) Their father gave each an assignment. One had a great attitude and immediately told his father, "No problem, I'm on it." The other brother moaned and complained and said, "No way." At the end of the day, the one with a great attitude had done a great job and the one with a bad attitude was still pouting and sullen. Right?

Wrong! The first brother got distracted and never got after it. The other brother thought better of his refusal and got the job done. Jesus asked, "Which one obeyed?" Easy answer. The one who got it done.

A good attitude is better than a bad attitude, but actions still speak louder than words. Have a bad attitude over a task God has placed before you? Just get busy and it'll disappear before you know it.

God, sometimes there's a certain joy missing in my efforts
to obey You. But I do want to live in a way that pleases You.
Teach me to obey whether or not I feel like it. Amen.

Joyful Obedience

Submit yourselves, then, to God. Resist the devil, and he will flee from you. Come near to God and he will come near to you.
JAMES 4:7–8

I know the power obedience has of making things easy which seem impossible.
TERESA OF AVILA

A Classic Devotional from Thomas à Kempis

It is a very great thing to obey, to live under a superior and not to be one's own master, for it is much safer to be subject than it is to command. Many live in obedience more from necessity than from love. Such become discontented and dejected on the slightest pretext; they will never gain peace of mind unless they subject themselves wholeheartedly for the love of God. Go where you may, you will find no rest except in humble obedience to the rule of authority. Dreams of happiness expected from change and different places have deceived many.

Lord, help me to find contentment in obeying You. Amen.

Be Fruitful

*Our people must learn to devote themselves to doing what is good, in order
that they may provide for daily necessities and not live unproductive lives.*

TITUS 3:14

An idle life and a holy heart are a contradiction.

THOMAS BROOKS

One of Paul's faithful coworkers in his missionary travels throughout the
Roman Empire was Titus. He left Titus on the island of Crete to encourage and
establish order in the churches there (1:5). He repeats a common theme that
salvation is not a matter of works but God's kindness: "But when the kindness
and love of God our Savior appeared, he saved us, not because of righteous
things we had done, but because of his mercy" (3:4–5).

But in verse 14 he appeals to an image from farming. Fruitfulness does not
happen unless seeds of good works and acts of love are planted: "Our people
must learn to devote themselves to doing what is good, in order that they may
provide for daily necessities and not live unproductive lives" (3:14).

Fall is coming and your fruitfulness will be in measure with the seeds of love
and obedience you've planted. What seeds will you plant today?

God, teach me to live well, bearing fruit of faithfulness to You. Amen.

The Wrong Kind of Pride

When pride comes, then comes disgrace,
but with humility comes wisdom.

PROVERBS 11:2

If you are humble, nothing will touch you, neither praise
nor disgrace, because you know what you are.

MOTHER TERESA

The sin of pride can be hard to define. Arrogance can be part of it, yes; but it's possible to have both pride and poor self-image at work in one's life at the same time. God doesn't want us to lack self-respect, either. Maybe it's best simply to be ever aware that all of us are vulnerable to vain pride and that it can find us at any time, anywhere.

Pride says, "I can do what I want," "I'm better than others," and "I'm looking out for number one." Above all, pride says, "I don't need God or anyone—I can make it on my own." But of course we do need God. And when we resist surrendering to Him, depending on Him, we experience damage to our souls.

Fortunately, we can resist our pride by simply praying and asking God to heal us from a prideful attitude and help us think rightly about ourselves, God, and others. When that happens, we can rest content in God's will and at peace with ourselves and others.

Lord, please heal me of a vain pride and set me
in right relationship with You. Amen.

An Obedient Surrender

Therefore everyone who hears these words of Mine and acts on them,
may be compared to a wise man who built his house on the rock. And the
rain fell, and the floods came, and the winds blew and slammed against
that house; and yet it did not fall, for it had been founded on the rock.
MATTHEW 7:24-25

Unless he obeys, a man cannot believe.
DIETRICH BONHOEFFER

A Classic Devotional from Andrew Murray

You know in daily life what absolute surrender is. You know that everything has to be given up to its special, definite object and service. I have a pen in my pocket, and that pen is absolutely surrendered to the one work of writing, and that pen must be absolutely surrendered to my hand if I am to write properly with it. If another holds it partly, I cannot write properly. This coat is absolutely given up to me to cover my body. The Temple of Solomon was absolutely surrendered to God when it was dedicated to Him. And every one of us is a temple of God, in which God will dwell and work mightily on one condition—absolute surrender to Him. God claims it, God is worthy of it, and without it God cannot work His blessed work in us. God not only claims it, but God will work it Himself.

Lord, today I choose to surrender to You completely. Amen.

Take the Right Path

We all, like sheep, have gone astray, each of us has turned
to his own way; and the Lord has laid on him the iniquity of us all.

ISAIAH 53:6

The word of God hidden in the heart is a stubborn voice to suppress.

BILLY GRAHAM

It's not that hard to take a wrong turn in life. Doing the wrong thing, if we're honest, has an allure. It's called temptation. When we look around, it's common to spot someone who has gone astray—wayward sons, daughters, friends, and acquaintances fill prisons and homeless shelters, church pews, and cubicles alike.

The good news is that when we repent, God can turn us around and help us find our way again. The better news is that He offers plenty of advice for how to live well in the world so that we can avoid going off the rails in the first place. The book of Proverbs alone is a treasure trove of principles for living: work hard, watch the time, don't live just for pleasure, make following God your primary concern. These aren't burdensome rules; they're simply guidelines for living the game of life well and effectively.

Open your Bible and let God lead you today. He'll show you the right path to take.

Dear Lord, thank You for picking me up and setting me on the right path. Give me understanding of Your principles for living. Amen.

Listen with Your Legs

*Whether you turn to the right or to the left, your ears will hear
a voice behind you, saying, "This is the way; walk in it."*
ISAIAH 30:21

*In many ways, the attitude of obedience is much more vital than
the act, because if the attitude is right, the act will naturally follow.*
JOHN MACARTHUR

Four-year-old Beverly was playing with her toys. Her mother, who was folding laundry across the room, noticed that Beverly's shirt was dirty and needed to be changed. She told Beverly to take it off and bring it to her so that she could wash it.

After telling her twice with no response, her mother finally gave her the full three-name call: "Beverly Elizabeth Provost, did you hear me?" Beverly answered, "Yes, Mama. My ears did, but my legs didn't."

Sometimes we don't hear God's directions because we're simply too busy; we're not listening with our whole being. What is God calling you to do today? Are you ready to listen with your legs as well as your ears?

Dear God, help me to be still and listen to You so
that I know what You want me to do. Amen.

The Benefits of Obedience

I lift up my hands to your commands,
which I love, and I meditate on your decrees.
PSALM 119:48

God's commands are designed to guide you to life's very best. You will not
obey Him, if you do not believe Him and trust Him. You cannot believe Him
if you do not love Him. You cannot love Him unless you know Him.
HENRY BLACKABY

We all know there are negative consequences to disobeying God, but do we ever stop to consider all the blessings and rewards that come to us through obedience? Have we made obedience a drudgery that steals the fun from life, rather than affirming how much sweeter and better it makes life? There are more rewards and blessings from obedience than can be listed on a single page, but consider the following as you look up the corresponding Bible verses.

Obedience gives us a clean conscience: Psalm 19:13
Obedience keeps us from danger: Psalm 119:10
Obedience brings material blessings: Deuteronomy 11:13–15
Obedience prolongs life: Deuteronomy 11:9
Obedience is a blessing to our family: Psalm 112:1–3
Obedience brings joy: Psalm 119:33–35
Obedience increases our faith: James 2:17

Lord God, thank You for enriching my life as I walk in Your ways. Amen.

The Power of Obedience

Then he took the Book of the Covenant and read it to the people. They
responded, "We will do everything the LORD has said; we will obey."

EXODUS 24:7

We ought not to be weary of doing little things for the love of God, who regards
not the greatness of the work, but the love with which it is performed.

BROTHER LAWRENCE

A Classic Devotional from Oswald Chambers

All God's revelations are sealed to us until they are opened to us by obedience.
You will never get them open by philosophy or thinking. Immediately you obey,
a flash of light comes. Let God's truth work in you by soaking in it, not by worrying into it. Obey God in the thing He is at present showing you, and instantly the
next thing is opened up. We read tomes on the work of the Holy Spirit when five
minutes of drastic obedience would make things clear as a sunbeam. We say, "I
suppose I shall understand these things some day." You can understand them
now: it is not study that does it, but obedience. The tiniest fragment of obedience and heaven opens up and the profoundest truths of God are yours straight
away. God will never reveal more truth about Himself till you obey what you
know already. Beware of being wise and prudent.

Lord, show me where I need to take a step of obedience to You.
And thank You for blessing me when I do so. Amen.

The Best Motivation

Whoever has my commands and obeys them, he is the one who loves me. He who loves me will be loved by my Father, and I too will love him and show myself to him.
JOHN 14:21

Obedience deepens our intimacy with Jesus. If we want to know the Father, we must not only love Him, but also obey Him.
JOHN WIMBER

As a parent, would you prefer that your child pick up his room because he knows he will be punished if he doesn't, or because he wants to please Mommy? As a husband, would you prefer your wife to shower you with affection because she is afraid you will be in a bad mood, or because she is crazy in love with you? As a manager, do you want your assistant to follow up on reports because he doesn't want to get a bad review in his personnel file, or because he enjoys what he does?

Now, getting a son to want to clean up his room may not be realistic, but in all these examples from everyday life, we prefer that people respond to us out of love, not fear. In the same way our Heavenly Father desires that we follow His will not because we are terrified of judgment—or because we want to earn His love—but because we love Him wholeheartedly.

Obedience to God is always a good thing, no matter what the motivation, but it is better for Him—and for you—when it is expressed out of a deep, enduring love.

Lord, thank You for Your goodness to me. Please deepen my love for You and make me ready and willing to serve You. Amen.

An Emergency Called Complacency

Let us throw off everything that hinders and the sin that so easily entangles.
HEBREWS 12:1

*Here lies the tremendous mystery—that God should be all-powerful,
yet refuse to coerce. He summons us to cooperation. We are honored
in being given the opportunity to participate in His good deeds.*
ELISABETH ELLIOT

Complacency is a blight that saps energy, dulls attitudes, and causes a drain on the brain. The first symptom is satisfaction with things as they are. The second is rejection of things as they might be. "Good enough" becomes today's watchword and tomorrow's standard. Complacency makes people fear the unknown, mistrust the untried, and abhor the new. Like water, complacent people follow the easiest course—downhill. They draw false strength from looking back.

But God has given us certain responsibilities that require attention and action on our part. Our lives need upkeep, and we must be careful not to neglect these matters that require a non-complacent vigilance of attitude. Priority one is making sure we are following God. He does not force us to choose Him. But when we do, we experience His blessing.

God, I want to keep my life in line with You. Fill me with Your Holy Spirit and grant me diligence to keep following Your will. Amen.

Losing to Gain

*The man who loves his life will lose it, while the man
who hates his life in this world will keep it for eternal life.*
JOHN 12:25

He is no fool who gives what he cannot keep to gain that which he cannot lose.
JAMES ELLIOTT

As he gained speed going down a hill, the young boy racing along on his bike saw a sharp turn just ahead. But the speed was exhilarating, so he paused a second—and then another and another—reluctant to apply the brakes. So he hit the curve at full speed. When he hit a bump, he lost control and found himself flying off the bike. Both he and the bicycle were a bit mangled, but survived. But he learned the simple truth that sometimes we must give up something we enjoy in order to get something better—or simply to survive. That is true in the physical realm, but even more so in the spiritual room.

Jesus said, "Whoever wants to save his life will lose it, but whoever loses his life for me and for the gospel will save it" (Mark 8:35). Giving something up in obedience to God might sting a little. But in the end, it's the only course for keeping our bike on the road and living our best possible life.

Lord, please nurture my character and give me
enough discipline to surrender to You. Amen.

Instant Obedience

*On that very day Abraham took his son Ishmael and all those
born in his household or bought with his money, every male
in his household, and circumcised them, as God told him.*

GENESIS 17:23

Obedience is the fruit of faith; patience, the bloom on the fruit.

CHRISTINA ROSSETTI

A Classic Devotional from Charles G. Trumbull

Instant obedience is the only kind of obedience there is; delayed obedience is disobedience. Every time God calls us to any duty, He is offering to make a covenant with us; doing the duty is our part, and He will do His part in special blessing.

The only way we can obey is to obey "in the selfsame day," as Abraham did. To be sure, we often postpone a duty and then later on do it as fully as we can. It is better to do this than not to do it at all. But it is then, at the best, only a crippled, disfigured, half-way sort of duty-doing; and a postponed duty never can bring the full blessing that God intended, and that it would have brought if done at the earliest possible moment.

It is a pity to rob ourselves, along with robbing God and others, by procrastination. "In the selfsame day" is the Genesis way of saying, "Do it now."

God, I choose to obey You in all things—right away. Amen.

The Ripples of Disobedience

A prudent man gives thought to his steps.
PROVERBS 14:15

The cost of obedience is nothing compared to the cost of disobedience.
AUTHOR UNKNOWN

When we are disobedient to God's will and ways, we create a negative impact not only for ourselves, but often for those around us. Ever since the sin of Adam and Eve in the Garden of Eden, the consequences of disobedience have been staggering. Cain's disobedience led to Abel's murder. David's infidelity led to the death of a trusted comrade—and ultimately the splitting of a kingdom. Judas' betrayal abetted Jesus' arrest.

There's a vital life-and-death lesson in these Bible stories for all of us. Even if some people seem to get away with wrongdoing—maybe even prosper in it—there is a price to pay for disobedience, and even if we swear we'll cover the whole bill ourselves, we can't necessarily protect those around us. If there is a temptation in your life right now that has become even more alluring because you've started to think that acting on it wouldn't hurt anyone else, ask God to check your spirit and provide you with the wisdom and perspective that will help you flee from the very idea of it. Some actions can't be taken back, nor can their consequences be contained or controlled.

God, I don't want my sin to affect the lives of others—or my own life. Teach me to bring my whole heart to You in obedience. Amen.

Listen Up!

Give me understanding, and I will keep your law and obey it with all my heart.
PSALM 119:34

*When God works in us, the will, being changed and sweetly breathed up
by the Spirit of God, desires and acts, not from compulsion, but responsively.*
MARTIN LUTHER

The idea of obedience has fallen on hard times in our culture. On one side are those who don't believe obedience in the traditional sense of following a set of moral guidelines is even possible. Another unhealthy view is that obedience is only for those who are not strong or smart enough to order their own lives.

Is there a better, healthier way of looking at obedience? One place to start is with the background of the English word. It is derived from the Latin *obaudire*, which means "to listen well." At the heart of obedience in the Bible is relationship. Obedience is based on the deepest level of communication where the other person is heard and understood. For Christians, this means that obedience cannot be reduced to a simple list of do's and don'ts, but is tantamount to an act of worship. We look so closely at God and listen so closely for His voice that we act in ways that show we are engaged in conversation and communion with God.

Obedience. Listening intently. Understanding the heart of another. When looked at that way, how obedient are you in hearing God's voice?

Lord, teach me to listen to Your voice
and follow You in loving obedience. Amen.

Obeying and Praying

*Dear friends, if our hearts do not condemn us, we have confidence
before God and receive from him anything we ask, because
we obey his commands and do what pleases him.*

1 JOHN 3:21–22

All true knowledge of God is born out of obedience.

JOHN CALVIN

A Classic Devotional from R. A. Torrey

The one who expects God to do as he asks Him must on his part *do whatever God bids him.* If we give a listening ear to all God's commands to us, He will give a listening ear to all our petitions to Him. If, on the other hand, we turn a deaf ear to His precepts, He will be likely to turn a deaf ear to our prayers. Here we find the secret of much unanswered prayer. We are not listening to God's Word, and therefore He is not listening to our petitions.

If we would have power in prayer, we must be earnest students of His Word to find out what His will regarding us is, and then having found it, do it. One un-confessed act of disobedience on our part will shut the ear of God against many petitions.

Father, help me to love You so deeply that I will always obey You.
Thank You for hearing my prayers. Amen.

The Good Shepherd

My sheep listen to my voice; I know them, and they follow me.
JOHN 10:27

I know not the way God leads me, but well do I know my Guide.
MARTIN LUTHER

In John 10, Jesus gives us plenty of reasons why we should trust Him and follow Him:

- Verse 11: He lays down His life for us. He always has our best interests at heart and serves us sacrificially.
- Verse 14: He knows us. He knows what's really best for us.
- Verse 10: He has come to give us abundant life. What awaits us when we follow Him are green pastures and abundant provision for our needs.
- Verse 28: He is strong enough to protect us.

We couldn't ask for a better Shepherd, always ready to guide and protect. Have you thanked Him today?

Lord, thank You for Your goodness to me. I love You. Amen.

Big Faith

*By faith Abraham, when he was called, obeyed by going out
to a place which he was to receive for an inheritance; and he
went out, not knowing where he was going.* HEBREWS 11:8

*One needs the sweetness to start one on the spiritual life but, once started,
one must learn to obey God for his own sake, not for the pleasure.*
C. S. LEWIS

God had promised to lead Abraham to a place called Canaan, a "land of
promise." Even when things looked bleak—enemies everywhere, a difficult
nephew, he and his wife's inability to have children—Abraham obeyed. And
ultimately, despite the obstacles to overcome, he received the promise.

You may feel like God is calling you into what looks like a forsaken desert. You
may not be sure how God's promises will be fulfilled. But like Abraham, you can
safely obey, because even though you might not know where you're going, you do
know who is leading you. And you know that He has never failed yet.

God, I know that You are trustworthy.
I choose to follow You today. Amen.

The Gift of Giving

Each man should give what he has decided in his heart to give,
not reluctantly or under compulsion, for God loves a cheerful giver.
2 Corinthians 9:7

Nothing is really ours until we share it.
C. S. Lewis

One of the true tests of our character is what we do with our money. Of course, God calls us to give a portion of our income to Him through ministry (Numbers 18:28) and also to give special sacrificial offerings to meet special needs as we feel directed in our hearts (Numbers 15:3). Paul does say that some people have a special gift of giving (Romans 12:8), but he also points out that God loves a cheerful giver (2 Corinthians 9:7).

When we are generous with our money above and beyond expectations, we experience a number of benefits: We are more aware that all good gifts come from God; we learn to trust and serve Him with a pure heart; and we receive the joy of helping someone in need. Besides all that, there is a strange paradox that the more we give, the more we seem to have.

As you practice giving generously, God will teach you the wonderful truth that whatever we grasp and hoard dries up and suffocates; but whatever we give freely and generously takes off and soars.

God, I want to be generous with my money and time.
Help me to serve You by serving others. Amen.

Obedience Brings Blessing

Be careful to obey all these regulations I am giving you, so that it may always go well with you and your children after you, because you will be doing what is good and right in the eyes of the Lord your God.

DEUTERONOMY 12:28

God is more anxious to bestow his blessings on us than we are to receive them.

ST. AUGUSTINE

A Classic Devotional from C. H. Spurgeon

Though salvation is not by the works of the law, yet the blessings which are promised to obedience are not denied to the faithful servants of God. The curses our Lord took away when He was made a curse for us, but no clause of blessing has been abrogated.

We are to note and listen to the revealed will of the Lord, giving our attention not to portions of it but to "all these words." There must be no picking and choosing but an impartial respect to all that God has commanded. This is the road of blessedness for the Father and for His children. The Lord's blessing is upon His chosen to the third and fourth generation. If they walk uprightly before Him, He will make all men know that they are a seed which the Lord has blessed.

God, thank You for the blessings that flow when I obey You.
I pray for a heart that longs to follow Your rules for living. Amen.

One Man's Faith

This book of the law shall not depart from your mouth, but you shall meditate on it day and night, so that you may be careful to do according to all that is written in it; for then you will make your way prosperous, and then you will have success. Joshua 1:8

When led of the Spirit, the child of God must be as ready to wait as to go, as prepared to be silent as to speak.
Lewis Sperry Chafer

In Exodus 14 we read that God commanded the children of Israel to turn on their journey toward the south, which would cause Pharaoh to think that they had lost their way in confusion and would be easy to overtake. As Pharaoh gathered his army of many men and rushed to catch up with the newly freed slaves, the Israelites grew fearful. But Moses obeyed God and stretched his hand over the sea, and it parted for the Israelites to cross to safety.

It's a familiar story, one with many life applications. It tells us of God's might in our weakness and His provision for His people. It also shows how a generation of people can be affected by one person's obedience to God. How can you help steer your generation into a bright future?

Lord, I want to be obedient to You in all things,
to gain blessings not just for myself, but for others. Show me
how I can faithfully follow You today. Amen.

Costly Grace

Anyone who does not carry his cross and follow me cannot be my disciple.

LUKE 14:27

Grace is never cheap. It is absolutely free to us, but infinitely expensive to God.

JERRY BRIDGES

A Classic Devotional from Dietrich Bonhoeffer

Costly grace is the treasure hidden in the field; for the sake of it a man will gladly go and sell all that he has. It is the pearl of great price to buy which the merchant will sell all his goods. It is the kingly rule of Christ, for whose sake of one will pluck out the eye which causes him to stumble; it is the call of Jesus Christ at which the disciple leaves his nets and follows him.

Such grace is costly because it calls us to follow, and it is grace because it calls us to follow Jesus Christ. It is costly because it costs a man his life, and it is grace because it gives a man the only true life. It is costly because it condemns sin, and grace because it justifies the sinner. Grace is costly because it compels a man to submit to the yoke of Christ and follow him; it is grace because Jesus says: "my yoke is easy and my burden light."

Lord, thank You for grace. May I never take it for granted; may I always remember with reverence what it cost You. Amen.

A Special Call

Then I heard the voice of the Lord saying, "Whom shall I send?
And who will go for us?" And I said, "Here am I. Send me!"
ISAIAH 6:8

The willing feet that go on errands of love, work for Christ.
ARTHUR INGRAM

Throughout Scripture we have accounts of men and women who were given special tasks, who received a special call on their lives from God. Abraham was called to leave his home country to become the father of God's people. Samson was called to be a Nazarite—a young man who would never touch fermented wine or have his hair cut—in order to show his commitment to God. James and John were two fishermen whom Jesus called to be His disciples. Paul was blinded and knocked off his horse when Jesus called him to be an ambassador of love. The list goes on and on.

God still calls people today. He asks young persons to prepare for a life of dedicated ministry—and some middle-aged and older persons to leave a career to serve Him in ministry. There are countless other tasks and calls that God gives that are not universal to all the world or everyone who is a believer, but to a specific person. Maybe even you.

When Isaiah worshipped in the temple and felt God's call on his life, his answer was simple: "Here am I. Send me!" (Isaiah 6:8). What will your answer be?

Lord, I want to go where You lead. Thank You
for the tasks You have placed before me. Amen.

Righteous Disobedience

Judge for yourselves whether it is right in God's sight to obey you rather than God. For we cannot help speaking about what we have seen and heard.
ACTS 4:19–20

Trust in God's promises comes to light in obedience to his commands.
SCOTT HAFEMANN

The Apostle Paul reminds us that if we obey our government's laws, we will save ourselves a lot of trouble in life (Romans 13:1–7). But from a biblical perspective, it also appears there is a time when disobedience to a governing body is the proper Christian response. When religious and civil rulers ordered John and Peter to stop preaching the gospel of Jesus Christ, their response was: "We must obey God rather than men!" (Acts 5:29). Even today, all over the world, more Christians are killed for their faith each year than in the first two thousand years combined.

Our freedom to express our faith sometimes seems under assault, but we still enjoy legal protection of worship and—for now, at least—don't have to defy our government to call ourselves Christians. But one thing all of us can do is reflect on our loyalty to God over our loyalty to earthly powers. And all of us can pray for Christian brothers and sisters all over the world whose faith has made them outlaws.

Lord, I know that I am a citizen of Your kingdom and owe You, first and foremost, my obedience. Please give me wisdom and discernment to follow You as I live in the world. Amen.

October

PRAYER

By Prayer

You do not have, because you do not ask God.
JAMES 4:2

*Prayer is the way and means God has appointed for the
communication of the blessings of His goodness to His people.*
ARTHUR W. PINK

God blesses us every day with things we don't necessarily ask for, things we might take for granted: a place to live, fresh air, the beauty of nature, friends and family. But for some blessings, He chooses to make us part of the process by encouraging us to ask for what we need and want. And the truth is that we experience life and blessings more fully when we look to God for all our wants and needs, either through expressing gratitude or petitioning Him for our needs.

If you're hurting for something today, ask God for it. And if you're not, thank Him for what you have. You'll find your life more richly blessed—even if only from an improved attitude. Best yet, your whole being will be permeated with an awareness of God's presence and goodness.

Lord, thank You for blessing me.
Help me open my heart and needs to You today. Amen.

When You Have No Words

The Spirit helps us in our weakness. We do not know what we ought to pray for, but the Spirit himself intercedes for us with groans that words cannot express. ROMANS 8:26

For the Holy Spirit is prayer's great Helper. We are incapable of ourselves to translate our real needs into prayer. The Holy Spirit does this for us. AUTHOR UNKNOWN

Prayer is so important to our spiritual life, but there's good news when we just don't seem to have the words to pray. First of all, we are told that Jesus Christ is at the right side of God the Father interceding for us. It's always great to have someone put in a good word for us, but think about it: right now, Jesus is doing just that for us. For you. What better reference could we have? But secondly, the Holy Spirit helps us as well. Paul tells us: "And he who searches our hearts knows the mind of the Spirit, because the Spirit intercedes for the saints in accordance with God's will" (Romans 8:27).

Is there a problem in your life you have prayed over for years and can no longer come up with words to pray for it? Are you watching a family member make bad decisions, and you don't know what else to say to God on his or her behalf? Do you feel a heaviness of heart and just can't muster the words to express what you're feeling? Maybe it's okay to just sit quietly and depend on the Holy Spirit to do your praying for you, to tell the Father what you can't quite say yourself.

God, You know my heart and thoughts before I can even form the words in my mind. Thank You for listening to the deepest parts of my life, even when I can't get the words out.

The Wish List

The prayer of the upright pleases him. Proverbs 15:8

Prayer is request. The essence of request, as distinct from compulsion, is that it may or may not be granted. And if an infinitely wise Being listens to the requests of finite and foolish creatures, of course He will sometimes grant and sometimes refuse them. C. S. Lewis

Scripture is full of assurances that God will hear and answer our prayers. Of course, there's a danger in taking this wonderful truth and turning God into a personal valet, ready to meet our every whim and fancy. In our praying, we have a responsibility to seek God's will. Our wish is not His command.

Perhaps the best way to avoid turning your prayer time into reciting a wish list is to remember that prayer is a real relationship. It's not magic. God has invited us into a relationship with Him and provided us the means to reach Him, through His Son. When we ask Him for good gifts—something He encourages us to do—we should remember that we're talking to someone who loves us, wants what's best for us, and knows what we really need.

Most importantly, when we go to God in prayer, we are communing with the One who seeks a relationship of love with us.

Lord, help me to pray not as an exercise of my will, but a surrender to Yours. Thank You for Your goodness to me. Amen.

A Good Listener

The eyes of the LORD are on the righteous
and his ears are attentive to their cry.

PSALM 34:15

All who call on God in true faith, earnestly from the heart, will
certainly be heard and will receive what they have asked and desired.

MARTIN LUTHER

A seventh grade teacher asked her students what action by their peers upset them most. One girl said that she hated to be talking to someone and have them walk away as if she was not there. Adults have learned at least to appear more polite and don't just walk off in mid-sentence. But we all know it doesn't feel good when someone subtly or obviously tunes us out. The feeling that someone is listening is encouraging; feeling ignored brings a distinct sting.

When we pray, God never turns away before we're finished. He is always watching out for us. We always have His attention. Since we know God listens to us, our prayer lives are enriched when we learn to be still and listen to Him.

Lord, thank You for Your ever-present attention and care.
Help me to direct my attention to You throughout the day. Amen.

Don't Let the Grass Grow

Be joyful in hope, patient in affliction, faithful in prayer.
ROMANS 12:12

Be sure no time is so well spent as that which a man spends on his knees.
J.C. RYLE

The story is told that in Africa, members of one tribe that had converted to Christianity staked out their own space in the thicket surrounding their village for prayer time. Gradually, they wore down paths in the grass that led to their prayer spot. If a believer began to neglect prayer, his fellow Christians would kindly point out, "Brother, the grass grows on your path."

Has the grass grown on your path? Do you struggle with the discipline of regular prayer? If you're willing to make the effort, you'll reap rewards of spiritual growth. Wherever you are—whether you already have a well-established prayer time or struggle just to whisper a few words a day—begin adding a little extra time in prayer to your day. Doing so will help you see everything else in your day through the lens of God's love and presence.

Lord, sometimes I struggle to make time to meet with You.
I pray that You would strengthen my resolve to spend
quality time with You in prayer. Amen.

Your Will Be Done

*Your kingdom come, your will be done
on earth as it is in heaven.*
MATTHEW 6:10

*We are trying not so much to make God listen to us as to make
ourselves listen to him; we are trying not to persuade God to do what
we want, but to find out what he wants us to do.* WILLIAM BARCLAY

A Classic Devotional from John Bunyan

As Christ has taught us, prayer must say, "Your will be done on earth as it is in heaven" (Matthew 6:10); therefore the people of the Lord in humility are to lay themselves and their prayers, and all that they have, at the feet of their God, to be disposed of by him as he in his heavenly wisdom sees best. And never doubting that God will answer the desire of his people in a way that will be most advantageous for them and for his glory. Therefore when the saints pray with submission to the will of God, they are not to doubt or question God's love and kindness to them. But because they are not always wise, and sometimes Satan may take advantage of them, so as to tempt them to pray for that which, if they had it, would neither be to God's glory nor for his people's good.

Lord, I know that You know what's best for me and that You care
about me. Please do what's good in my life. Amen.

Never Give Up

*I prayed for this child, and the LORD has granted me what I
asked of him. So now I give him to the LORD.* 1 SAMUEL 1:27–28

*In all moods and in all seasons pour out the soul in prayer and
supplication with thanksgiving, and if the Spirit groans in intercession do not
be afraid of the agony of prayer. There are blessings of the Kingdom that are
only yielded to the violence of the vehement soul.* BRUCE WILKINSON

Hannah loved the Lord and was a woman of good report. But she was barren, which in her culture made her something of an outcast. She prayed faithfully and diligently for years, crying out to God for a child. And then one day it happened. She bore a son and named him Samuel. Soon she did something that seems counterintuitive: she took Samuel to the priest in Shiloh and left him there. Because God had blessed her with a child, she gave him back to God. In the end, God gave Hannah and her husband other children, and Samuel became one of the greatest figures in Israel's history.

Often we have to wait for the things we most deeply want. There are times when we have to accept "no" as an answer to prayer; but there are other times when we'll be blessed if we keep knocking, seeking, and asking. And what we receive will be a blessing not only for ourselves, but for others as well.

God, I know that You see the desires of my heart.
Today I bring them before You and determine to continue
doing so, knowing that You are good. Amen.

A Prayer for Our Children

Come, my children, listen to me; I will teach you the fear of the LORD.
PSALM 34:11

The greatest gift we can give to others is our prayers.
AUTHOR UNKNOWN

A Classic Devotional from Jeremy Taylor

O almighty and most merciful Father, who hast promised children as a reward to the righteous, and hast given them to me as a testimony of thy mercy, and an engagement of my duty, be pleased to be a Father unto them, and give them healthful bodies, understanding souls, and sanctified spirits, that they may be thy servants and thy children all their days. Let a great mercy and providence lead them through the dangers and temptations and ignorances of their youth, that they may never run into folly and the evils of an unbridled appetite. So order the accidents of their lives, that by good education, careful tutors, holy example, innocent company, prudent counsel, and thy restraining grace, their duty to thee may be secured in the midst of a crooked and untoward generation. Amen.

God, thank You for my children.
Teach me to pray for them and care
for them as You care for me. Amen.

Good Things Come to Those Who Wait

Be still before the LORD and wait patiently for him.
PSALM 37:7

You're in a hurry. God is not. Trust God.
MARIE T. FREEMAN

They were a young couple in love, and they knew they wanted to be together. But there were a few things standing in the way. She waited for him until he completed his stint in the Army, and then he waited for her while she finished college. Then she waited for him a second time, this time waiting out his years in the Navy. A total of thirteen years passed before they got married. But by all accounts, theirs was a sweet and contented marriage, one that lasted almost forty-five years.

Some of the best things in life don't happen in an instant and require waiting. If you're waiting and hoping for God to provide something, don't give up. What He has for you is worth the wait.

God, I know You have good plans for me.
I choose to wait for Your best. Amen.

Listen for His Voice

*After the earthquake came a fire, but the L*ORD *was not in the fire.*
And after the fire came a gentle whisper.

1 KINGS 19:12

Why is it important that you are with God and God alone
on the mountain top? It's important because it's the place in which
you can listen to the voice of the One who calls you the beloved. To pray
is to let that voice speak to the center of your being, to your guts,
and let that voice resound in your whole being.

HENRI NOUWEN

Do you know someone who is a chronic interrupter? Someone who you know isn't really listening to you or others but thinking of what to say next? Has that someone ever been you? How about in your prayer life? Do you ever present your needs and thanksgiving and then just pause to listen?

Does God still speak directly today? Many of us will never know because we don't stop, quiet our hearts, and listen. When was the last time you truly prayed—without speaking a word? Is today that day for you?

Lord, I quiet my heart and mind before You and listen.
Thank You for speaking to me. Amen.

Until the End

*Let us not become weary in doing good, for at the proper time
we will reap a harvest if we do not give up.* GALATIANS 6:9

*Always respond to every impulse to pray. The impulse to pray may come
when you are reading or when you are battling with a text. I would make an
absolute law of this—always obey such an impulse.* MARTYN LLOYD-JONES

While very ill, John Knox, the founder of the Presbyterian Church in Scotland, called to his wife and said, "Read me that Scripture where I first cast my anchor." After he listened to the beautiful prayer of Jesus recorded in John 17, he seemed to forget his weakness. He began to pray, interceding earnestly for his fellow men. He prayed for the ungodly who had thus far rejected the gospel. He pleaded on behalf of people who had been recently converted. And he requested protection for the Lord's servants, many of whom were facing persecution. As Knox prayed, his spirit went home to be with the Lord. The man of whom Queen Mary had said, "I fear his prayers more than I do the armies of my enemies," ministered through prayer until the moment of his death.

There are many needs around us—our neighbors, family, friends, and coworkers could all use a touch from God in some area or another. We have the privilege of bringing those needs to God in prayer. And we are blessed when we do so.

Lord, open my heart so that I can see the
needs around me and bring them to You. Amen.

Meaningful Prayer

I call on you, O God, for you will answer me;
give ear to me and hear my prayer. PSALM 17:6

Prayer keeps us in constant communion with God,
which is the goal of our entire believing lives. BETH MOORE

A Classic Devotional from R. A. Torrey

Stop a moment and think. Is it not often the case, when men stand up to pray in public, or kneel down to pray in private, that they are thinking far more of what they are asking for than they are of the great God who made heaven and earth, and who has all power? Is it not often the case that in our prayers our thoughts are wandering off everywhere? We take the name of God on our lips, but there is no real conscious approach to God in our hearts.

If there is to be any power in our prayer, if our prayer is to get anything, the first thing to be sure of when we pray is that we really have come into the presence of God, and are really speaking to Him. Oh, let those two words, "to God," "to God," "to God," sink deep into your heart; and from this time on never pray, never utter one syllable of prayer, until you are sure that you have come into the presence of God and are really talking to Him.

Father God, it is a privilege to come into Your presence.
Give me a reverence for You as I sit down to pray. Amen.

A Call to Prayer

Every day they continued to meet together in the temple courts.
They broke bread in their homes and ate together with glad and sincere hearts,
praising God and enjoying the favor of all the people. And the Lord added
to their number daily those who were being saved. ACTS 2:46–47

I had rather stand against the cannons of the wicked than
against the prayers of the righteous. THOMAS LYE

In September of 1857, Jeremiah Lanphier, a city minister, began a weekly noon prayer meeting in New York that by October had grown into a daily prayer meeting attended by hundreds of businessmen. By March of the next year newspapers carried front-page reports that over 6,000 were attending daily prayer meetings in downtown New York and Pittsburgh, and similar meetings were being held in Washington at five different times to accommodate the crowds. By May 1859, 50,000 New Yorkers had reported accepting Christ through these meetings.

It might be hard to envision a similar resurgence of faith in our own time. But the biggest movements often begin with the smallest steps of prayer. What would happen if you began meeting with just a few friends to pray? Why not try it and see?

Lord, I'm amazed at what You do in response to the prayers of Your people. Today I bring the concerns of my community before You, and I ask for Your guidance as I seek out friends to pray with. Amen.

An Eternal Impact

*I have been reminded of your sincere faith, which first
lived in your grandmother Lois and in your mother Eunice and,
I am persuaded, now lives in you also.* 2 TIMOTHY 1:5

*Personal working for souls is good. Giving money is good.
But praying is best of all.* J.C. RYLE

What a wonderful heritage in the faith Timothy had. Paul considered this young man more than a protégé, he looked at Timothy as a son (1 Corinthians 4:17). But Paul knew that Timothy's godly heritage began long before he took him under his wing on his missionary journeys. Timothy had a mother and grandmother who prayed for him from his childhood (2 Timothy 1:5). Did you grow up in that kind of family? Even if you didn't, there is a good chance someone prayed for you and was instrumental in your relationship with God.

Even if you can't answer that question, it raises an even more important question for you to consider right now. For whom are you praying regularly? Who will say that your prayers gave them the encouragement they needed in a tough time to draw even closer to God? Whom might you meet in heaven because you would not stop praying for their very soul here on earth?

You have the power to make a difference in the kingdom of God simply by praying for those close to you. Don't miss out on seeing blessings in their lives.

Lord, show me whom I can pray for not just today,
but every day as they grow to know You. Amen.

Change of Plans

But he took note of their distress when he heard their cry;
for their sake he remembered his covenant and out of
his great love he relented. PSALM 106:44–45

God does nothing but in answer to prayer. JOHN WESLEY

It is true to say God never changes. "Jesus Christ is the same yesterday and today and forever," Hebrews tells us (13:8). But that verse is referring to His nature: He is always good and holy and loving and merciful. It is also true to say that often what changes most when we pray, is us. We ask God to change a situation and instead He changes us. He doesn't always make our burdens smaller; sometimes He makes us stronger.

But sometime our prayers convince God to intervene in a situation in a way He would not have had we not prayed. Because of the Hebrew children's flagrant disobedience, God intended to destroy them (Exodus 32:9). But Moses prayed that God would not do so, and God changed His mind (vv. 11–14). Have you ever considered that you can convince God to act in a brand new way in a situation because He responds to the urgency of your heart and prayers? This in no way makes God less or smaller than He is. But it does show that He responds to the prayers of His children.

Father God, thank You for loving me so much that
You take time to listen to my heart, my prayers,
what's on my mind—and You respond! Amen.

Consistently and Persistently

*Then Jesus told his disciples a parable to show them that
they should always pray and not give up.*
LUKE 18:1

Prayer is not overcoming God's reluctance, but laying hold of His willingness.
MARTIN LUTHER

Jesus spoke in many parables to teach His followers about living in the Kingdom of God. In one parable, He told them about a widow who came before a judge with a grievance. She constantly, continually requested that the judge protect her from her adversary. The judge always refused to grant the widow's request, but she was persistent until finally the judge said, "Even though I don't fear God or care about men, yet because this widow keeps bothering me, I will see that she gets justice, so that she won't eventually wear me out with her coming!" (Luke 18:4–5).

Salespeople know you have to knock on doors persistently and consistently to close a sale. Teachers know repetition is a necessary ingredient if students are to retain what they learn. Constantly coming to God doesn't pester Him; but it does keep our own focus on Him.

Heavenly Father, thank You for the invitation to come to You in prayer on a daily, hourly, and even moment-to-moment basis. Amen.

The Prayer of St. Francis

Delight yourself in the LORD; and he will give you the desires of your heart.
PSALM 37:4

Prayer is not intended to change God's purpose, nor is it to move Him to form fresh purposes. God has decreed that certain events shall come to pass through the means He has appointed for their accomplishment. ARTHUR W. PINK

A Classic Devotional from St. Francis of Assisi

A PRAYER FOR PEACE, GROWTH, AND RECOVERY

Lord, make me an instrument of your peace. Where there is hatred, let me sow love; Where there is injury, pardon; Where there is doubt, faith; Where there is despair, hope; Where there is darkness, light; Where there is sadness, joy.

O Divine Master, grant that I may not so much seek to be consoled as to console; To be understood as to understand; To be loved as to love. For it is in giving that we receive. It is in pardoning that we are pardoned. It is in dying that we are born to eternal life.

Your heart, O Lord, is open to Your children.
Help me to be willing to learn from You. Amen.

Hearing God's Voice

Very early in the morning, while it was still dark, Jesus got up,
left the house and went off to a solitary place, where he prayed.
MARK 1:35

Most of man's trouble comes from his inability to be still.
BLAISE PASCAL

Music. Television. Traffic and other background noises. The ticking of a clock. Is there ever a moment of quiet and silence for the modern soul? How about you? How do you do without sound? Are you distracted when there are no distractions?

Perhaps we never hear God's voice because we always have some other sound turned on. How would you feel if you were trying to say something to someone with earbuds in their ears connected to a tiny music player? How easy is it to have a conversation when the other person keeps texting or picking up other calls?

Jesus Christ Himself pulled away from crowds for some alone time with His Father. How much more important is that for us?

Lord, help me to shut off the noise of everyday
life so I can hear Your voice. Amen.

Hindrances to Prayer

Devote yourselves to prayer, keeping alert in it with an
attitude of thanksgiving. COLOSSIANS 4:2

When a Christian shuns fellowship with other Christians,
the devil smiles. When he stops studying the Bible, the devil laughs.
When he stops praying, the devils shouts for joy. CORRIE TEN BOOM

What keeps you from prayer? Is it worry? Demands on your attention? Boredom? An abundance of entertainment?

Nothing is more important to our spiritual lives than prayer. Jesus taught us to seek the Kingdom first (Matthew 6:33), and Paul instructed us to pray without ceasing (1 Thessalonians 5:17). If we desire to follow God, we must pray. So how can you beat those distractions and hindrances?

Try a little separation. Physically remove yourself from your phone, the TV, reading material. You might choose a verse of Scripture and concentrate on it for a few moments before starting to pray. The hard truth is that all the tricks in the world won't make prayer a piece of cake. Sometimes the choice to direct our attention to talking to God is simply an act of the will. But take heart: God wants us to pray, and He can help us overcome any obstacles.

Lord, I do want to pray actively, consistently.
Help me clear the clutter that keeps me from You. Amen.

Praying for Others

*Therefore confess your sins to each other and pray for
each other so that you may be healed. The prayer of a
righteous man is powerful and effective.* JAMES 5:16

*I have benefited by my praying for others; for by making an errand to God for
them, I have gotten something for myself.* SAMUEL RUTHERFORD

The old religious cliché is true: we can't out-give God. Whatever we do for Him
comes back in much greater measure. One way to experience a deep fellowship with God—the greatest gift of all—is to pray for others. In the next few
moments, turn your heart toward God and pray for a loved one who might be

- experiencing job or career difficulties;
- struggling with a health issue;
- dealing with marital difficulties;
- attempting a new venture;
- wandering in their spiritual life.

You might be facing some tough needs right now; but there are also plenty of
needs in the lives of those around you. You can't pray for them without being
blessed yourself.

Father, thank You that as I pray for others, my own problems
fade into the background and I am blessed. Amen.

All I Need

*And my God will meet all your needs according to his
glorious riches in Christ Jesus.* Philippians 4:19

*People, places, and things were never meant to give us life. God alone
is the author of a fulfilling life.* Gary Smalley and John Trent

A Classic Devotional from George Mueller

All believers, according to the will of God concerning them in Christ Jesus, may cast, and ought to cast, all their care upon Him who careth for them, and need not be anxiously concerned about anything.

My Lord is not limited; He can again supply. How truly precious it is that every one who rests alone upon the Lord Jesus for salvation, has in the living God a father, to whom he may fully un-bosom himself concerning the most minute affairs of his life, and concerning everything that lies upon his heart! Dear reader, do you know the living God? Is He, in Jesus, your Father? Be assured that Christianity is something more than forms and creeds and ceremonies: there is life, and power, and reality, in our holy faith. If you never yet have known this, then come and taste for yourself.

God, I know that You can provide all I need.
Today I bring all my worries to You. Amen.

Personal Interaction

*Trust in him at all times, O people; pour out
your hearts to him, for God is our refuge.*
PSALM 62:8

In prayer it is better to have a heart without words than words without a heart.
JOHN BUNYAN

An anonymous author recounted the story of a traveler in China who visited a temple on a feast day, joining many pilgrims in gathering around a sacred shrine. He noticed that many of them were pulling out strips of paper, rolling them in mud, and tossing them at the idol. When he asked what they were doing, he was told that the pieces of paper were written prayers. They believed that if the mud-wrapped paper stuck to the idol, it would serve as a promise that the prayer would be answered. If it fell off, it meant the prayer had been rejected.

There's no easy way to know how God will respond to our prayers. But would we really want there to be? We grow through prayer and communing with God through His Word and connections with fellow believers. If we interacted with God through anything but personal means, would that experience be as rich and engaging?

God is listening. And if we pay attention, we will hear Him speak back, even if our prayers aren't immediately answered.

God, thank You for interacting with us so personally.
Help me to more fully engage in a relationship of prayer. Amen.

Be Specific

This is the confidence we have in approaching God: that if we ask anything according to his will, he hears us. And if we know that he hears us—whatever we ask—we know that we have what we asked of him. 1 JOHN 5:14–15

Don't pray when you feel like it. Have an appointment with the Lord and keep it. A man is powerful on his knees. CORRIE TEN BOOM

A Classic Devotional from C. H. Spurgeon

There is no need for us to go beating about the bush, and not telling the Lord distinctly what it is that we crave at His hands. Nor will it be seemly for us to make any attempt to use fine language; but let us ask God in the simplest and most direct manner for just the things we want. I believe in business prayers. I mean prayers in which you take to God one of the many promises which He has given us in His Word, and expect it to be fulfilled as certainly as we look for the money to be given us when we go to the bank to cash a check. We should not think of going there, lolling over the counter chattering with the clerks on every conceivable subject except the one thing for which we had gone to the bank, and then coming away without the coin we needed; but we should lay before the clerk the promise to pay the bearer a certain sum, tell him in what form we wish to take the amount, count the cash after him, and then go on our way to attend to other business. That is just an illustration of the method in which we should draw supplies from the Bank of Heaven.

God, thank You for the assurance that You hear my prayers.
I lay my needs before You today. Amen.

Teach Us to Pray

Lord, teach us to pray, just as John taught his disciples.
LUKE 11:1

*Prayer is not so much an act as it is an attitude—an
attitude of dependency, dependency upon God.*
ARTHUR W. PINK

One day when Jesus had just finished praying, one of His disciples came to Him with a request. He wanted Jesus to teach them how to pray. At that moment, Jesus gave His disciples the Lord's Prayer, the model for Christian prayer throughout the centuries. He went on to teach them more about prayer, saying, "Ask and it will be given to you; seek and you will find; knock and the door will be opened to you. For everyone who asks receives; he who seeks finds; and to him who knocks, the door will be opened" (Luke 11:9–10).

There is no one better than Jesus Christ to teach us how to relate to and interact with God. He offers us teaching about how to pray, and in the Gospels He models for us a diligent and dedicated prayer life. If we ask Him to, He can show us how to pray effectively.

Thank You, Jesus, for being such a good Teacher.
Teach me to live closely with You. Amen.

Right Motives

*When you ask, you do not receive, because you ask with wrong
motives, that you may spend what you get on your pleasures.*
JAMES 4:3

Prayer does not change God; it changes me.
C. S. LEWIS

No other biblical writer is more pragmatic and in-your-face than James. In
his letter, he puts great emphasis on faith in action. Does this mean he was a
legalist who didn't believe in salvation as a gift? Was he calling for us to base our
relationship with God on our good works? Not at all. He simply believed that the
person who has experienced God's grace will evidence it in his or her daily walk.

On the topic of prayer, James extols the power of prayer—"The prayer of a
righteous man is powerful and effective" (5:16)—but he also challenges us to
check our motives. Is our prayer focused on an easy life or on doing great things
for God? Never stop taking your needs before God, but do pause and check your
heart from time to time.

God, make my prayer life a powerful force to do great things
for You and the building of Your kingdom. Amen.

Keep It Simple, Keep It Secret

*When you pray, do not be like the hypocrites, for they love to pray
standing in the synagogues and on the street corners to be seen by men.
I tell you the truth, they have received their reward in full.*
MATTHEW 6:5

*We should speak to God from our own hearts
and talk to Him as a child talks to His father.*
C. H. SPURGEON

In the Sermon on the Mount, Jesus advises His listeners not to pray for show, and not to pray with endless repetition. He tells us to keep it simple, and to pray in secret, not flaunting our spirituality before other people. Prayer is meant to be communion with God. When we pray for show, our hearts and minds are on what others think, not what God thinks. And when we pray with many words, we get caught up in the action of prayer and forget to direct our thoughts to God.

There are many simple prayers that can be said quietly and quickly, but deeply express our need for God: "Lord, help." "Lord, have mercy." "Your will be done." All it takes to pray meaningfully is to bring our whole hearts to God. And that can be done in very few words.

Lord, I need You. Teach me to bring my needs before You. Amen.

Fasting

After fasting forty days and forty nights, he was hungry. MATTHEW 4:2

Christian fasting, at its root, is the hunger of a homesickness for God.
JOHN PIPER

Prayer should be as natural as breathing in and out, a seamless part of our everyday lives. But many of us also find that pulling away for a time of focused prayer is incredibly beneficial. Reading a short devotion and then having a brief time of prayer is part of morning preparation for many Christians, and some go on retreats to spend an entire weekend in prayer.

There is another special practice that has been used with prayer through the centuries. The discipline of fasting is modeled for us by Jesus Christ Himself. (See Matthew 4:1–11 for the account of Jesus fasting in the wilderness.) Fasting is the choice to give something up—usually food—in order to focus all our attentions and energies on communing with God. Many have sought prayer and fasting when an urgent need arises. For Jesus, facing the beginning of His ministry, a forty-day fast provided a way to face every temptation that Satan would throw His way in the years to come.

Is there an urgent need in your life? In your family? Your church? Your business? Consider a time of prayer and fasting to lay your heart bare before God and find His will and answers for you.

Lord Jesus, teach me to fast in a way that
brings me closer to You. Amen.

Rejoice

Sing and make music in your heart to the Lord. EPHESIANS 5:19

*When we bless God for mercies, we usually prolong them. When we bless God
for miseries, we usually end them. Praise is the honey of life which a devout
heart extracts from every bloom of providence and grace.* C. H. SPURGEON

Some days find us more eager to rejoice than others. Some days, something big
and wonderful happens in our lives, and joyful feelings flow freely. Other days are
difficult, and other days are simply ordinary. Nothing to write home about.

But Paul admonishes us to rejoice always. And whether we realize it or not,
we have good reason to. We have the promise of God's love and salvation and
His grace to pull us through any circumstance. We also have the promise of His
Spirit working within us to make us more like Him and more able to live joyful,
productive lives.

When we know God and walk closely with Him, every day can be extraordi-
nary. So rejoice throughout the day!

God, Your presence is the best thing in my life. Today I want to pray
prayers of rejoicing and thanks throughout the day. Amen.

Listening Hard for God

*Call to me and I will answer you and tell you great
and unsearchable things you do not know.*
JEREMIAH 33:3

Surrender your mind to the Lord at the beginning of each day.
WARREN WIERSBE

A Classic Devotional from Dr. Pardington

Waiting upon God is necessary in order to see Him, to have a vision of Him. The time element in vision is essential. Our hearts are like a sensitive photographer's plate; and in order to have God revealed there, we must sit at His feet a long time. The troubled surface of a lake will not reflect an object.

Our lives must be quiet and restful if we would see God. There is power in the sight of some things to affect one's life. A quiet sunset will bring peace to a troubled heart. Thus the vision of God always transforms human life.

Lord, teach me to be still before You and listen for Your voice. Amen.

The Heart Behind the Words

*Whoever humbles himself like this child is
the greatest in the kingdom of heaven.*
MATTHEW 18:4

When you can't put your prayers into words, God hears your heart.
AUTHOR UNKNOWN

"God is grape. God is goo," intoned the little boy before mealtime. Over and over, his mom would stop him and explain the proper way to say the words in the blessing. But sure enough, before the next meal she would hear the boy's usual prayer, "God is grape. God is goo."

After a while, it finally dawned on this mom that God was probably amused. He may have even called the angels over to hear her son as he prayed. More than likely, God wasn't as concerned about him pronouncing the words correctly as He was that her son stopped long enough to thank God for the food He had provided.

When we pray, we don't have to impress God. In fact, we can't impress God. All that matters is that we come to Him with childlike wonder and thanksgiving. Even if our words aren't impressive, the heart behind them moves God's heart.

Lord, thank You for the gift of coming to You in prayer,
and thank You that You delight in my feeble attempts. Amen.

Bless My Family

But as for me and my household, we will serve the LORD. JOSHUA 24:15

Consider family religion not merely as a duty imposed by authority, but as your greatest privilege granted by divine grace. SAMUEL DAVIES

One of the greatest blessings you can give to your family is a heritage of prayer. That means your children and spouse know that you have a committed prayer life that includes them, and that there are times when the whole family gathers together for prayer. Of course it's great to pray together before a meal. But in our fast-paced, media-saturated, activity-filled culture, it is difficult to get a whole family together for a meal in the first place. So establishing prayer as a part of life in your home is not easy; you'll have to be deliberate and intentional if you want to make it a reality.

What's required is a commitment on your part to see it happen. That means first of all that you believe family prayer is important. Secondly, it means you won't be turned aside by distractions and obstacles. Third, it means you will have a plan. How about posting a new verse around the house each day, and before everyone gets out the door in the morning or goes to bed in the evening, you read the verse together and say a short prayer based on it. Ask others—even young children—to pray aloud as well.

Prayer is a personal blessing—and a family blessing.

Father, I am part of Your family and enjoy all the blessings that come from You being my Abba—Daddy. I ask for guidance to create a climate of prayer in my family.

November

THANKSGIVING

Be Glad in the Lord

Therefore, since we are receiving a kingdom that cannot be shaken,
let us be thankful, and so worship God acceptably with reverence and awe.
HEBREWS 12:28

Thou who has given me so much, give me one more thing: a grateful heart.
GEORGE HERBERT

A Classic Devotional from Dietrich Bonhoeffer

We prevent God from giving us the great spiritual gifts He has in store for us, because we do not give thanks for daily gifts. We think we dare not be satisfied with the small measure of spiritual knowledge, experience, and love that has been given to us, and that we must constantly be looking forward eagerly for the highest good. Then we deplore the fact that we lack the deep certainty, the strong faith, and the rich experience that God has given to others, and we consider this lament to be pious. We pray for the big things and forget to give thanks for the ordinary, small (and yet really not small) gifts. How can God entrust great things to one who will not thankfully receive from Him the little things?

Lord, today I choose to notice all the things You do for me—for Your spiritual blessings as well as temporal ones. Amen.

Remember to Remember

I will remember the deeds of the LORD; yes,
I will remember your miracles of long ago. PSALM 77:1

Memory keeps gratitude fresh and gratitude keeps faith fruitful.
DALE RALPH DAVIS

The concept of remembering is an important biblical theme. The command not to forget is given more than four hundred times. We are to remember:

- The wonders of God's creation and works of His hands: "Ask now about the former days, long before your time, from the day God created man on the earth; ask from one end of the heavens to the other" (Deuteronomy 4:32);
- That the world belongs to God: "For every animal of the forest is mine, and the cattle on a thousand hills" (Psalm 50:10);
- The deliverance of His people from captivity: "Remember that you were slaves in Egypt and that the LORD your God brought you out of there with a mighty hand and an outstretched arm" (Deuteronomy 5:15);
- The sacrificial gift of Jesus Christ on the cross: "In the same way, after supper he took the cup, saying, 'This cup is the new covenant in my blood; do this, whenever you drink it, in remembrance of me'" (1 Corinthians 11:25).

Remembering keeps us from the sin of ingratitude. It also helps us face the future with confidence. Today have you remembered to remember?

God, You have done so much for me. Today I
choose to reflect on Your goodness in my past
with hope for the present and future. Amen.

The Ant and the Dove

*Make sure that nobody pays back wrong for wrong, but always try
to be kind to each other and to everyone else.* 1 Thessalonians 5:15

*Be thankful for the smallest blessing, and you will deserve to receive greater.
Value the least gifts no less than the greatest and simple graces as especial
favors. If you remember the dignity of the Giver, no gift will seem small
or mean, for nothing can be valueless that is given by the Most High God.*

Thomas à Kempis

In one of Aesop's Fables, an ant went to the bank of a river to drink, fell into
the stream, and found itself on the brink of drowning. A dove sitting on a tree
overhanging the water plucked a leaf and let it fall into the stream close to the
drowning ant. The ant climbed onto it and floated in safety to the bank. Shortly
afterward, a bird catcher came and stood under the tree and began laying a trap
for the dove. The ant, seeing his intent, seized the opportunity to sting him in
the foot. In pain the bird catcher threw down the trap, and the noise alerted the
dove to fly away.

It is wonderful to be blessed by random acts of kindness. It's even more
wonderful when we can return the favor. Who has helped you get by? Is there a
way you can show them your gratitude?

Lord, thank You for the people who have helped me in life.
Show me how I can be a blessing to others today. Amen.

A Gift of Gratitude

Give thanks to the God of heaven.
His love endures forever.
PSALM 136:26

Blessings hemmed with praise will not unravel.
ANONYMOUS

Mother Teresa told the story of finding four starving people on a Calcutta street. She told the other nuns with her to take care of three of them while she attended to a woman who looked to be in the worst condition. They got them back to their clinic and Mother Teresa put the woman in bed and attended to her needs. The woman took hold of Mother Teresa's hand, smiled, and said only two words, "Thank you," before passing into eternity. Mother Teresa was deeply moved and blessed.

In the most tender and delicate moments of our lives, gratitude is often the most precious gift we can give. It affirms; it heals; it forgives. It's important to remember, though, that we can give that gift anytime. There might be some people in our lives who desperately need it sooner rather than later.

Lord, I pray that You would help me show kindness and thankfulness to someone close to me today. Amen.

A Debt of Gratitude

How can we thank God enough for you in return for all the joy we have
in the presence of our God because of you? 1 THESSALONIANS 3:9

There is as much greatness of mind in acknowledging
a good turn, as in doing it. SENECA

Years ago a wealthy English family was entertaining friends at their home. As the children swam, one ventured into the deep water and began to drown. The gardener heard the other children screaming, jumped into the water, and saved the child. That youngster was none other than Winston Churchill. Deeply grateful to the gardener, when the Churchills learned that he wished his son to go to medical school, they vowed to pay his way.

Years later when Sir Winston was Prime Minister, he became ill with pneumonia. The best physician the king could find was called to the bedside of the ailing leader. His name was Sir Alexander Fleming, the developer of penicillin—and the son of that gardener who long ago saved his life. Churchill later said, "Rarely has a man owed his life twice to the same person."

Gratitude is a wonder. It not only improves our attitudes, it also has a way of bringing rewards later down the line. Never miss an opportunity to give thanks.

Father, I want to show thanks to the people in my life who help me.
Please nurture my relationships. Amen.

Sing Praises

*As they began to sing and praise, the LORD set ambushes against
the men of Ammon and Moab and Mount Seir who were invading
Judah, and they were defeated.* 2 CHRONICLES 20:22

*When I give thanks, my thoughts still circle about myself to some extent.
But in praise my soul ascends to self-forgetting adoration, seeing and praising
only the majesty and power of God, His grace and redemption.*
OLE KRISTIAN O. HALLESBY

A Classic Devotional from Mrs. Charles E. Cowman

Those men that ponder, and meditate, and weigh the affairs of life, and study
the mysterious developments of God's providence, and wonder why they should
be burdened and thwarted and hampered—how different and how much more
joyful would be their lives, if, instead of forever indulging in self-revolving and
inward thinking, they would take their experiences, day by day, and lift them up,
and praise God for them.

We can sing our cares away easier than we can reason them away. Sing in the
morning. The birds are the earliest to sing, and birds are more without care than
anything else that I know of.

Dear God, teach me to praise You and unburden myself by
remembering Your goodness to me. Amen.

Thankfulness in Tough Times

Though there are no sheep in the pen and no cattle in the stalls,
yet I will rejoice in the LORD, I will be joyful in God my Savior.
The Sovereign LORD is my strength. HABAKKUK 3:17–19

Gratitude as a discipline involves a conscious choice. I can choose to be
grateful even when my emotions and feelings are still steeped in hurt and
resentment. It is amazing how many occasions present themselves in which I
can choose gratitude instead of a complaint. HENRI NOUWEN

Habakkuk 3 describes an economic nightmare: the vines are not bearing fruit, the fields are not producing food, livestock is not thriving. When the right (or wrong) conditions conspire, we find ourselves scrambling to get by, staving off desperation, and dreading the future.

Yet even in the midst of crisis, Habakkuk exulted in God. Why? Because God gives strength to keep going. He gives us hinds' feet on high places—He enables us to trod rough terrain as nimbly as a deer.

Unhappy with today and fearful about tomorrow? Stop for a minute, take a deep breath, and consciously express praise and thanks to God. He is at work even if you can't see it. And with eyes of gratitude, you'll probably begin to see more blessings than you did before.

God, even when I'm scared and frustrated, I want to praise You.
Strengthen my heart and give me joy in You. Amen.

Overcome Grumbling with Gratitude

*The LORD said to Moses, "How long will these people treat me
with contempt? How long will they refuse to believe in me, in spite of all the
miraculous signs I have performed among them?"* NUMBERS 14:11

*The careless soul receives the Father's gifts as if it were a way
things had of dropping into his hand. Yet he is ever complaining,
as if someone were accountable for the problems which meet him at every
turn. For the good that comes to him, he gives no thanks—who is there to
thank? At the disappointments that befall him he grumbles—there
must be someone to blame!* GEORGE MACDONALD

"That's not fair!" seems to be written into our DNA, because almost every
child has loudly lodged this protest with the proper authorities, usually Mom or
Dad. But it's not just children who cry, "Unfair!" Teens can do so with style and
adults with subtlety.

After being delivered safely from captivity and given free food each morning
on their journey, the Hebrew children began a pattern of grumbling, to the point
some said slavery was better than eating manna every day (Numbers 11:4–6).
Apparently few things bother God as much as ungrateful grumblers. And had it
not been for Moses' intercession, he would have been done with them.

There is a huge price tag on grumbling for you and everyone around you. The
antidote is always gratitude.

Lord, I know that You provide so richly for me. Help
me never to take Your goodness for granted. Amen.

The Prodigal Son

*Let's have a feast and celebrate. For this son of mine was dead
and is alive again; he was lost and is found.* Luke 15:23–24

*We need deliberately to call to mind the joys of our journey. Perhaps we should
try to write down the blessings of one day. We might begin; we could never end;
there are not pens or paper enough in all the world.* George A. Buttrick

Remember the story of the prodigal son? Most retellings of the parable focus closely on the wayward son. But there's another son in the parable, the resentful and grumpy older brother. As the party rang in the distance, he sulked that even though he had never asked his father for anything, he now had to watch him lavish gifts on his ungrateful brother.

Have you ever been the older brother? Have you wondered why God chose to bless someone else, someone who didn't appear to deserve it? If so, the father's words to his son might be meaningful for you as well: "You have always been with me, and all that I have is yours. But we had to celebrate and rejoice, for this brother of yours was dead and has begun to live, and was lost and has been found" (Luke 15:31–32).

Like the father in the parable, God richly blesses us every day. When He throws a party for someone else, we should celebrate too, knowing what a good God we have.

Thank You, God, for the blessing of being Your son or
daughter. I choose today to be happy for the blessings I
see in the lives of others. Amen.

Always Giving Thanks

Speak to one another with psalms, hymns and spiritual songs. Sing and make music in your heart to the Lord, always giving thanks to God the Father for everything, in the name of our Lord Jesus Christ. EPHESIANS 5:19–20

Gratitude is the mother of all the virtues.
G. K. CHESTERTON

A Classic Devotional from Albert Barnes

We can always find something to be thankful for, and there may be reasons why we ought to be thankful for even those dispensations which appear dark and frowning. A man owes a debt of obligation to him for anything which will recall him from his wanderings, and which will prepare him for heaven. Are there any dealings of God towards men which do not contemplate such an end? Is a man ever made to drink the cup of affliction when no drop of mercy is intermingled? Is he ever visited with calamity which does not in some way contemplate his own temporal or eternal good? Could we see all, we should see that we are never placed in circumstances in which there is not much for which we should thank God. And when, in his dealings, a cloud seems to cover his face, let us remember the good things without number which we have received, and especially remember that we are in the world of redeeming love, and we shall find enough for which to be thankful.

God, You have given me so many gifts. Thank You. Amen.

Unrecognized Blessings

Let them give thanks to the LORD for his unfailing love and his wonderful deeds
for men, for he satisfies the thirsty and fills the hungry with good things.
PSALM 107:8–9

How many times do we miss God's blessings
because they are not packaged as we expected?
AUTHOR UNKNOWN

A poverty-stricken elderly woman in Europe complained that her wealthy son in America was cruel and ungrateful. "Does he never send you any money?" a friend asked. "Never a penny," she replied. "He sends me pictures quite often, but I do not need pictures; I need money." The friend said, "Do you have any of these pictures?" "Oh, yes, I have them all. They are here in the old Bible." When she pulled them out, her friend gasped. The "pictures" were fresh, crisp fifty- and hundred-dollar bills, a huge and generous gift at the turn of the nineteenth century.

In order to enjoy our blessings, we first have to realize what we have. We might be sulking in squalor while we are surrounded by abundance. Are you missing any blessings in your life? Have you allowed misplaced values to rob you of the abundance God has given you?

Lord, open my eyes to see the gifts You have given me. Amen.

We Get What We Give

*Give, and it will be given to you. A good measure, pressed down,
shaken together and running over, will be poured into your lap.
For with the measure you use, it will be measured to you.* LUKE 6:38

*As base a thing as money often is, yet it can be transmuted into everlasting
treasure. It can be converted into food for the hungry and clothing for the poor.
Any temporal possession can be turned into everlasting wealth. Whatever is
given to Christ is immediately touched with immortality.* A. W. TOZER

There's a principle in life that seems oxymoronic at first glance: we get what
we give. But a second look shows the wisdom of the principle. When we bless
others, we are blessed; when we love, we are loved; when we give—even in the
midst of our own needs—we greatly receive. It's possible to give beyond our
resources and find ourselves burned out and broke. But over time, if we're
willing to give, we'll receive a lot more in return.

Gratitude unlocks the doors of generosity. Even if you're in need, gratitude
helps you give to others sacrificially, just like the poor widow Jesus praised (Mark
12:41–44). Do your own soul a favor by sharing generously from the abundance
of your life. You'll be grateful you did!

Father, show me where I can give today and
help me to do so out of gratitude. Amen.

All His Benefits

Praise the LORD, O my soul, and forget not all his benefits. PSALM 103:2

*Love is the child of gratitude. Love grows as gratitude is felt, and then
breaks out into praise and thanksgiving to God: "I love the Lord because
he hath heard my voice and my supplication."* E. M. BOUNDS

In Psalm 103, the psalmist urges us to praise God for all the things He does for
us. And the list is long:

- He forgives our sins and heals our sicknesses (v. 3);
- He saves us from the messes we get into (v. 4);
- He gives us good gifts (v. 5);
- He has compassion on us as His children (v. 13).

One possible cause of feelings of anxiety and lack in our lives is that we trust
in something—ourselves, money, another person—more than we trust in God.
In times like these, we need to let the truth sink into our hearts: God is more
than enough. He lovingly meets our every need. Step one to living joyfully and
thankfully in His grace is acknowledging His goodness.

Lord, You do so much for me. You are all I need. Amen.

The Secret of True Wealth

*But may the righteous be glad and rejoice before God;
may they be happy and joyful.* PSALM 68:3

*You say, "If I had a little more, I should be very satisfied."
You make a mistake. If you are not content with what you have,
you would not be satisfied if it were doubled.* C. H. SPURGEON

A man lives in a mansion in a zip code known for wealth, his garage filled with expensive automobiles. And yet he lives in poverty, for he is miserable—a word that shares its origin with the word *miser*—in his heart and poor in spirit. Never satisfied, nothing seems to make him happy.

Contrast him with the man who works hard every day—including half days on Saturday for the overtime pay—and barely makes ends meet, despite living in a small, tidy home in a neighborhood that has seen better days, a car that makes funny noises parked out front. But he is wealthy. Life is good. He wishes some business decisions had turned out better, but he has a roof over his head and his family is fed and happy.

How can the man with so much be poor and the man with so little be rich? The difference is simple. One man is grateful for nothing. The other sees blessings everywhere. What is the secret to true wealth? A wealth that can never be taken away on the ups and downs of the stock market and business cycle? Gratitude.

Lord, help me to see the wealth around me. Help me find my
satisfaction in Your love and provision, not in earthly wealth. Amen.

Count Your Blessings

Since my youth, O God, you have taught me, and to this day I declare your marvelous deeds. PSALM 71:17

No duty is more urgent than that of returning thanks.
ST. AMBROSE

How many ways have you been blessed by God? Relationally? Materially? Spiritually? Physically? His blessings are all around us, but we are too easily distracted. Consider an activity where you write in your journal or on a sheet of paper all the different ways God has blessed you. Not only can you divide it by category, but you can also do this for different stages of your life: childhood blessings, teen blessings, young adult blessings, and so on until you hit your age. If this sounds too simplistic, remember that many people have started a gratitude list with skepticism, only to be delightfully surprised by how much the list brightened their outlook.

King David said, "I will meditate on all your works and consider all your mighty deeds" (Psalm 77:12). Another Psalm echoes, "Come and listen, all you who fear God; let me tell you what he has done for me" (66:16). Whatever God has done for you, stop to remember His blessings in detail. And say a word of thanks.

Lord, when I look back, I can see that You have been with me all my life. Thank You for Your goodness to me. Amen.

Thankful Service

*He touched her hand and the fever left her, and she got
up and began to wait on him.* MATTHEW 8:15

*We should spend as much time in thanking God for His benefits
as we do asking Him for them.* St. VINCENT DE PAUL

A Classic Devotional from John Henry Jowett

May we not with advantage accept the suggestion which is contained in these words? The fever-stricken woman was healed by the Saviour; and then, when she was delivered from her fever, "She arose and ministered unto Him." She had been lifted out of sickness into sanity, out of aches and pains into peace, out of feverishness into comfort, out of unrest into a healthy calm, and now she uses her restored strength to minister to her Saviour. It is ever the way of the healed and invincible life. We shall best preserve our health by serving our Lord. As to what that service shall be, He has given us a broad and spacious conception in His own Word. "I was an hungred, and ye gave Me meat." "Lord, when saw we Thee an hungred?" When did we minister unto Thee? "Inasmuch as ye did it unto one of the least of these, ye did it unto Me."

Lord, You have done so much for me. I want to
serve You each day out of gratitude. Amen.

The Ten Percent Club

One of them, when he saw he was healed, came back,
praising God in a loud voice. He threw himself at Jesus' feet
and thanked him—and he was a Samaritan. Luke 17:15–16

God is worthy of our praise and is pleased when we come
before Him with thanksgiving. Shirley Dobson

Ten were healed. Only one returned to say thank you to the miracle worker. Does that percentage, only 10 percent, represent those in everyday life who stop to notice and express thanks for the miracles and ordinary blessings bestowed on them? Maybe. But this Scripture passage (Luke 17:11–19) is not about percentages. It's not about numbers—though it is about a number. The number one. The one Samaritan leper who expressed the gratitude of his heart.

Are you numbered with the ten percent? Are you a kindred spirit with the one who gave thanks? Are you a person who sees miracles and blessings, or who wonders why things never go your way? Join an elite—though not exclusive—group. The ten percent, the one who savors God's goodness and shouts out praise as a result.

God, I never want to neglect to praise You for the ways
You bless me. Open my eyes to Your miracles today. Amen.

Thanking God

Keep me safe, O God, for in you I take refuge. I said to the LORD,
"You are my Lord; apart from you I have no good thing." PSALM 16:1–2

Nothing taken for granted; everything received with gratitude;
everything passed on with grace. G. K. CHESTERTON

When a mother in a drunken stupor lit up a cigarette, not coherent enough to think of her children's safety, she set fire to their little shanty home. When she escaped, she abandoned it—and the children. Fortunately, all of the children made it out of the house alive and actually lived in the yard near the charred remains of their home for several days until the police found them. They were taken to a Christian children's home to live. And there their lives were turned around. Notably, these children—now grown and married—are marked by a deep sense of gratitude. They have endured more heartbreak than most, and having escaped and moved on to a better life, they are grateful to God for seeing them through.

Your life's tragedies may not be as difficult and dramatic as what this family faced. But if you have a relationship with God, your life has been touched for the better. Have you said thank you today?

God, I have seen You turn around even the
worst situations. Thank You for Your work in
our lives, and thank You for saving me. Amen.

Our First Love

I remember the devotion of your youth.

JEREMIAH 2:2

God thirsts to be thirsted after.

AUGUSTINE

A Classic Devotional from Oswald Chambers

Am I as spontaneously kind to God as I used to be, or am I only expecting God to be kind to me? Am I full of the little things that cheer His heart over me, or am I whimpering because things are going hardly with me? There is no joy in the soul that has forgotten what God prizes. It is a great thing to think that Jesus Christ has need of me—"Give Me to drink." How much kindness have I shown Him this past week? Have I been kind to His reputation in my life?

God is saying to His people—You are not in love with Me now, but I remember the time when you were—"I remember . . . the love of thine espousals." Am I as full of the extravagance of love to Jesus Christ as I was in the beginning, when I went out of my way to prove my devotion to Him? Does He find me recalling the time when I did not care for anything but Himself? Am I there now, or have I become wise over loving Him?

Lord, I pray that I would never lose my love for You.
Help me remember what first drew me to You, and renew
the gratitude I felt when You first saved me. Amen.

The Way to Worship

Worship the Lord with gladness; Come before him with joyful songs.
PSALM 100:2

*Just as an indescribable sunset or a breath-taking mountaintop
vista evokes a spontaneous response, so we cannot encounter the
worthiness of God without the response of worship.* DONALD WHITNEY

When we recognize all that God has done for us and given us—not least of which is the gift of salvation and promise of His presence—the right response is to worship. Psalm 100 offers us a powerful primer for true worship:

"Shout for joy to the LORD" (v. 1). Worship should be enthusiastic and engage our whole hearts and minds.

"It is he who made us, and we are his" (v. 3). Here David affirms that God is our creator and we depend on Him; he also affirms that God has taken us on as our Father, a truth which should fill our hearts with joy.

"For the LORD is good and his love endures forever; his faithfulness continues through all generations" (v. 5). True worship expresses gratitude to God for His goodness and praises Him for His wonderful character.

Now might be a good time to read slowly through all of Psalm 100 as a reminder of how to worship and why God deserves our praise. One of the joys of knowing God is the privilege of entering "his gates with thanksgiving and his courts with praise" (v. 4).

God, You are so good. Teach me to express
praise and worship to You. Amen.

Praise for God's Goodness

But you are a chosen people, a royal priesthood, a holy nation,
a people belonging to God, that you may declare the praises of him
who called you out of darkness into his wonderful light.
1 PETER 2:9

Jesus loves us with fidelity, purity, constancy,
and passion, no matter how imperfect we are.
STORMIE OMARTIAN

A Classic Devotional from Adam Clarke

As there is no end to the merits of Christ incarnated and crucified; no bounds to the mercy and love of God; no hindrance to the almighty energy and sanctifying influence of the Holy Spirit; no limits to the improvability of the human condition; so there can be no bounds to the saving influence which God will dispense to the heart of every genuine believer.

We may ask and receive, and our joy shall be full! Well may we bless and praise God, "who has called us into such a state of salvation"; a state in which we may be thus saved; and, by the grace of that state continue in the same to the end of our lives.

God, thank You for Your boundless love and grace. Help me to experience the fullness of You today. Amen.

Say Thanks

I thank God . . . as night and day I constantly remember you in my prayers.
2 TIMOTHY 1:3

Silent gratitude isn't much use to anyone. G. B. STERN

Everyone wants to feel appreciated. How do you feel when it seems your contributions at home, at work, or in a church or civic group are taken for granted? Just as importantly, how well do you say thank you to those who make a difference in your life? Colleagues? Friends? Family members? Mentors?

Paul began and ended all his New Testament letters by expressing his gratitude for the co-laborers who helped him spread the gospel of Jesus Christ. One letter, Philemon, is a very practical epistle written to a church leader. He says to Philemon: "I always thank my God as I remember you in my prayers, because I hear about your faith in the Lord Jesus and your love for all the saints" (vv. 4–5). Paul knew to express appreciation to his fellow workers meaningfully and often.

To whom can you say thanks today? And how would your thank-you be most effective? Do you need to write an extended letter, purchase a meaningful gift, or make a special visit? Ask God to give you a spirit of gratitude—and the ability to express it well.

Lord, so many people have contributed to my life and
success over the years. Please show me who deserves my
thanks and help me bless them with my gratitude. Amen.

Happy Thanksgiving

And do not forget to do good and to share with others,
for with such sacrifices God is pleased. HEBREWS 13:16

No matter how little you have, you can always give some of it away.
CATHERINE MARSHALL

"When you go grocery shopping, will you pick up some extra food for a needy family?" Martin asked. "There is a family of eight who needs something to eat for Thanksgiving."

Jean considered her limited funds. Eight people? With the dozen-plus people she would be feeding at her own house that year, she wasn't sure she could afford two Thanksgiving dinners. "I'll do the best I can," she answered. "But on our budget, it is probably an impossible mission."

With her coupons, several buy-one-get-one-free specials, and God's help, Jean bought two carts filled with groceries. Later that day, six gleeful children paraded from the car to their kitchen with enough groceries to feed an army.

Even when we're struggling ourselves, with a little creativity we can often do more than we think we can for someone else. One of the best ways to show our gratitude to God is to help Him help those around us. Who needs your help today?

God, I know that You care about the needs around me. Show
me how I can serve You with gratitude by serving others. Amen.

The Eye of the Beholder

I will extol the Lord at all times; his praise will always be on my lips.
PSALM 34:1

Pride slays thanksgiving, but a humble mind is the soil out of which thanks naturally grow. A proud man is seldom a grateful man, for he never thinks he gets as much as he deserves. HENRY WARD BEECHER

In Depression-era America, a lawyer successfully handled a difficult case for a wealthy friend. Following the happy outcome of the case, the friend went to the lawyer's office, expressed his appreciation of his work, and handed him a handsome Moroccan leather wallet. The lawyer looked at the wallet in astonishment and handed it back with a sharp reminder that a wallet could not possibly compensate him for his services. "My fee for that work," acidly snapped the attorney, "is five hundred dollars."

The client opened the wallet, removed a one-thousand dollar bill, replaced it with a five-hundred dollar bill, and handed it back to the lawyer with a smile.

We can easily be too quick to assess what life gives us and demand more. Greed can squash gratitude. But an attitude of contentment turns everything into a gift.

God, help me to see the best in others
and in what You give me. Amen.

Good Soil

*Let the word of Christ dwell in you richly as you teach and admonish
one another with all wisdom, and as you sing psalms, hymns and spiritual
songs with gratitude in your hearts to God.* Colossians 3:6

*The unthankful heart discovers no mercies; but let the thankful
heart sweep through the day and, as the magnet finds the iron, so it will find,
in every hour, some heavenly blessings!* Henry Ward Beecher

A colloquial story is told of a man who found the barn where Satan stores the seeds he sows in the human heart: envy, greed, anger, hatred, lust, and so on. The man noticed that Satan had more seeds of discouragement than any other kind, and he learned that those seeds were hardy and fruitful and could be made to grow almost anywhere. But when Satan was questioned, he reluctantly admitted that there was one place in which he could not get them to grow. "Where is that?" asked the man. Satan replied, "In the heart of a thankful man."

When we choose a thankful attitude, our spirits resist the cynicism, discouragement, and pessimism that weigh life down. We're better able to thrive and survive no matter what life throws at us. And our love for God blooms.

God, I pray for a thankful heart.
Please nurture in me a spirit of gratitude. Amen.

A Thanksgiving Prayer by Scott Wesemann

*Give thanks to the LORD, call on his name; make known
among the nations what he has done.* 1 CHRONICLES 16:8

*Thankfulness to God is a recognition that God in His
goodness and faithfulness has provided for us and cared for us,
both physically and spiritually.* JERRY BRIDGES

Lord, so oftentimes, as any other day, when we sit down to our meal and pray we hurry along and make fast the blessing— "Thanks, Amen. Now please pass the dressing."

We're slaves to the olfactory overload. We must rush our prayer before the food gets cold. But Lord, I'd like to take a few minutes more to really give thanks for what I'm thankful for.

For my family, my health, a nice soft bed, my friends, my freedom, a roof over my head. I'm thankful right now to be surrounded by those whose lives touch me more than they'll ever possibly know.

Thankful, Lord, that You've blessed me beyond measure, thankful that in my heart lives life's greatest treasure, that You, dear Jesus, reside in that place, and I'm ever so grateful for Your unending grace.

So please, heavenly Father, bless this food You've provided and bless each and every person invited. Amen!

Lord, this Thanksgiving, help me reflect
on what really matters. Amen.

Victory Begins With a Thankful Heart

*Grace and peace be yours in abundance through
the knowledge of God and of Jesus our Lord.* 2 PETER 1:2

*Strength, rest, guidance, grace, help, sympathy, love—all
from God to us! What a list of blessings!* E. STENBOCK

A Classic Devotional from D. L. Moody

We ought to be more thankful for what we receive from God. Here we are, getting blessings from God day after day, yet how little praise and thanksgiving there is in the church of God!

It is said that in a time of great despondency among the first settlers in New England, it was proposed in one of their public assemblies to proclaim a fast. An old farmer arose. He spoke of their provoking heaven with their complaints. He reviewed their measures, showed that they had much to be thankful for, and moved that instead of appointing a day of fasting, they should appoint a day of thanksgiving. This was done, and the custom has been continued ever since.

Even if we had nothing else to be thankful for, we would always have ample cause for giving thanks in that Jesus Christ loved us and gave Himself for us (Gal. 2:20).

Lord, thank You for being in my life. I choose
today to be grateful to You all day. Amen.

A Day Set Aside

*Now, our God, we give you thanks,
and praise your glorious name.*
2 CHRONICLES 29:13

*It is therefore recommended to set apart Thursday the eighteenth day of
December next, for solemn thanksgiving and praise, that with one heart and
one voice the good people may express the grateful feelings of their hearts and
consecrate themselves to the service of their divine benefactor.* SAMUEL ADAMS

The Founding Fathers of the United States of America saw the need for the
nation to celebrate the new beginnings of the country, and they instituted the
first national day of thanksgiving. Although the Thanksgiving we know—the
fourth Thursday of November—wasn't made official by Congress until 1941,
many presidents between Washington and Franklin D. Roosevelt understood the
value of a national day of gratitude. Canada set its Thanksgiving on the second
Monday of every October. Other countries celebrate similarly.

This Thanksgiving, as you gather with family and friends, why not adopt that
age-old tradition of asking each guest at your table to name something he or she
is thankful for? No matter what country you call home, as you ponder your own
list of things to be grateful for individually, don't forget about the blessings your
nation has received collectively. All of us have much for which to give thanks.

God, thank You for Your provision for me,
my family, and my country. Amen.

Our Lot in Life

The boundary lines have fallen for me in pleasant places;
surely I have a delightful inheritance. Psalm 16:6

How completely satisfying to turn from our limitations to a God who
has none. God never hurries. There are no deadlines against which He must
work. Only to know this is to quiet our spirits and relax our nerves.
A. W. Tozer

At nineteen months old, Helen Keller was stricken with a rare infection that
caused her to lose both her sight and her hearing. The road ahead was long and
difficult. She had to blaze new trails in living life with disabilities. Yet she was
able to express her gratitude to God by saying: "I thank God for my handicaps,
for, through them, I have found myself, my work, and my God."

Our lot in life may not be what we would have picked for ourselves. Some days
we might wish we could do away with this flaw or that difficulty—a physical
problem, a complicated background, a troublesome quirk or tendency. But what
we so often forget is that God has a plan and purpose for each of us. He knows
what is best and can use even the worst of our problems for good. View yourself
and your life prayerfully and gratefully. If you keep yourself open to God's plan,
you will see His great purposes will be fulfilled.

God, I know that You have a plan, and I thank You for
it in advance. Help me to cooperate with You. Amen.

A Deep River

Thanks be to God for his indescribable gift!
2 CORINTHIANS 9:15

Grace is always given to those ready to give thanks for it.
THOMAS À KEMPIS

A Classic Devotional from C. H. Spurgeon

Every attribute of God should become a fresh ray in the sunlight of our gladness. That he is wise should make us glad, knowing as we do our own foolishness. That he is mighty should cause us to rejoice who tremble at our weakness. That he is everlasting, should always be a theme of joy when we know that we wither as the grass. That he is un-changing, should perpetually yield us a song, since we change every hour. That he is full of grace, that he is overflowing with it, and that this grace in covenant he has given to us; that it is ours to cleanse us, ours to keep us, ours to sanctify us, ours to perfect us, ours to bring us to glory—all this should tend to make us glad in him. This gladness in God is as a deep river; we have only as yet touched its brink, we know a little of its clear sweet, heavenly streams, but onward the depth is greater, and the current more impetuous in its joy.

Lord, I know that You are good. Help me to experience Your goodness more deeply each day of my life. Amen.

December

Faith

The Right Path

Trust in the Lord with all your heart and lean not on your own understanding.
PROVERBS 3:5

*Trust the past to God's mercy, the present to God's love,
and the future to God's providence.* ST. AUGUSTINE

We rightfully teach our children—and attempt to live our own lives—by the credos of responsibility, self-control, and mature self-reliance. And yes, being responsible is a very good thing. But when our attitude reaches the point where we trust more in ourselves than in God, twin temptations, both that lead to spiritual shipwreck, suddenly confront us.

One temptation is pride, an unhealthy arrogance that slips (or roars) into our thinking when things are going great in our lives. We become convinced that we are in control of our own world. The second temptation, despair, works itself into our hearts when we face the inevitable difficulties and setbacks of life that are outside of our control.

Daily trusting in God—acknowledging that He is the one source of all good gifts and success and the only safe refuge when life is difficult—steers us from these twin dangers. The good news is that with complete and total trust in Him, He directs our steps in the most fulfilling paths for our lives.

God, I know that You are in control. Help me trust
in You day by day, moment by moment. Amen.

Practice Makes Perfect

*Whatever you have learned or received or heard from me, or seen in
me—put it into practice. And the God of peace will be with you.*
PHILIPPIANS 4:9

Faith is an activity; it is something that has to be applied.
CORRIE TEN BOOM

You're not really a soccer player unless you actually play soccer. You're not a
writer if you don't put ink on a page or start typing at a keyboard. And you're
not a pianist if you never play the piano. In much the same way, faith is a practice. It is active. And it can be strengthened or weakened, depending on how
little or much we practice it.

There are many ways to practice faith, like attending church or joining a Bible
study; serving the needy or visiting prisoners; tithing and even giving sacrificially when the economy is tough. Spiritual disciplines like prayer and fasting
can also nurture your faith and spirit. Practicing your faith doesn't have to be
complicated or a long list of regulations. All it takes is a little effort and initiative
on your part.

Practice makes perfect because that is when we live as God intended us to live.

God, please teach me to discipline myself
and practice my faith. Amen.

Watch Your Faith

[Abraham] did not waver through unbelief regarding the promise
of God, but was strengthened in his faith and gave glory to God.
ROMANS 4:20

The true, living faith, which the Holy Spirit
instills into the heart, simply cannot be idle.
MARTIN LUTHER

A Classic Devotional from C. H. Spurgeon

Christian, take good care of thy faith; for recollect faith is the only way whereby thou canst obtain blessings. If we want blessings from God, nothing can fetch them down but faith. Prayer cannot draw down answers from God's throne except it be the earnest prayer of the man who believes. Faith is the angelic messenger between the soul and the Lord Jesus in glory. Let that angel be withdrawn, we can neither send up prayer, nor receive the answers. Faith is the telegraphic wire which links earth and heaven—on which God's messages of love fly so fast, that before we call He answers, and while we are yet speaking He hears us. O, then, Christian, watch well thy faith; for with it thou canst win all things, however poor thou art, but without it thou canst obtain nothing.

Lord, teach me to grow in my faith. Amen.

In the Fiery Furnace

When you walk through the fire, you will not be scorched,
Nor will the flame burn you. Isaiah 43:2

Faith does not operate in the realm of the possible. There is no glory for God in
that which is humanly possible. Faith begins where man's power ends.
GEORGE MUELLER

In the biblical story of Shadrach, Meshach, and Abednego—three young men abducted into Babylonia during King Nebuchadnezzar's reign—we literally see grace under fire. (Look up Daniel 3 for the story.) The three young men refused to bow to any idol or serve any god other than the God of their fathers. When the king decreed that anyone who would not bow to an idol would be thrown into a furnace, Shadrach, Meshach, and Abednego stayed true to their principles. And the king had them bound and dragged into a fiery furnace. Amazingly, the three emerged from the furnace not only unscathed, but without even the smell of smoke on them.

They believed that God would rescue them from the flames. But just as importantly, they determined, even if He did not, they would not bow down to an idol. They had faith in God and faithfulness to Him. One tends to feed the other. Maybe you aren't facing a fiery furnace today, but you probably have your own tests of faith. If you cultivate faithfulness like Shadrach, Meshach, and Abednego's, your faith will grow. And you just might witness the impossible.

Lord, please give me the faith and confidence in
You that I will always exhibit faith under fire. Amen.

Sincere Faith

*The goal of this command is love, which comes from a
pure heart and a good conscience and a sincere faith.*

1 TIMOTHY 1:5

It is just as important to trust God as it is to obey Him.

JERRY BRIDGES

Yes, faith is active; there are steps we can take to express and nurture our faith.
But is it possible to go through all the motions—read Scripture, serve others,
faithfully attend church services—and not have a drop of authentic, internal
faith? Possibly. Though probably not—there are simply some seasons when we
"feel" our faith more than others.

But it's still a good idea to audit our own heart. What is our sincerity level
today? Have we let our hearts and minds wander? Why do we do what we do?
Is it out of duty or faith? Remember that God prizes our service; but more than
that, He wants to be known and loved.

Lord, thank You for revealing Yourself to me. Rekindle
my love for You and my passion to do Your will. Amen.

Bold Faith

*I tell you the truth, if you have faith as small as a mustard seed,
you can say to this mountain, "Move from here to there"
and it will move. Nothing will be impossible for you.*
MATTHEW 17:20

*Faith and works are bound up in the same bundle. He that obeys
God trusts God; and he that trusts God obeys God. He that is without
faith is without works; and he that is without works is without faith.*
C. H. SPURGEON

A Classic Devotional from Martin Luther

Faith is a living, bold trust in God's grace, so certain of God's favor that it would risk death a thousand times trusting in it. Such confidence and knowledge of God's grace makes you happy, joyful and bold in your relationship to God and all creatures. The Holy Spirit makes this happen through faith. Because of it, you freely, willingly, and joyfully do good to everyone, serve everyone, suffer all kinds of things, love and praise the God who has shown you such grace. Thus, it is just as impossible to separate faith and works as it is to separate heat and light from fire! Ask God to work faith in you, or you will remain forever without faith, no matter what you wish, say or can do.

Lord, I pray that my faith would show up in
my life through good works for You. Amen.

Pulling Through

Everything is possible for him who believes. MARK 9:23

Faith in faith is pointless. Faith in a living, active God moves mountains.
BETH MOORE

His football career was legendary. He played for one of the most tradition-rich high schools in the state and even the nation. Even before his first college game, he ended up pictured on the front of a Wheaties box. He was a two-time All-American for Ohio State and went on to a long, award-filled NFL career, even overcoming a broken neck to extend his playing days.

But the biggest challenge of his life came when doctors diagnosed his wife with an aggressive malignant cancer. With the same passion he showed on the football field, he prayed and stood by his wife—leaving professional football for a year to be by her side. When she lost her hair to chemotherapy, he went with his two children to the barber so that all members of the family had shaven heads in a display of team solidarity. With faith and determination, the family pulled together as Mom pulled through for more than a decade before finally succumbing to the disease.

Life will very often call for us to respond with strength and perseverance. Fortunately, when we put our faith in God, He can supply all the strength we need.

Lord, help me to tackle my life's challenges and
responsibilities with unshakable faith in You. Amen.

By Faith Alone

For in the gospel a righteousness from God is revealed, a righteousness that is by faith from first to last, just as it is written: "The righteous will live by faith." Romans 1:17

> *Faith is a living, bold trust in God's grace, so certain of God's favor that it would risk death a thousand times trusting in it. Such confidence and knowledge of God's grace makes you happy, joyful and bold in your relationship to God and all creatures.* Martin Luther

A Classic Devotional from C. H. Mackintosh

To live by faith is to walk with God: to cling to Him; to lean on Him; to draw from His exhaustless springs; to find all our resources in Him; and to have Him as a perfect covering for our eyes and a satisfying object for our hearts—to know Him as our only resource in all difficulties, and in our trials.

Such is the life of faith. Let us see that we understand it. It must be a reality or nothing at all. It will not do to talk about the life of faith; we must live it; and in order to live it we must know God practically—know Him intimately, in the deep secret of our own souls. It is utterly vain and delusive to profess to be living by faith and looking to the Lord, while in reality our hearts are looking to some creature resource. How often do people speak and write about their dependence upon God to meet certain wants, and by the very fact of their making it known to a fellow-mortal they are, in principle, departing from the life of faith!

Lord, I want to live a life of faith in You. Teach me to focus my heart and mind on following You. Amen.

The Armor of God

*For our struggle is not against flesh and blood, but against the rulers,
against the authorities, against the powers of this dark world and against
the spiritual forces of evil in the heavenly realms.* EPHESIANS 6:12

*There are two equal and opposite errors into which our race can
fall about the devils. One is to disbelieve in their existence. The other
is to believe, and to feel an excessive and unhealthy interest in them.
They themselves are equally pleased by both errors.* C. S. LEWIS

Among people of faith, there is some variation in doctrine about spiritual
warfare. Some see demons in everything; others have more or less eliminated
a personal devil from the equation of their spiritual practice. While we can go
astray by devoting too much thought and care to Satan, the Bible does tell us
that we must be on our guard against spiritual attacks.

Fortunately, we are never in the battle alone. God always arms us with His
strength and enables us to defeat temptation and assaults on our Christian walk.
In Ephesians 6, Paul tells us to take up the armor of God, including the shield of
faith and the sword of the Spirit. We can deflect the attacks that would wound
our souls by diligently nurturing our faith in God.

God, help me to be vigilant and protective of my spiritual life.
Guard me from the attacks of the devil today. Amen.

The Right Motivation

But God demonstrates his own love for us in this:
While we were still sinners, Christ died for us. ROMANS 5:8

Get yourself into the presence of the loving Father. Just place yourself before
Him, and look up into His face; think of His love, His wonderful, tender love.
ANDREW MURRAY

Following Marie's doctor's advice, the couple purchased a treadmill. For several days she walked faithfully. Before long, however, she quit. When her husband confronted her, she unfurled a list of excuses. "It's boring" was the first. Her husband purchased a television and mounted it on the wall above the treadmill. "It's too hot," Marie further complained. Her husband purchased a fan on a stand and placed it near the exercise equipment. "My feet are hurting," she moaned. Together, they went shopping and bought her a pair of walking shoes.

Marie finally understood her husband's deep concern for her—he only wanted her to be healthy. She decided to walk faithfully and quit using lame excuses. The time on the treadmill passed quickly when she thought about how much her husband must love her.

Somehow it's easier to persevere when we're doing so for someone we love. Whatever God has asked you to do, remember that He loves you. Reflecting on His abundant love will make the task at hand lighter and easier.

Lord, I know that You love me. Help me to see
Your love in each circumstance of my life. Amen.

Riches of Grace

In him we have redemption through his blood, the forgiveness of sins,
in accordance with the riches of God's grace. Ephesians 1:7

Grace is something you can never get but can only be given. There's no way to
earn it or deserve it or bring it about anymore than you can deserve the taste of
raspberries and cream or earn good looks. Frederick Buechner

Did you know God favors you? He does. God favors you out of His deep, abiding love for you, a love that is not contingent upon any effort you put forth.

Here are some aspects of grace that just might be what you need to hear today:

- Grace provides the gift of salvation, a gift that can't be earned. Paul says: "For it is by grace you have been saved, through faith—and this not from yourselves, it is the gift of God— not by works, so that no one can boast" (Ephesians 2:8–9).
- Grace is available to us when we are weak. Paul says: "Therefore I will boast all the more gladly about my weaknesses, so that Christ's power may rest on me" (2 Corinthians 12:9).
- Grace is sufficient for absolutely any need we have—whether health, finances, relationships, temptations, or any other need. Paul says: "My grace is sufficient for you" (2 Corinthians 12:9).

Whatever need you have in your life today, be assured, God is on your side. He is ready and able to help you as you respond to Him with faith.

Lord, thank You for grace. It amazes me to know I am Your
beloved child. Help me to live in Your grace today. Amen.

Do We Really Have a Choice?

We were therefore buried with him through baptism into death in order that, just as Christ was raised from the dead through the glory of the Father, we too may live a new life. ROMANS 6:4

When we come to the end of ourselves, we come to the beginning of God.
BILLY GRAHAM

For centuries, people have debated what makes us who we are—are we born the way we are, or do we become this way through the things that happen to us? Though our genes and life experiences have a huge impact on us, aren't you glad that there is a miraculous, powerful God who is able to change even the most stubborn, damaged, sinful heart? Paul goes so far as to say, "Therefore, if anyone is in Christ, he is a new creation; the old has gone, the new has come!" (2 Corinthians 5:17).

But you don't understand how I've been brought up. You don't know the mistakes I've made. You don't understand how hard it is for me to break certain negative patterns.

With grace, with faith, with the help of godly friends, you can say along with Paul: "Forgetting what is behind and straining toward what is ahead, I press on toward the goal to win the prize for which God has called me heavenward in Christ Jesus" (Philippians 3:13–14). Because of His forgiving, life-changing power, God's ultimate concern with your life is not where you've been, but where you are going.

God, thank You for making me new, day by day.
I'm so grateful for Your life-changing power. Amen.

Faith and Trust

*May your whole spirit, soul and body be kept blameless at the coming of our
Lord Jesus Christ. The one who calls you is faithful and he will do it.*

1 Thessalonians 5:23–24

*God is God. Because He is God, He is worthy of my trust and obedience. I will
find rest nowhere but in His holy will, a will that is unspeakably beyond my
largest notions of what He is up to.* Elisabeth Elliot

We operate by faith every day. When we sit on a chair, we trust that it will hold us; when we get behind the wheel of our car, we put faith in the brakes to work; we accelerate after a green light, believing cross traffic will stop for reds; we drink bottled water because we believe it has been purified and is safe. Without thinking or questioning, we act as if the objects and many of the circumstances in our lives will come through for us, will be safe for us, because they almost always have.

Putting trust in an invisible God is different and can be a scarier proposition. We can't physically see Him the way we see a chair or a car or the clarity of water or the smiles on neighbors' faces. But when we seek to know Him, we can know His character. And we find that He will always come through for us. With that thought firmly in our minds, we can trust Him.

Lord, help me to know You and overcome any doubts.
I want to trust You more than anything. Amen.

Faith Shows Love

The only thing that counts is faith expressing itself through love.
GALATIANS 5:6

Love is an attribute of God. To love others is evidence of a genuine faith.
KAY ARTHUR

A Classic Devotional from Martin Luther

He who does not firmly believe in God's grace assuredly will not extend kindness to his neighbor, but will be tardy and indifferent in aiding him. In proportion to the strength of his faith will be his willingness and industry in helping his neighbor. Thus faith incites love, and love increases faith.

All Christian doctrines and works, all Christian living, is briefly, clearly and completely comprehended in these two principles, faith and love. They place man as a medium between God and his neighbor, to receive from above and distribute below. Thus the Christian becomes a vessel, or rather a channel, through which the fountain of divine blessings continuously flows to other individuals.

God, please fill me with Your love and
increase my faith in You. Amen.

Worry and Faith

*I pray that out of his glorious riches he may strengthen you
with power through his Spirit in your inner being, so that Christ
may dwell in your hearts through faith.* Ephesians 3:16–17

*I am inwardly fashioned for faith, not for fear. Fear is not
my native land; faith is. I am so made that worry and anxiety are
sand in the machinery of life; faith is the oil.* E. Stanley Jones

Fear and faith are diametrically opposed. When we live in fear, it erodes our faith in God. When worries creep in and dominate our thinking, we start to feel far from God.

How can we overcome the force of worry and choose faith instead? One simple discipline that will help is choosing to let problems and worries drive you to God instead of away from Him. Instead of mulling incessantly over the mortgage payment, pray and thank God for His provision. When someone you love is sick, meditate on verses that celebrate God as a healer. If work pressures are constantly gnawing at you, commit your work to God and begin each day with prayer.

The only way to grow spiritually is to bring more and more of ourselves to our relationship with God. Don't suppress or deny your fears. Let them lead you to God.

Lord, sometimes I get so anxious. I pray that You would
heal me and help me keep my mind on You. Amen.

Family Time

*And over all these virtues put on love, which binds
them all together in perfect unity.* Colossians 3:14

*The blessing of an earthly family gives only a hazy picture
of the blessing in God's heavenly family.* Janette Oke

Families that sweat together, stick together. Okay, that may not be a pleasant thought, but the point is crystal clear. Healthy family interaction enriches each family member's emotional and spiritual health. The holiday season is a time for family interaction. Board games. Backyard football. Touring the city to see Christmas lights. Delivering turkey dinners to needy families. Christmas Eve candlelight service. A fun seasonal movie night. Opening gifts together. Meals with everyone at the table. Reading the Christmas story (Luke 2) out loud on Christmas morning.

If this hasn't been the experience of your family, select one activity from the list above and do all you can to make it happen. If this is how your family interacts during the holidays, thank God for the blessing of time together. If you are living on your own and away from family right now, create holiday traditions with a group of friends—or become an "adopted" member of a family at your church or in your neighborhood. Ask God to make this a season of togetherness for you and those you love.

God, thank You for the people in my life. Be close to us this
Christmas and draw us near to You and near to each other. Amen.

Ready for a Surprise

*Because Joseph her husband was a righteous man and did not want
to expose her to public disgrace, he had in mind to divorce her quietly.*
MATTHEW 1:19

*Have your heart right with Christ, and He will visit you often,
and so turn weekdays into Sundays, meals into sacraments, homes
into temples, and earth into heaven.* C. H. SPURGEON

Christmas is full of surprises each year. But perhaps no one faced a greater surprise than Joseph did in the months before that first Christmas when Jesus was born. What was his surprise? The news that his betrothed, whom he had never slept with, was pregnant. How did he handle it? With a cautious, respectful decision to cancel the wedding with as little embarrassment and shame to Mary as possible. But then Joseph received another surprise. An angel visited him and gave him the news of a miracle. Joseph's response was immediate, simple, selfless obedience.

What prepared Joseph to handle these surprises with such grace? We are told that Joseph was a righteous man. Righteousness: in the Old Testament world of Joseph, this was defined as being innocent and doing right; for Matthew, the most Jewish of the gospel writers, it was being ethical and doing the will of God. What's the best preparation for any surprise that comes your way in life? Righteousness.

Heavenly Father, work in my heart today to give me a righteousness that will allow me to do Your will in every area of my life. Amen.

His Birth and Our New Birth

The virgin will be with child and will give birth to a son,
and will call him Immanuel. Isaiah 7:14

When Christ entered our world, he didn't come to brighten our Decembers, but
to transform our lives. Rich Miller

A Classic Devotional from Oswald Chambers

His Birth in History. "Therefore also that holy thing which shall be born of thee shall be called the Son of God" (Luke 1:35). Jesus Christ was born into this world, not from it. He did not evolve out of history; He came into history from the outside. Our Lord's birth was an advent.

His Birth in Me. "Of whom I travail in birth again until Christ be formed in you" (Gal. 4:19). Just as Our Lord came into human history from outside, so He must come into me from outside. Have I allowed my personal human life to become a "Bethlehem" for the Son of God? I cannot enter into the realm of the Kingdom of God unless I am born from above by a birth totally unlike natural birth. The characteristic of the new birth is that I yield myself so completely to God that Christ is formed in me. Immediately Christ is formed in me, His nature begins to work through me.

God manifest in the flesh—that is what is made profoundly possible for you and me by the Redemption.

Lord, thank You for coming to earth. Please be
born in my heart this Christmas. Amen.

The Wise Still Seek

Where is the one who has been born king of the Jews? We saw his
star in the east and have come to worship him. Matthew 2:2

Lord Jesus, master of both the light and the darkness, send your Holy Spirit
upon our preparations for Christmas. We are your people, walking in
darkness, yet seeking the light. To you we say, "Come Lord Jesus!"
Henri Nouwen

What does the world seek in life? Many seek riches. Others chase fame. Still others race after success. Some pursue pleasure.

Who were these magi of the East? We don't know a lot about them, not even how many there were, but we do know that they were men of goodwill who wanted to discover spiritual truth. The cost of their journey and the gifts they carried would have been staggering, so they weren't in this for personal gain. Their first concern wasn't their own safety or they would have let Herod know the location of the Child on their return home. If it was comfort they sought, they would have never begun the journey in the first place.

No, these men had sincere hearts. They knew there was something greater than they already knew and they were willing to pay the cost to discover it. In the same way, if we are wise, we still seek to know God in His fullness today. And that trip begins with a visit to a manger.

Father, help me to know You and Your ways
and Your truth as never before. Amen.

God with Us

*She will give birth to a son, and you are to give him the name Jesus,
because he will save his people from their sins.* MATTHEW 1:21

*If we could condense all the truths of Christmas into only three words,
these would be the words: "God with us." We tend to focus our attention at
Christmas on the infancy of Christ. The greater truth of the holiday is His
deity. More astonishing than a baby in the manger is the truth that this
promised baby is the omnipotent Creator of the heavens and the earth!*

JOHN F. MACARTHUR, JR.

The hundred-mile journey to Bethlehem might have taken as many as eight
or ten days by donkey and foot. The road ahead was full of rocks and steep
upgrades, not to mention the danger of thieves. When Mary and Joseph reached
their destination, Mary gave birth to the baby they named Jesus.

Sometimes life gets hard. We can't see exactly where we're going; we face
formidable obstacles. But just as the star shone down over Bethlehem that night,
a beacon of hope shines over our own lives—all because of the Baby in the
manger. With the birth of Jesus came the promise that God is with us, for us,
willing to do whatever it takes to save us.

So no matter what happens around us, we have the comfort of the angels
proclaiming, "Peace on earth and good will toward men."

Lord, thank You for the abundant hope You offer in Jesus.
Help me never lose faith in Your goodness. Amen.

Not Just Another Day

*And there were shepherds living out in the fields nearby, keeping watch over
their flocks at night. An angel of the Lord appeared to them, and the glory of
the Lord shone around them, and they were terrified.* LUKE 2:8–9

*Their night watch had been interrupted by an explosion of light from heaven
and a symphony of angels. God goes to those who have time to hear him—and
so on this cloudless night he went to simple shepherds.* MAX LUCADO

Can you think of anything more boring than watching sheep eat and sleep?
Well, it might be pleasant on a vacation in Scotland, but that will only last so
long. It wouldn't be interesting hour after hour, day after day, night after night,
and week after week. Oh, undoubtedly there were moments of excitement for a
shepherd when keeping a wolf or lion away from his flock, but the job undoubtedly was filled with drudgery.

Do you ever wake up knowing that this day will be the same as all others? Isn't
that probably what the shepherds felt that first Christmas Eve more than two
thousand years ago? Do you ever feel like nothing ever changes? Even Christmas
and the holidays are the same every year? Maybe we've all gotten into a rut and
feel that way. But what if this year a new star shines in the night sky and the
evening is filled with angels?

It happened to some simple shepherds. It could happen to you.

Lord, keep my sense of wonder alive. Help me to see what
great thing You are doing in my world and life. Amen.

Room in the Inn

*She wrapped him in cloths and placed him in a manger,
because there was no room for them in the inn.* LUKE 2:7

*In the same manner in which we clean and prepare our homes in the
anticipation of welcomed guests and family members this Christmas season,
let us also prepare our hearts in anticipation of the Lord's coming.*
KATHERINE WALDEN

How many blessings and miracles have we missed because we didn't have room in our hearts and homes to receive them? Too often we fill our lives to over brimming with activities and entertainment—much of it good, but much of it unimportant and distracting—so that we couldn't hear God's voice even if He spoke audibly to us.

Bethlehem was not a large town, but there were numerous inns and many homes. Any one of them could have welcomed the birth of the Christ child. The innkeepers obviously wanted to make as much money as possible and would have loved to have another room or space for a paying guest. But only one innkeeper, the one who first said he had no room, found a warm, dry place for the Baby Jesus to be born.

Out of room in your life? No more time, money, energy, and other resources to make a difference? To welcome Jesus? Look around your home. Search your heart. Is there a warm, dry space for Jesus to visit you?

Gracious God, thank You for sending Christ to
my home and my heart. I welcome Him now. Amen.

A Heart Filled With Worship

From now on all generations will call me blessed, for the Mighty One has done great things for me— holy is his name. LUKE 1:48–49

This is Christmas: not the tinsel, not the giving and receiving, not even the carols, but the humble heart that receives anew the wondrous gift, the Christ.

FRANK McKIBBEN

All mothers feel a sense of joy at the moment of birth. The day has been arduous and often painful, but the miracle of birth fills the hearts of all witnesses, including medical professionals who have "been there and done that" hundreds of times, first-time fathers who sometimes are a bit weak in the knees, and grandparents and siblings who are outside the room anxiously awaiting word.

Shepherds. Magi. Joseph. Maybe an innkeeper's wife or servant. All were filled with wonder and delight at the birth of Jesus. But no one experienced the birth like the Baby's mother. Mary, weary from a journey on the back of a donkey and the delivery in a primitive stable, listening to the shepherds' testimony about the angels' song and the significance of this child, "treasured up all these things and pondered them in her heart" (Luke 2:19).

When a baby is born, all those close to the family celebrate. When Jesus was born, something happened that gives the whole world reason to celebrate and worship.

Father God, my heart is filled with worship and adoration to You for the gift of salvation that You gave to me through the birth of Jesus Christ. Amen.

A Baby Changes Everything

Glory to God in the highest,
and on earth peace to men on whom his favor rests.

LUKE 2:14

Love came down on Christmas Day so many years ago and brought
the greatest happiness the world would ever know. Peace came down on
Christmas Day to fill the hearts of men with all the sweet tranquility each
Christmas brings again. Joy came down on Christmas Day as angels
came to earth heralding the miracle of our Messiah's birth.

AUTHOR UNKNOWN

A mentally disturbed king. A powerful conqueror. A tumultuous engagement. A new marriage. A pregnancy that generated whispers and rumors. An arduous journey. The wrong setting to deliver a child.

But a baby is born, and this Baby changes everything. Angels sing. Shepherds and wise men worship. A mother's prayer of praise is heard throughout generations.

No matter what circumstances surround you this Christmas, never forget. A Baby changes everything.

I praise You, Heavenly Father, for the gift of a Baby. Amen.

A Prayer for Christmas Morning

I pray that you, being rooted and established in love,
may have power, together with all the saints, to grasp how wide
and long and high and deep is the love of Christ. Ephesians 3:17–18

God grant you the light in Christmas, which is faith; the warmth
of Christmas, which is love; the radiance of Christmas, which is purity; the
righteousness of Christmas, which is justice; the belief in Christmas, which
is truth; the all of Christmas, which is Christ. Wilda English

A Classic Devotional from Henry Van Dyke

The day of joy returns, Father in Heaven, and crowns another year with peace and good will. Help us rightly to remember the birth of Jesus, that we may share in the song of the angels, the gladness of the shepherds, and the worship of the wisemen. Close the doors of hate and open the doors of love all over the world. Let kindness come with every gift and good desires with every greeting. Deliver us from evil, by the blessing that Christ brings, and teach us to be merry with clean hearts. May the Christmas morning make us happy to be thy children, and the Christmas evening bring us to our bed with grateful thoughts, forgiving and forgiven, for Jesus' sake.

Amen.

Lord, this Christmas, please let Your kingdom
come in me and make me more like You. Amen.

The Holy of Holies

I will listen to what God the LORD will say;
he promises peace to his people, his saints. PSALM 85:8

It is not thy hold on Christ that saves thee; it is Christ. It is not thy joy
in Christ that saves thee; it is Christ. It is not even thy faith in Christ, though
that be the instrument; it is Christ's blood and merit. C. H. SPURGEON

A Classic Devotional from A. W. Tozer

The interior journey of the soul from the wilds of sin into the enjoyed presence of God is beautifully illustrated in the Old Testament tabernacle. Though the worshiper had enjoyed so much, still he had not yet entered the presence of God. Another veil separated from the Holy of Holies where above the mercy seat dwelt the very God Himself in awful and glorious manifestation. While the tabernacle stood, only the high priest could enter there, and that but once a year, with blood which he offered for his sins and the sins of the people. It was this last veil which was rent when our Lord gave up the ghost on Calvary, and the sacred writer explains that this rending of the veil opened the way for every worshiper in the world to come by the new and living way straight into the divine Presence.

Ransomed men need no longer pause in fear to enter the Holy of Holies. God wills that we should push on into His presence and live our whole life there.

God, thank You for sending Your Son so
that I might live in Your presence. Amen.

Focus On Christ

There is but one God, the Father, from whom all things came and for whom we live; and there is but one Lord, Jesus Christ, through whom all things came and through whom we live. 1 Corinthians 8:6

Christ is the desire of nations, the joy of angels, the delight of the Father. What solace then must that soul be filled with, that has the possession of Him to all eternity! John Bunyan

December is a month that draws our attention back to Christ. We are reminded that Christ was with God the Father from the very beginning of eternity (John 1:1); that His appearance as Savior and Redeemer has been anticipated and prophesied for centuries (Isaiah 9:6–7); that His birth as the Baby Jesus has brought salvation to the world and to each one of us (John 3:16–17). This is a good thing. When we keep our eyes on Christ we are able to handle any challenge, any disappointment, any heartache with an incredible sense of grace and peace.

Because the scenery and images are so different, we usually think of Christmas and Easter as two very separate events. After all, one observance is about a birth and the other about a death. But in the divine picture of life, the birth of Jesus is woven together with the death and resurrection. All are acts of grace from God.

No matter what life holds for you right now, whether peaceful and easy or rigorous and stressful, there is still only one true Source for experiencing the life God has planned for us: Jesus Christ. Focus on Him today.

Lord Jesus, I am so glad I know You. In the coming new year, help me focus on You. Amen.

Praying Hands

He has made everything beautiful in its time. ECCLESIASTES 3:11

In God's faithfulness lies eternal security. CORRIE TEN BOOM

Two friends, Albrecht and Franz, both very poor, but both showing great promise as artists, made a deal: they would draw lots; the winner would continue in art school, while the other would work to support both of them. Once the one finished school and began to make money as an artist, he would in turn support the other in his education and work.

Albrecht won the drawing, finished his training, and went on to have a wildly successful career as an artist. Tragically, however, it was no longer possible for Franz to be an artist—his fingers were stiff and twisted from the manual labor. A true friend, Franz did not succumb to bitterness, but was thrilled for Albrecht's success.

One day Albrecht found his friend kneeling, his misshapen hands intertwined in prayer. Struck by sudden inspiration, he grabbed his sketch pad and began work on what was to become his greatest masterpiece.

Five hundred years later, none of Albrecht Durer's works are more famous and loved than "The Praying Hands" he sketched that day.

God can make a work of art out of any circumstances.

Father God, teach me to remain faithful to
You and keep my eyes open for miracles. Amen.

Belief As Commitment

I believe that you are the Christ, the Son of God,
who was to come into the world. JOHN 11:27

When we are engaged in His work we are very close to Christ.
We are expending our anxiety and affections on the same
objects on which His heart is set. JAMES STALKER

A Classic Devotional from Oswald Chambers

Martha believed in the power available to Jesus Christ; she believed that if He had been there He could have healed her brother. But—she needed a closer personal intimacy with Jesus. Martha's theology had its fulfillment in the future. But Jesus continued to attract and draw her in until her belief became an intimate possession. It then slowly emerged into a personal inheritance— "Yes, Lord, I believe that You are the Christ . . ." (John 11:27).

Is the Lord dealing with you in the same way? Is Jesus teaching you to have a personal intimacy with Himself? Allow Him to drive His question home to you— "Do you believe this?" Are you facing an area of doubt in your life? Have you come, like Martha, to a crossroads of overwhelming circumstances where your theology is about to become a very personal belief? This happens only when a personal problem brings the awareness of our personal need.

To believe is to commit. In intimate personal belief I commit myself spiritually to Jesus Christ and make a determination to be dominated by Him alone.

Lord, I commit myself to You. Amen.

Keep Going

*Let us draw near to God with a sincere heart in full assurance of faith,
having our hearts sprinkled to cleanse us from a guilty conscience
and having our bodies washed with pure water.* HEBREWS 10:22

*A true faith in Jesus Christ will not suffer us to be idle. No, it is
an active, lively, restless principle; it fills the heart, so that it cannot be
easy till it is doing something for Jesus Christ.* GEORGE WHITEFIELD

During a long race, it's easy to get discouraged. But what most runners know is that being familiar with the course helps to keep up momentum and motivation. When you know what to expect, you're able to pace yourself and not become discouraged when the road seems endless.

God doesn't map out for us the exact course of our lives. But there are some things we can know without a shadow of a doubt. We know troubles will come. We know that God will never abandon us. We know that He has good plans for us. And we know that He will ultimately overcome evil in the world. That knowledge and faith helps us persevere when the going gets tough and the race gets long.

God, give me greater confidence in You so
that I might persevere in the race of life. Amen.

Another Year

See, the former things have taken place, and new things I declare;
before they spring into being I announce them to you. Isaiah 42:9

We will open the book. Its pages are blank. We are going to
put words on them ourselves. The book is called Opportunity and
its first chapter is New Year's Day. Edith Lovejoy Pierce

Another year has come and gone. How will this one go down in the books for you? Did you meet new friends? Did you start or finish any new projects? Did you take a class or learn anything new? Did you read any books? Did you bless those around you? Your family? Your neighbors? Did you serve at your church? Did you share your faith? Did you pray more or less? Did you draw closer to God?

Years come and go. Are we growing and making a difference in the time God has given us? The questions raised above are not intended to elicit guilt, but they are the kind of questions that help us determine how much we are making our life count.

Consider writing down a highlight of your year before you even begin thinking about goals for next year. Do this thoughtfully and prayerfully. Ask God to convict you in areas that need to change. Let Him affirm you in areas where He is pleased with your life. Let this account of your year challenge and encourage you to live your best life yet in the days ahead.

God, as I sit down to take stock of the year, I want to
thank You for Your blessings and ask for Your guidance.
Help me to make this year count for You. Amen.

Inspired Faith
365 Days a Year

*T*O SHARE HOW THIS BOOK has encouraged you or someone close to you, send us an email at: *feedback@simpletruths.com*

To read more heartfelt stories, view life-inspiring movies, enjoy daily devotionals, quotes and Scriptures to strengthen and inspire your faith— and to share with a friend—visit us at *www.simpletruths.com*

simple truths®
Motivational & Inspirational Gifts